# BUSINESS & COMMERCE

Gerry Gorman

TEACH YOURSELF BOOKS

Hodder and Stoughton

*First published 1984*
*Second edition 1990*

*Copyright © 1990*
*G. Gorman*

All rights reserved. No part of this publication may be
reproduced or transmitted in any form or by any means,
electronic or mechanical, including photocopy, recording
or any information storage and retrieval system, without
permission in writing from the publisher.

*British Library Cataloguing in Publication Data*
Gorman, Gerry
Business and commerce. – 2nd ed
1. Business enterprise
I. Title   II. Warson, Ronald
338.6

ISBN 0 340 49136 1

*Printed in Great Britain for*
*Hodder and Stoughton Educational,*
*a division of Hodder and Stoughton Ltd,*
*Mill Road, Dunton Green, Sevenoaks, Kent,*
*by Richard Clay Ltd, Bungay, Suffolk.*
*Photoset by Rowland Phototypesetting Ltd,*
*Bury St Edmunds, Suffolk.*

# Contents

**Acknowledgements** vi
**Preface to the Second Edition** vii

1 **Introduction to the Economic System** 1
   What is commerce? The economic system. The free-market economy. The planned economy. The mixed economy. Industry and commerce.

2 **Private Sector Firms – Legal Structure** 9
   Limited liability. Sole trader. Partnership. Private limited company. Public limited company. Joint-stock companies. Registration of joint-stock companies. Co-operatives.

3 **Private Sector Firms – Organisation of Production** 22
   Internal organisation of a typical business. The size of firms. Location of industry.

4 **Private Sector Firms – Finance** 30
   Why firms need capital. Retained profit. Borrowing. Share issues. Government grants and loans. The Stock Exchange. Factors affecting share prices. A typical share issue.

5 **Public Sector Production** 42
   The public sector. Local government. Nationalised industries. Control of public corporations. Privatisation.

iv *Business and Commerce*

**6 Business Documents** 54
A typical business transaction on credit. Value added tax.

**7 Business Accounts** 62
The balance sheet. Gross and net profit. Stock turnover.

**8 Retailing** 71
The organisation of retailing. Types of shop. Other types of retailer.

**9 Wholesaling** 89
Types of wholesaler. Services provided by the wholesaler. Is the wholesaler necessary? Bypassing the wholesaler.

**10 Money and Finance** 95
The importance of money. The Bank of England. Specialist financial institutions. Commercial banks. Types of bank account. Cheques. The credit transfer (giro credit) system. Direct debiting. Other banking services. Building societies.

**11 Communications** 115
The importance of communications. The Post Office. British Telecommunications PLC. Mercury Communications Ltd.

**12 Transport** 128
The importance of transport. Factors affecting the choice of transport. Road. Rail. Sea. Inland waterways. Air. Pipelines. Containerisation. The Channel Tunnel.

**13 Insurance** 138
The statistical basis of insurance. Principles of insurance. Personal insurance. Insurance for business. Organisation of British insurance. Lloyds of London. Insurance and the economy.

**14 Advertising** 149
Types of advertising. Arguments for advertising. Arguments against advertising. Advertising media. Control of advertising.

**15 Consumer Protection** 158
Principles of consumer law. Consumer legislation. Consumer organisations.

**16 Overseas Trade** 167
The advantages of foreign trade. Protectionism. The Balance of Payments. Difficulties facing exporters. Assistance for exporters. Financing of international trade. Britain and the European Community.

| | |
|---|---|
| **Commercial Abbreviations** | 184 |
| **Glossary of Commercial Terms** | 189 |
| **Multiple-choice Test** | 200 |
| **Answers to Multiple-choice Test** | 207 |
| **Examination Questions** | 208 |
| **Sources of Information** | 241 |
| **Index** | 245 |

# Acknowledgements

I would like to thank the following organisations for providing information and material for the book:

Advertising Standards Authority; Asda PLC; Association of British Insurers; Bank of England; Banking Information Service; Bradford City Council; Bradford *Telegraph and Argus*; British Standards Institute; Building Societies Association; Consumers Association; Co-operative Development Agency; Co-operative Wholesale Society; European Community Information Office; HM Treasury; Lloyds Bank; Mercury Communications Ltd.; Next PLC; Post Office; Stock Exchange; *Trader*; West Yorkshire Trading Standards Department; *Yorkshire Post*.

# Preface to the Second Edition

The aim of this book is to provide the reader with a general picture of the business world, particularly in the United Kingdom. It is a useful summary of the commercial system for students sitting introductory RSA, BTEC and GCSE examinations. It is also recommended as preliminary reading for students at GCE 'A' and BTEC National level.

The book starts with a short survey of the British economic system and then deals with the different forms of business organisation in the private and public sectors. It then describes the major 'aids to trade' such as banking, advertising and transport.

Since the original edition of this book was published, there have been tremendous changes in business and commerce in Britain. The text has been substantially revised to cover these changes, and new examination questions, particularly for GCSE, have been included. The rapid pace of change in the economy means that the student must always attempt to keep his or her knowledge up to date. A list of addresses of organisations providing suitable material can be found at the end of book.

I am grateful to the late Ronald Warson, author of the first edition, for creating the structure and much of the material in the book. Any errors or omissions in this new edition are, however, my responsibility.

# 1
# Introduction to the Economic System

...h the study of trade and the aids to
...vhich provide goods and services, and
...nd its agencies in making such produc-
...and producers rely upon commercial
...banking, communications, transport,

...g goods from the manufacturer to the
...*etailing* (Chapter 8) and *wholesaling*
...ticated systems for storing goods and
...would be impossible for firms to find

... 10) is one of the UK's fastest growing
...institutions provide loans and other
...sses to function and invest in future
...mers to purchase goods and services.
... 11), in both written and electronic
...and sell their goods efficiently and
cheaply. They also provide services for people, enabling them to
keep in touch with family and friends over long distances.

*Transport* (Chapter 12) is linked with distribution because it is
necessary to have efficient means for physically moving goods.
Good transport links are also needed for people and documents
such as letters and contracts.

*Insurance* (Chapter 13) allows risks to be taken without fear of

loss. People and firms can protect themselves financially against disasters such as fire or burglary. Without adequate insurance, many enterprises would be too risky to undertake.

*Advertising* (Chapter 14) enables firms to let potential customers know what they have to offer. It covers many forms from hand-distributed leaflets to sophisticated television campaigns.

# The economic system

Any economic system has to solve the problem of scarce resources. 'Scarce' in this context means that all resources such as land, raw materials, labour and machinery are limited in supply. On the other hand, the uses to which such resources can be put are unlimited.

For example, a plot of land might be used for farming, car-parking, playing-fields, a factory site or simply unused open space. However, using it for one purpose prevents its use for any other. A decision has to be made about which of the alternative choices is best.

Any economy, however it is governed, has to make such decisions about how resources are to be used. There are three basic decisions to be made:

1 *What is to be produced?* For example, should there be more soldiers and fewer nurses? Should more goods be transported by road rather than rail?
2 *How is it to be produced?* Should electricity be produced by nuclear rather than coal-fired power stations? Should machinery replace labour in a particular manufacturing process?
3 *How is it to be distributed?* Who gets the goods and services? (Note that 'distribution' used in this way means something different from its commercial definition.)

Depending upon the particular type of economy, these decisions may be made by private individuals, the Government, or a combination of the two. Economies are often divided into three types, which vary according to who makes these decisions. Figure 1.1 illustrates the three types.

### The free-market economy
In a free-market economy, decisions about production are made by private individuals and firms. The Government interferes as little as

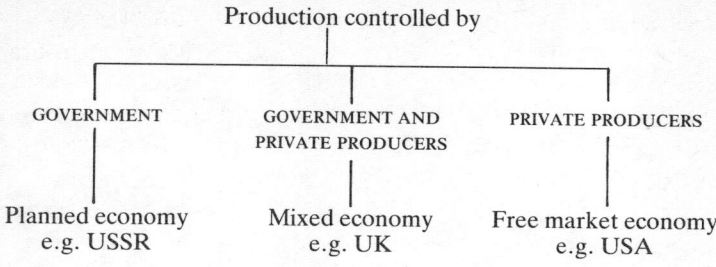

**Fig. 1.1** The three types of economy

possible in business affairs, providing only those services such as defence and the legal structure which are necessary to protect the country's citizens. This policy is sometimes called *laissez-faire* meaning 'let be'.

The basic principle of the free-market economy is that production is based upon free enterprise. People and firms produce goods and services in order to make money. Firms are continually attempting to make as much profit as possible. They can only achieve this by producing goods and services that their customers want, and by producing as cheaply and efficiently as possible.

Prices are the mechanism by which a free-market system works. The price of a good or service depends upon its *demand* (the amount that consumers wish to buy) and its *supply* (the amount that producers are willing to sell). Demand and supply are constantly changing, and this affects prices and amounts produced.

In a free-market economy, the consumer decides what is to be produced by buying goods and services. Businesses which satisfy consumer wants will be profitable – those which don't will not survive. Even those industries which manufacture *producer goods* depend upon consumer tastes. For example, a fall in the demand for beer will also lead to a fall in the demand for brewing equipment.

The supporters of free enterprise make several arguments for the non-intervention of Government in business affairs:

(a) Producers have to satisfy the consumer in order to make a profit.
(b) Free enterprise encourages efficient production because firms

have an incentive to cut costs and produce good quality goods and services.
*(c)* Initiative and effort are encouraged because people have the incentive of making money.
*(d)* There is minimal Government intervention in the economy, which leads to more freedom for people to make their own decisions.

The free-market system can have disadvantages, however:

*(a)* The demand for products depends upon people's ability to pay for them. Poorer people may not be able to afford essential goods and services, and resources may be allocated to the luxuries demanded by the rich.
*(b)* Some public services such as universal education would not be provided.
*(c)* Monopolies may occur which exploit consumers.
*(d)* Private producers may ignore the bad effects of their activities such as pollution and traffic congestion if they are allowed complete freedom.

**The planned economy**
A planned or *command* economy is one where decisions about production are taken by the Government, usually through a central planning department such as Gosplan in the Soviet Union. The Government sets out plans for the economy, usually for several years ahead. The plans set targets for production of different goods and services, prices, wages and other variables.

Centrally-planned economies are generally associated with Communist governments, which believe in state control of the economy in order to organise production for everybody's benefit rather than for private profit. However, during wartime many non-Communist governments take control of production. During the Second World War the British Government directed labour and factories to military use.

Planning a modern economy is a very complex process. To take a simple example, suppose the Government wants to produce a particular number of tractors over the next few years. In order to do this it will have to ensure that sufficient labour, steel, machinery and equipment are available to achieve this production. This involves issuing orders for production of steel, coal, tractor components and so on.

Taking this a stage further, the coal industry will have to plan for extra production, which will require inputs of labour, machinery and other resources. Every decision about what to produce in turn means that other adjustments have to be made by the central planners. This is a massive task, too big for even the most sophisticated computer.

Several advantages are claimed for the centrally-planned economy:

*(a)* The Government can plan for the production of essential goods and services.
*(b)* Central planners can take into account social costs such as pollution which might be ignored by private producers.
*(c)* The Government can aim to make the distribution of income more equal.

Opponents of central planning point to several possible disadvantages:

*(a)* Planning a large economy is very complicated, and it is impossible to do it without making mistakes. Changes in demand or production problems often lead to shortages and surpluses.
*(b)* A large and expensive bureaucracy is needed to make and carry through the Government's plans.
*(c)* Because there is no private profit, there may be little incentive for people and firms to work hard or develop new products.
*(d)* If prices are fixed in advance, the advantages of the price system as a signal to producers are lost.

These problems have caused severe difficulties for centrally-planned economies such as the Soviet Union and China. During the 1980s, these countries have gradually loosened the central control of the economy, allowing more private enterprise.

**The mixed economy**
A mixed economy is one in which production is controlled by both the Government and private producers. A good example is the United Kingdom. To some extent, all economies are mixed economies, since none is completely dominated by private or

Government production, but the term is usually applied to countries where there is substantial production by both sectors.

In the UK, private firms account for the largest share of production, but the Government intervenes in the economy in several ways:

1  The *public sector* (central and local Government and nationalised industries) produces many goods and services. Some of these, such as coal and steel, are sold commercially at or near their full cost. Others, such as education and health services, are provided 'free' to users, although they are of course paid for by the taxpayer (it is estimated that the National Health Service costs the average British family £30 per week in taxes). The role of public sector production is examined in Chapter 5.

2  The Government influences spending on particular goods and services through its taxation and spending policies. It may discourage consumption through heavy taxes such as those on alcohol and cigarettes. Other goods and services are exempted from tax, for example food, or subsidised directly or through tax reliefs, for example house purchase. Many goods and services are licensed, such as guns and drugs, or can only be provided by qualified people, such as legal representation and medical care.

3  Through social services such as social security, health care and education, the Government attempts to eliminate poverty and guarantee a minimum standard of living to all citizens. These services are often called the *Welfare State*, which has been described as the care of people 'from the cradle to the grave'.

4  The Government regulates the economy in various ways, for example by influencing factors such as interest rates, investment and the location of industry. Although political parties have different priorities and policies, they share basic aims such as the reducing of inflation and unemployment, and the growth of the economy and living standards.

5  Workers are protected by various Acts of Parliament which stipulate hours of work, minimum wages for some jobs, health and safety procedures and workers' rights such as maternity leave and redundancy pay.

6 There are many laws which protect consumers when they buy goods and services. These include rules about weights and measures, quality of food and safety of goods. Consumer protection is discussed in Chapter 15.

## Industry and commerce

Many people use the term 'industry' to mean what should more accurately be described as 'manufacturing'. However, industry includes the production of services as well as that of goods. The driver who transports a radio to the shop and the assistant who sells it are helping as much towards the satisfaction of a need as the factory employee who assembles it.

Production can be classified as *primary*, *secondary*, and *tertiary* industries. Figure 1.2 shows the major industries in the UK.

*Primary* or *extractive* industries are those which produce food and raw materials. They include agriculture, mining, forestry and fishing.

| Main sectors of economic activity | Employees '000 (Dec. 1986) | Volume change in output % pa (1976–85) | % share of gdp at current factor cost (1985) |
|---|---|---|---|
| Agriculture, forestry, fishing | 313 | 3.6 | 1.8 |
| Energy and water supply | 514 | 8.2 | 11.3 |
| Manufacturing | 5,153 | −0.1 | 25.4 |
| Construction | 1,007 | 0.0 | 6.2 |
| Distribution, hotels and catering | 4,319 | 1.4 | 13.4 |
| Transport and communications | 1,399 | 0.8 | 6.9 |
| Financial services | 2,166 | 6.5 | 14.1 |
| Ownership of dwellings | 120 | 1.5 | 5.9 |
| Education and health | 2,942 | 1.6 | 8.7 |
| Public administration | 1,599 | 0.0 | 7.1 |
| Other services | 1,798 | 3.2 | 6.0 |
| Adjustment and residual | — | — | −6.8 |
| Gdp at factor cost | 21,270 | 1.9 | 100.0 |

**Fig. 1.2** Major UK industries – employment and output

*Secondary* or *manufacturing* industries are involved in producing goods, such as televisions and cars. The construction trades (building and civil engineering) are included in this category.

*Tertiary* industries are those producing services. They may be *commercial services*, such as banking and retailing, which are used to assist the manufacture and distribution of goods. These are the *aids to trade*. Other services such as education and entertainment are *direct services* which are enjoyed for their own sake. They are sometimes described as *quaternary* production.

As an economy becomes more developed, the proportion of production and employment tends to shift away from primary and secondary production towards the tertiary sector. In the seventeenth century, over 80 percent of British workers were employed in agriculture. During the Industrial Revolution the emphasis moved away from agriculture to manufacturing industry such as textiles.

In the twentieth century there has been a further shift from manufacturing to service industries such as tourism and banking. Agriculture now provides only 3 percent of employment, and over 60 percent of workers are involved in producing services. This type of change is normal for an industrial economy and has also occurred in the USA and Western Europe.

# 2
# Private Sector Firms – Legal Structure

A private sector firm is one which is not owned by the Government. The other feature which distinguishes it from public sector firms such as the nationalised industries is that its main objective is to make profits for its owners. Whilst some nationalised industries do make profits, they may also have other aims such as providing services to rural areas.

Leaving aside *co-operatives*, which are dealt with in a separate section in this chapter, there are four types of legal structure for privately-owned business:

1 Sole trader
2 Partnership
3 Private limited company (Ltd)
4 Public limited company (PLC)

Generally, this order reflects the usual size of the types of business in terms of turnover. Sole traders are usually small businesses and public limited companies are invariably large firms, including household names such as Boots, National Westminster and Amstrad. There are, however, exceptions to this rule of thumb – for example, some partnerships in accountancy and law are bigger businesses than many private limited companies.

## Limited liability
There are various differences between the four types of firm, but one of the most crucial is that private and public limited companies have *limited liability*. This means that if the firm goes bankrupt, the

owners of the company can only lose the money that they have paid for shares.

Sole traders and partnerships do not have limited liability. If the business cannot pay its debts, the owners have to pay them out of their own pockets. They may have to sell their house and other personal possessions to pay the business's creditors.

The importance of limited liability is that people can put money into a firm by buying shares, without risking the loss of all their money if the company fails. If limited liability did not exist, people would be less willing to risk investing in firms. This would make it extremely difficult to raise money for large-scale projects.

## Sole trader

The sole trader (sometimes called *sole proprietor*) is a business owned by one person. This type of business is usually small, and is common in industries such as farming, hairdressing, window cleaning and retailing. It is most common where personal service is important, and where little capital is needed for machinery and equipment.

As well as owning the business, the sole trader controls it and receives the profits. The owner is also responsible for all of the firm's debts. Capital is usually obtained from personal savings, borrowing and putting profit back into the business.

An important feature of this type of organisation is that the business is not a separate legal entity, even if it trades under a title such as 'West Street Stores' or 'Best Books'. Under the Companies Act 1981, a sole trader using such a title must also display the name and address of the owner on its premises and stationery. Although it is not now compulsory to register a business name, titles which include terms such as 'British' or 'Royal' are not allowed. Whatever title is used, the owner is the business for legal, financial and tax purposes.

Advantages of the sole trader:

1. The business is easy to set up. Apart from any necessary licences or planning permission, there are very few legal formalities. Although accounts will be inspected by tax authorities, they do not have to be made public, unlike those of limited companies.

2  The firm is usually small, and the owner manages the day-to-day business. Decisions can be made quickly.
3  Because the owner gets all of the profit from the business, there is an incentive to work hard.
4  Being small, the firm can provide personal attention for its customers.

Disadvantages of the sole trader:

1  Prices may be higher. The business is usually too small to get the benefits of large-scale production. However, if overhead expenses are kept down, for example by using the owner's home as premises, a sole trader may be able to keep prices low.
2  The business may find it difficult to raise finance to expand.
3  The sole trader has unlimited liability, and is personally responsible for the business's debts. He or she may have to risk home and savings to start the business.
4  The business depends very heavily upon the owner's ability. He or she may be good at some parts of running the business, but poor at others. For example, a person may be very capable at a craft such as bricklaying or pottery, but find it difficult to cope with accounts or staff when given responsibility for an entire business. If the owner is ill, the business may have difficulty in continuing.
5  Sole traders often have to work very long hours, particularly when setting up a business.

## Partnership

To avoid some of the disadvantages of the sole trader, a partnership may be formed. This is merely an association of two or more persons 'carrying on a business in common with a view to profit' (Partnership Act 1890). This definition excludes non-profit-making organisations such as youth and sports clubs.

The maximum number of partners is normally twenty, but some partnerships such as solicitors and accountants can now exceed this limit (these are usually professions where members are not allowed to form limited companies). It is likely that in the future the Department of Trade and Industry will allow more exceptions, and that formation of limited companies (called *incorporation*) will be allowed in such professions. For example, since 1986 companies have been allowed to be members of the Stock Exchange.

Setting up a partnership can be fairly simple. It is possible to establish a partnership without any legal formalities, although this is often inadvisable. If there is no legal agreement, the provisions of the Partnership Act 1890 apply. These are basically that profits and losses are shared equally, all partners have an equal say in the running of the business, and all must agree before new partners can be admitted.

If a Partnership Deed or Agreement is drawn up it is likely to cover matters such as:

*(a)* The amount of capital to be contributed by each partner.
*(b)* The proportion in which profits and losses are to be shared.
*(c)* The management responsibilities of each partner.
*(d)* The maximum drawings of cash for personal use by each partner.
*(e)* Provisions for introducing new partners and the ending of the partnership.

The Partnership Agreement may stipulate that some partners receive a larger share of the profits than others. This need not necessarily be in proportion to the amount of capital invested in the partnership. A partner who invests 30 percent of the capital may receive 50 percent of the profits if he or she is giving more time or has more ability than other partners. As an alternative arrangement, partners may be allowed a fixed salary in addition to their share of the profits.

Even if there is a Partnership Agreement, there may be cases of dispute which are not properly covered by the Agreement. In these cases, the dispute will be settled by reference to the provisions of the Partnership Act.

Partnerships are not allowed to sell shares in the same way as limited companies, although new partners or *limited partners* may contribute capital. Capital tends to come from partners' personal savings, borrowing and retained profit.

Advantages of partnerships:

1   Compared to a sole trader, there are more people to put money into the business.

2 A partnership can include people with different skills. For example, a building partnership may include a surveyor, accountant and architect, each specialising in their own trade.
3 Partnerships are fairly easy to set up, with few legal formalities. As with sole traders, accounts do not have to be made public.
4 Partners are generally involved in the day-to-day running of the business, and have an incentive to see that it works efficiently.
5 Small partnerships can provide personal service.

Disadvantages of partnerships:

1 The business is usually too small for large-scale production, although there are exceptions to this.
2 The partners have unlimited liability (except for *limited partners*).
3 Because there are more people involved in management, decisions may take longer than for the sole trader.
4 Small partnerships may find it difficult to raise cash for expansion.
5 Each partner is legally and financially liable for the actions of every other partner. If one partner makes a mistake or is reckless, all the others suffer.
6 Unless the Partnership Agreement is very carefully drafted, there may be problems if one of the partners leaves or dies. It is, however, possible to insure against the death of a partner, so that his or her capital can be paid out without damaging the business.

## Limited partners

The Limited Partnership Act 1907 allows for a person to put money into a partnership, but retain limited liability. This type of partner is a *limited partner* (sometimes called a *sleeping partner*, because he or she is not allowed to participate in the management of the business). There must, however, still be at least one ordinary partner with unlimited liability.

In practice, very few limited partnerships have been registered under this Act – a few thousand at most since it was passed. It is generally more satisfactory to form a limited company if limited liability is required.

## Private limited company

A private limited company issues shares and is a *joint-stock* company. It must have at least two shareholders, and since the Companies Act 1980 there has been no maximum number of shareholders. The shareholders own the company, and in smaller companies may have a significant part to play in running the business.

A proportion of the business's profits are distributed to shareholders every six or twelve months as *dividends* (see Chapter 4). The remainder will be retained by the firm to finance future investment. Private limited companies can also raise capital from borrowing, and sometimes Government grants and loans.

Private limited firms cannot appeal to the public to buy shares, and are not quoted on the Stock Exchange. New shareholders are allowed to put capital into the company, although there may be restrictions upon entry of new shareholders into the business; for example a shareholder who wishes to sell may be required to allow first option to existing shareholders.

A private limited company has limited liability, and is required to use the term 'limited' in its title (the abbreviation 'Ltd' is acceptable). Until 1981 both private and public limited companies used this term, but under European Community regulations the two types of limited company must be distinguished. Public limited companies now use the abbreviation 'PLC' in their name.

Advantages of private limited companies:

1. Limited liability makes it easier to raise capital than for an unincorporated business.
2. Many private limited companies are large enough to obtain the benefits of large-scale production.
3. As a separate legal entity, it is easier to maintain continuity despite death or retirement of shareholders.
4. They gain certain tax advantages compared to unincorporated businesses.

Disadvantages of private limited companies:

1. They have to register with the Registrar of Companies, and comply with other regulations.

2   Accounts have to be filed with Companies House, and it is therefore difficult to retain privacy.
3   Shares cannot be sold to the public or on the Stock Exchange.
4   It may be difficult for shareholders to sell their shares and get their investment back.

## Public limited company

Public limited companies are the largest of all the types. Although they number only about 1 in 40 of Britain's joint-stock companies, they include most of the well-known firms and account for a very high proportion of total production.

A public limited company (which carries the letters PLC after its name) is owned by at least two shareholders. Most, of course, have hundreds or even thousands of shareholders.

The PLC's distinguishing feature is that its shares can be issued to the public, and can be sold through the Stock Exchange if the company applies for a 'listing'. They should therefore be freely transferable, without the restrictions imposed by some private companies.

The most common way for a public limited company to be formed is for an existing private company to *go public*. This involves applying to the Stock Exchange (see Chapter 4) to be *listed* or *quoted* on the Exchange. The company will have to satisfy the Council of the Stock Exchange that it is soundly based and a reasonable investment for the public.

Public limited companies are controlled by a Board of Directors elected by the shareholders. The Board manages the running of the firm, although some members will not be heavily involved in its actual administration. The firm is obliged to hold an Annual General Meeting (AGM) to report to shareholders and elect directors. As a high proportion of many firms' shares are owned by insurance companies and pension funds, however, the influence of the small shareholder at the AGM is very seldom significant.

The profits of PLCs (after deduction of dividends) are used to finance future investment by the company. Capital may also be obtained by further share issues, borrowing (often from international banking consortia) and Government grants and loans.

Advantages of public limited companies:

1 They have limited liability.
2 They are large and can get the benefits of large-scale production.
3 They can raise large amounts of capital through share issues and borrowing. Banks and other lenders will lend at lower rates of interest to larger firms.
4 Shares are easily transferable, so shareholders can recover their investment (subject to changes in share prices).
5 They can afford specialist workers such as lawyers, accountants and personnel staff.

Disadvantages of public limited companies:

1 They are expensive to register, because the regulations before and after going public are very complicated.
2 Because of the size of the firm, there may be bureaucracy and 'red tape' with decisions taking a long time to make.
3 As a large firm, the company may seem impersonal to customers and employees. One result of this is that the larger a firm is, the more likely it is to suffer from strikes and absenteeism.
4 Many shares in PLCs are owned by people who buy them in order to make a profit (the average large shareholding is kept for less than two years). This makes PLCs vulnerable to takeovers by other firms.

## Joint-stock companies

Limited companies are sometimes called *joint-stock* companies because their shares or 'stock' is held jointly by a number of people.

Unlike the sole trader or partnership, a limited company is an *incorporated body* having a legal existence independent of its owners. Contracts can be signed in its name and it has legal rights and liabilities independent of its owners. Its owners also enjoy limited liability.

Joint-stock companies with limited liability were first allowed by the Companies Act 1855. The advent of the factory system and other large-scale enterprises such as the railways had created the need for raising large sums of money. People were naturally unwilling to risk all their possessions in such speculative ventures, but

| | No of members | Capital | Control | Profits | Liability of members | Acts of Parliament |
|---|---|---|---|---|---|---|
| SOLE TRADER | 1 owner | Provided by owner | Wholly by owner | Belong to owner | Unlimited liability for business debts | None |
| PARTNERSHIP | 2–20 with a few exceptions | Subscribed by partners in agreed proportions | Divided among partners by arrangement – partnership share only transferable by agreement | Divided equally unless agreement to the contrary | Unlimited liability – partners bear losses usually in profit-sharing ratio. Limited partnerships possible but uncommon – at least one partner must accept unlimited liability | Partnership Act 1890. Limited Partnership Act 1907 |
| PRIVATE LIMITED COMPANY (Ltd) | Minimum 2; no maximum | Public issue forbidden, but raising of additional capital now easier | Shareholders elect board of directors (minimum of 1). Right to transfer shares *may* be restricted by Articles of Association | Preference shareholders – fixed % dividend. Ordinary shareholders – variable % dividend | Shareholders have no additional liability after shareholding fully paid (small number of unlimited companies) | Companies Acts 1948/1985 |
| PUBLIC LIMITED COMPANY (PLC) | Minimum 2; no maximum | May be raised by public issue or offer for sale. Minimum capital £50 000 | Shares transferable without restriction (Stock Exchange). Shareholders elect board of directors | Preference shareholders – fixed % dividend. Ordinary shareholders – variable % dividend | Shareholders have no additional liability after shareholding fully paid | |

**Fig. 2.1** Comparison of different business units

were prepared to invest some capital when given the protection of limited liability.

The general rules for the running of joint-stock companies are laid down by various Companies Acts dating from 1844 onwards. There are also regulations laid down by Government ministers and bodies such as the Stock Exchange and the Takeovers Panel. Many of these rules are 'non-statutory' and are based upon 'gentleman's agreements' and 'codes of conduct'. In general, compared to other countries such as the USA, the supervision of business in the UK has been based upon voluntary co-operation rather than legislation and court decisions.

The purpose of these Acts and accompanying regulations is to provide safeguards for shareholders and company creditors, whilst allowing companies to be created, expand, change ownership and dissolve.

## Registration of joint-stock companies

Anyone wishing to start a limited company must submit certain documents to the Registrar of Companies, a Government department. The two most important documents are the Memorandum of Association and the Articles of Association.

A private limited company needs a Certificate of Incorporation before it can commence business, and a public limited company needs to receive a Certificate of Trading. To qualify for this, it must have sold shares up to a certain minimum. This is to ensure that the company will have sufficient capital to start trading. A public limited company must also satisfy the conditions laid down by the Council of the Stock Exchange (see Chapter 4).

**The Memorandum of Association**
This governs the firm's external relationships with other people and organisations, and provides the world at large with certain basic information about the company. It contains several items.

**1 Name Clause** A company is free to choose its own name, within certain bounds. The Department of Trade will not allow a name which is too similar to that used by an existing company, especially one in the same type of business. Names which imply royal approval or a link with famous people are not permitted; for example, 'Paul Daniels Magic Tricks Ltd' could not be used unless there was a real connection with the celebrity himself.

The title must also include the word 'limited', although exemption from this requirement may be allowed to non-trading bodies such as the Red Cross.

**2 Registered Office** It is necessary to state whether this is in England and Wales, or Scotland, as the latter has different laws.

**3 Objects Clause** This states the type of business that the company will undertake. Acting outside the stated objects is *ultra vires*, i.e. outside the powers of the company (and therefore illegal). This is to protect investors from putting their money into a company which then uses it in a different manner. It is usual to state the objects in a general way (e.g. 'general retailing' rather than 'grocery retailing'). This saves the trouble of having to change the objects, for instance if the grocery firm decided to diversify by opening off-licences.

**4 Limitation Clause** This shows whether the company is limited by shares or guarantee. All commercial companies are limited by shares, which means that people have put capital into the business. Some non-profit-making bodies, however, such as professional associations, are limited by guarantee. This means that they are responsible for the organisation's debts up to a fixed amount (often £1).

**5 Capital Clause** This gives details of the proposed amount of share capital and the different categories of shares.

**6 Association Clause** This includes the names of the founder members and the number of shares for which each has subscribed.

**Articles of association**
These are the rules governing the internal affairs of a company – voting rights of shareholders, election of directors, conduct of general meetings of shareholders, etc. The Companies Acts contain a set of model rules which can be used, or the founders of the company can draw up their own special articles.

## Co-operatives

Co-operatives are private sector businesses in the same way as sole traders, partnerships and joint-stock companies. They are less common in Britain than in some other countries, but it has been estimated that in 1986 there were 1500 co-ops employing 14 000 workers.

In the UK, there is no legal definition of a co-operative, but the Co-operative Development Agency (CDA) suggests certain features which distinguish them from other types of firm:

---

**Producer co-ops.** Agricultural, horticultural and fishery co-ops are linked through Food from Britain.

**Consumer co-ops**: the popular retail societies with membership open to all shoppers, which with their associated Wholesale, Insurance and Banking organisations are co-ordinated by the Co-operative Union.

**Credit Unions** which are self-help savings and loan co-operatives formed by groups of members with a common bond. They are promoted by the Association of British Credit Unions.

**Housing co-operatives**, of tenants that maintain and manage communal property. They are linked through the National Federation of Housing Co-operatives. More and more councils are encouraging housing co-operatives because members care about the environment in which they live, the upkeep of their homes, and the surroundings.

**Community co-operative** businesses sponsored by all aspects of community life to provide local services and create local jobs.

**Worker co-ops**, where ultimate ownership and control rests with the people who work in the business.

**Equity Participation Co-operatives (EPCs)** through which the employees of a company participate in or even control the running of the business but can also attract and use outside finance.

**Marketing, Service and Secondary co-ops**, designed to bring together co-operatives, small businesses and individuals, to provide themselves with a level of services and marketing which they would be unable to afford individually.

---

Fig. 2.2  Types of co-operative

*(a)* Each member has one vote, whatever the work or capital that he or she puts into the co-op.
*(b)* Shares do not alter in value.
*(c)* Any profits made belong to the members. After some have been held back for investment, the rest are distributed to members in some previously agreed way.
*(d)* The business should have limited liability.

The CDA lists several types of co-operative (see Fig. 2.2). *Retail* co-operatives are discussed in Chapter 8. *Producer* co-operatives involve a central organisation such as the Milk Marketing Board buying and selling products on behalf of its members. In the UK these are very common in agriculture.

*Worker* co-operatives, in which workers own the business in which they are employed, are very common in some European countries (notably the Mondragon co-operatives in Spain). In Britain they are a comparatively small proportion of businesses (less than 1 percent), although their number has increased rapidly during the 1980s. Amongst the benefits claimed for worker co-ops are:

*(a)* There is no conflict between the owners of a business and its workers, because they are the same people.
*(b)* Workers have an incentive to work hard and contribute to the business.
*(c)* Because of the motivation and sense of ownership generated in worker co-ops, the quality of goods and services is generally higher.

Co-operatives have had some problems, however. They may find it difficult to raise finance, and their managers often have little experience of running a business.

# 3

# Private Sector Firms – Organisation of Production

## Internal organisation of a typical business

As can be seen from Chapter 2, private firms are of different types and sizes, from sole traders with one owner-worker to multinational companies with thousands of employees. However, whatever the size of the firm, there have to be procedures for making decisions about production and location.

Any well-managed organisation must operate within a framework. This includes arrangement of staffing and allocation of duties. If properly run, all the parts of the enterprise will work together. Important considerations are:

1   The need for good communication both within the firm and with the outside world. The importance of this can be illustrated by considering the prime function of the 'office' within a business as the place where information is received, recorded, sorted or re-arranged, acted upon, filed and passed on.

A simple example is a complaint received by telephone. The information will be received verbally, rearranged on a memo pad to make it easier to deal with and linked with other information (e.g. a copy of an order). A copy of the memo will be retained in a complaints file, with the original being passed to the relevant department for action.

The complaint will then be dealt with according to a procedure laid down by the management – it will involve contacting the customer for example. If necessary the problem will be notified to other departments to ensure that it is not repeated.

Even if the business is a small one, and the owner takes care of all this work personally, the basic procedures of recording and acting are the same.

2 The business must have the services of specialists such as accountants and solicitors. Large firms may well have their own specialist staff working full-time – small businesses will pay for advice when they need it.

3 The degree of central control is important. For example, in some retailing chains individual store managers may have little power, in others they may have the authority to make important decisions quickly.

4 The span of control, i.e. the number of staff over whom each manager or supervisor has immediate and direct control. There is no ideal figure for this – between five and fifteen is considered appropriate in many organisations.

**Organisation charts** In a small business with just a few employees, everybody knows his or her role and there is usually direct contact between the employer and staff. A formal written structure is not needed. However, as a business grows larger the need for a formal framework tends to emerge. Many organisations draw up charts showing those in authority and the people under their supervision.

Figure 3.1 illustrates an organisation chart which might be used for the head office of a large group retailing electrical and other household goods through a chain of High Street branches. There is a central warehouse at the head office and four area distribution depots each supplying a number of shops. Ordering is carried out from head office (an example of centralised management). The firm is carrying out the wholesaling function (see Chapter 9) itself.

The head office departments in this example are controlled by:

*The Company Secretary*, who has responsibility for administrative work in connection with shareholders, directors, company meetings and legal duties imposed by various Acts of Parliament. The Secretary also deals with the legal aspects of business functions connected with matters such as properties, insurance and contracts.

*The Chief Accountant*, who is responsible for all accounting operations. One Deputy Accountant looks after finance, auditing and

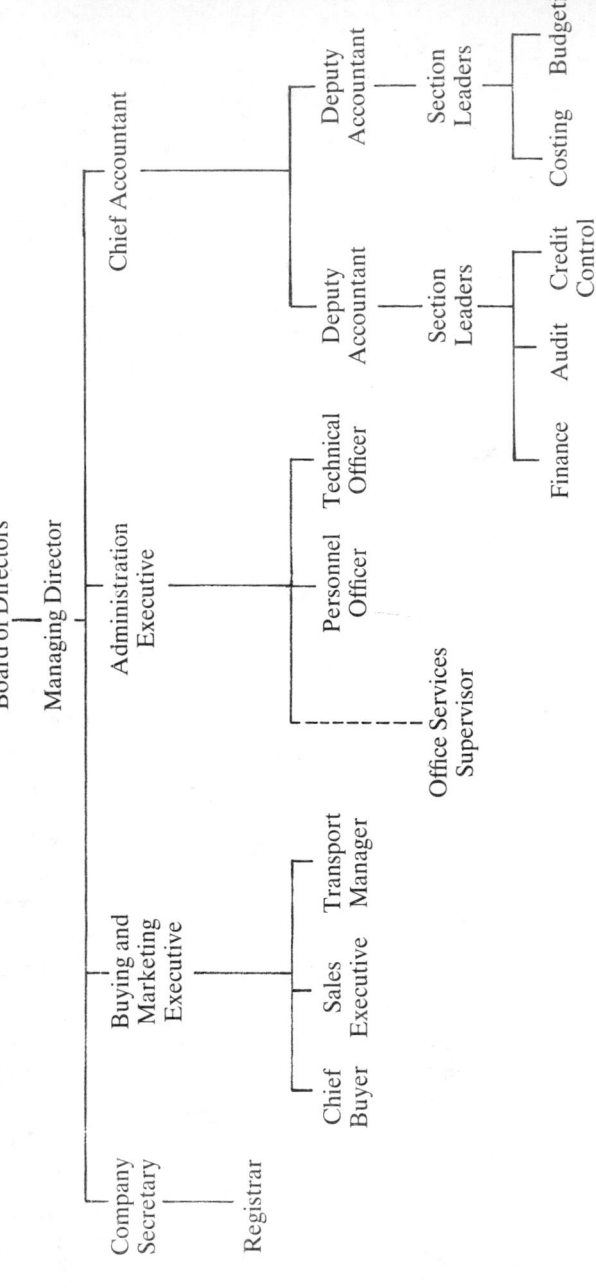

**Fig. 3.1** Organisation chart

credit control. The other Deputy Accountant deals with costing, estimating and budgeting. There are section leaders with responsibility for each of the functions of the Deputy Accountants.

*The Administration Executive* is in charge of the Personnel Office and general services such as the mail room, reception, security and buildings. He or she has two deputies, the Personnel Officer and the Technical Officer. An Office Services Supervisor is in charge of general office services such as the switchboard and mail room.

*The Buying and Marketing Executive* has responsibility for buying, selling, warehousing, transport operations, advertising and research.

Obviously, this is only an example, and many large firms would have completely different structures – for example the Personnel Officer might be a director. However, the principles of specialisation in different functions and of lines of management are similar for most big companies.

## The size of firms

Firms in Britain come in many different sizes – even within a single industry there may be firms ranging from one-man (or one-woman) businesses to huge multinationals. In some industries there are many firms; in others a few large firms dominate the market.

Large firms have many advantages over small firms. These are referred to as *economies of scale*. They can allocate their workers to very specialised functions, as in a car assembly line. Their size allows them to buy specialised machinery and equipment such as oil-rigs or mainframe computers. In some industries such as drugs and aeroplanes, millions of pounds have to be spent researching and developing a product before even one item can be sold.

As well as these technical advantages, large firms benefit from their size when buying and selling. They can buy in large quantities, obtaining lower prices and better credit and delivery terms. They can afford extensive advertising and often have their own outlets for their products; for example, most oil companies own petrol stations.

Some large firms are 'holding companies' which own shares in many different businesses. For example, the Granada organisation currently has interests including television and radio stations, TV rental, newspapers, motorway service stations and other leisure activities.

Because of these advantages, it is usually possible for large firms to cut costs and produce more cheaply than their smaller rivals. This is particularly true in industries such as car manufacture and chemicals.

In some cases, however, size may have disadvantages (called *diseconomies of scale*). They may have very high overheads and waste time and effort with excessive paperwork as communications within the business become more complicated. Also, the larger the firm the higher is the likelihood of labour problems such as strikes and absenteeism.

Despite their inability to benefit from economies of scale, many small firms are very successful. There are a number of reasons for this. Small firms do particularly well in industries where specialised labour and personal service are important, for instance, garages, hairdressing and accountancy. Many such types of production do not require large-scale investment in buildings or equipment. Small firms often sell goods or services to larger firms, who find it easier to buy in supplies rather than produce themselves.

There are also personal reasons for the large number of small businesses. People wish to become their own boss by starting a business, and many owners are happy to run a small concern without the effort and worry involved in expansion. Other changes in the economy such as Government assistance and the formation of co-operatives (Chapter 2) help to maintain the existence of small businesses.

## Location of industry

The choice of location for a firm or industry can be affected by many factors. It has been estimated that about half of British firms are *footloose* because they could locate in almost any part of the country without significantly affecting their costs of production. However, there are a number of factors which have determined the location of particular industries in the past – some of which are still important today.

## Raw materials

Primary industries such as mining obviously have to be located at the source of supply. In the past, industries which rely upon particular materials tended to locate near to natural resources; for example, Sheffield became a major iron and steel-making area because it was convenient for coal-fields, iron-ore deposits and limestone quarries.

When the metal industries expanded during the Industrial Revolution, transport was still very primitive and it made sense to manufacture iron and steel near to raw material supplies. Nowadays most iron ore is imported, and the location of large steelworks has shifted to coastal areas such as Port Talbot and Redcar.

## Power

Early industries requiring power for machinery were set up near fast-flowing water. With the coming of steam power, access to coal was more important. Most areas of Britain now have plentiful supplies of power, which is not such a crucial feature as it used to be.

## Transport

It has always been important to get raw materials into the factory, and transport them out. Many towns have grown rapidly around a railway line, motorway or airport (e.g. Swindon, Warrington and Crawley respectively). Good transport links are still stressed by towns trying to attract industry.

## Nearness to markets

Until comparatively recently, many industries were forced to be near their main markets (e.g. market gardens in Warwickshire served Birmingham). This was particularly important for heavy low-value goods such as beer and bricks. Similarly, suppliers of components for the car industry were located in the Midlands near to the major manufacturers.

Because of improved transport this factor is no longer as crucial for firms producing goods, but it is vital for service industries such as retailing and banking, which have to be convenient for their customers.

## Climate and landscape

This is vital for producers of food and drink, who need particular

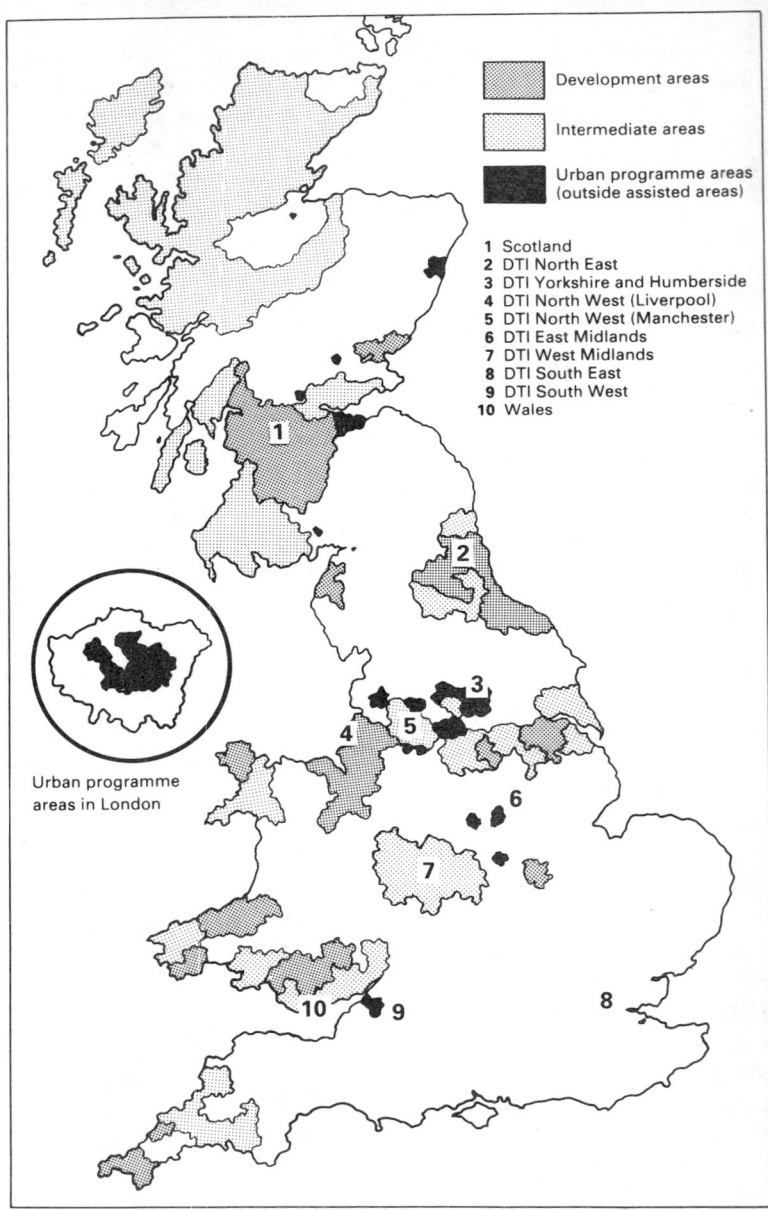

**Fig. 3.2** Assisted Areas in 1988

combinations of soil and weather. It was one of the reasons for the cotton industry's location in Lancashire, where the damp climate kept threads moist so that they did not become brittle and snap.

With new technology and production methods, climate and landscape are less important for many producers, but they still affect industries such as tourism.

**Labour force**
Many areas have a ready supply of labour with particular skills, such as engineering in the West Midlands, financial analysts in the City of London. It may also be possible for a firm which is new to an area to adapt existing skills from another industry. For example, the precise techniques involved in textile manufacture are also suitable for assembling electronic goods.

**Government influence**
The Government will often give grants, cheap loans and tax reliefs to firms locating in areas of high unemployment such as Merseyside or Northern Ireland. This type of *regional policy* has been run down in the last decade, but firms are still given incentives to set up in certain areas, shown in Figure 3.2.

**Industrial inertia**
This is the tendency of industries to remain in a particular area after the original advantages have disappeared. For example, the pottery industry grew in North Staffordshire because of deposits of china-clay in that area. These ran out many years ago, but the firms have remained because of tradition. A more recent example is that of financial services. With the introduction of computerised dealing there is little reason for many stockbrokers or financial institutions to pay high wages and rents in London, but there has not yet been significant movement away from the capital.

**Economies of concentration**
Some areas contain concentrations of particular industries, such as textiles in West Yorkshire, electronics in Berkshire. Once an industry becomes established in an area, firms there gain many advantages such as skilled workforce, local school and college courses and a reputation for a particular product.

# 4
# Private Sector Firms – Finance

## Why firms need capital

All firms need capital to stay in business. As well as money for running costs such as wages, materials and rent, they need to have financial reserves. Extra capital may be needed to expand, by buying new premises or developing new products. Firms may also need working capital to preserve cash-flow through the business, for instance if there is a time-lag between producing goods and services and getting paid for them.

There are four main ways of obtaining capital. In order of the amounts raised by British firms they are:

1. Retained profit
2. Borrowing
3. Share issues
4. Government grants and loans

### Retained profit

This is by far the most importance source of capital for firms, accounting for over two-thirds of the total. For smaller businesses it may be the only source of capital. Retained profit is also referred to as *ploughed-back profit*, *internal finance* or *undistributed profit*.

When the business assesses its profits at the end of the financial period (usually every 6 or 12 months), it will divide it in three ways, as shown in Figure 4.1.

An *incorporated* firm will pay corporation tax to the Government, assuming that the profits are more than the tax-free allow-

```
                                          Corporation
Retained        ┌─────────┐              tax
profit          │ PROFIT  │
                └─────────┘              Shareholders'
                                          dividends
```

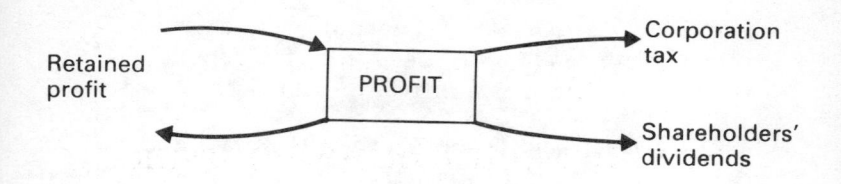

**Fig. 4.1** Allocation of profit by a public limited company

ance. Sole traders and partnerships will pay income tax on the proceeds. Part of the profit will be paid as dividends or personal income to the owners. The remainder will be put back into the business for future capital. A more detailed example is given later in this chapter.

**Borrowing**

Borrowing money usually accounts for 20–30 percent of firms' capital. There are several different types of lender to business.

**1 Commercial banks** These are the major High Street banks such as Barclays and Midland, who lend to firms of many different types and sizes. They offer two major types of loans to firms;

a) *Overdraft* This allows the firm to spend more than it has in its account, up to an agreed limit. The period of the overdraft may be fixed, but is often continued indefinitely. This is the cheapest form of borrowing, as the bank only charges interest upon the actual sum owing on a daily basis.

Overdrafts are suitable in cases where a business wants money to cover a temporary deficit (such as a retailer stocking up for a peak sale-time or a manufacturer supplying goods on credit). However, an overdraft is an insecure form of borrowing from the business's point of view, since the bank can insist upon immediate full repayment at any time.

b) *Fixed-term loan* This is more suitable for a business wishing to invest in fixed assets such as premises or machinery. A fixed amount is borrowed and paid back in instalments over a definite period (or sometimes in a lump sum at the end of the repayment period).

Apart from these basic loans, banks are continually developing new schemes for lending to firms, often specially designed for particular types of business such as farms or franchises.

**2 Specialist banks and finance houses** There are a number of banks and other institutions which specialise in lending to commercial borrowers. A well-known example is Investors in Industry (3i). These institutions are often involved in leasing arrangements.

**3 International banks and consortia** Large public limited companies may need to borrow millions of pounds for investment in projects such as the Channel Tunnel. No single bank would be willing to risk lending all of this money, so an international bank such as Chase Manhattan or Barclays International will arrange for a number of lenders to share the loan and risks. An example of a consortium loan arrangement is shown in Figure 4.2.

**4 Leasing** If a firm needs expensive equipment or vehicles it may consider leasing them through a bank or finance house. The leasing house buys the equipment and hires it out to the user over an agreed period. In effect, leasing is a form of borrowing money.

Leasing has some advantages over outright purchase of equipment. The firm does not have to commit large amounts of capital, there are tax reliefs and the leasing house is responsible for repairs and maintenance (this is usually done through an agent, e.g. a car manufacturer for company cars).

**5 The Stock Exchange** As well as shares, public limited companies can issue *debentures* on the Stock Exchange (see below). A debenture is basically an IOU from the firm, which promises to repay it in a few years' time. Meanwhile the holder of the debenture receives interest every year. Debentures are usually secured upon the assets of the company and in effect are similar to mortgages.

Debentures are *negotiable* and can therefore be bought and sold. They are not shares, and their holders have no say in the running of the firm. However, debenture holders are entitled to preference in payment before all shareholders.

This advertisement appears as a matter of record only

# TI Group plc

# £300,000,000
# Multiple Option Facility

ARRANGED BY

**Manufacturers Hanover Limited**  **National Westminster Bank Group**

LEAD MANAGED BY

Barclays Bank PLC
Credit Suisse
Lloyds Bank Plc
Midland Bank plc

Continental Illinois National Bank and Trust Company of Chicago London Branch
International Westminster Bank PLC
Manufacturers Hanover Trust Company
The Mitsubishi Bank, Limited

MANAGED BY

The Sanwa Bank, Limited

Société Générale London Branch

CO-MANAGED BY

Algemene Bank Nederland N.V.
Banque Nationale de Paris London Branch
Canadian Imperial Bank of Commerce
Mellon Bank
The Royal Bank of Canada
Westpac Banking Corporation

Amsterdam-Rotterdam Bank N.V.
Bayerische Landesbank Girozentrale London Branch
The Fuji Bank, Limited
Rabobank Nederland London Branch
Westdeutsche Landesbank Girozentrale

ADDITIONAL TENDER PANEL MEMBERS

Banca Nazionale del Lavoro London Branch
Bankers Trust Company
Baring Brothers & Co., Limited
Credito Italiano London Branch
Den Danske Bank

Grindlays Bank plc
Philadelphia National Limited
The Toyo Trust and Banking Company, Limited

Banco di Napoli
Banque Belge Limited
Crédit Lyonnais London Branch
The Dai-Ichi Kangyo Bank, Limited
First Republic Bank Dallas, N.A. London Branch
Hambros Bank Limited
Swiss Bank Corporation
S. G. Warburg & Co. Ltd.

AGENT BANK

**International Westminister Bank PLC**

February, 1988

**Fig. 4.2** An international bank consortium loan

### Share issues

Limited companies can attract new capital by issuing shares. Private limited companies cannot advertise publicly for new shareholders, but are allowed to admit new shareholders – often from banks and finance companies. A private company also has the option of 'going public' by seeking a listing on the Stock Exchange.

Public limited companies issue two main types of shares – *preference* and *ordinary* shares. *Preference* shareholders receive their dividend before other shareholders. Their shares carry a fixed dividend rate; for example, the holder of £100 7% preference stock would receive £7 per year. Most preference shares are *cumulative*; if profits are too low to pay a dividend in one year, they get double dividends the next year. Preference shares provide a steady and safe income. They are often non-voting shares, but some companies issue *participating* preference shares which do carry a vote.

*Ordinary* shares form the majority of company shares. The rate of dividend varies from year to year, depending upon the level of profits. Ordinary shareholders only receive their dividend after the preference shareholders have been paid. However, in a good year they will usually receive a higher return than preference shareholders. Ordinary shares also generally give the holder a vote for each share held.

### Government grants and loans

The Government has a variety of schemes which give grants or cheap loans to firms for certain purposes such as investing in particular regions or types of production. For example, a large firm building a factory in an area of high unemployment might get a grant from the Government, or be exempted from paying rates or other taxes for a certain period.

## The Stock Exchange

The Stock Exchange acts as a market for both new and second-hand shares and securities. About 80 percent of its business is actually in Government securities. These work in a similar way to debentures, being bought and sold freely.

The Stock Exchange is responsible for supervising *new issues* of shares when firms become public limited companies, but most of its share transactions (30 000 a day at the end of 1987) are in existing securities. By providing a market for second-hand shares, the Stock Exchange makes it possible for investors to convert their shares into cash. Without this facility it would be more difficult for companies to persuade people to invest their money in new issues.

In December 1987 there were 3062 companies listed on the Stock Exchange. Four hundred of these were quoted only on the *Unlisted Securities Market* (USM) and the *Third Market*. These exist to allow companies which cannot satisfy the requirements for a full listing to be traded on the Exchange. The value of all listed companies in 1987 was over £1000 billion.

## The Big Bang
Until October 1986 there were two distinct types of members of the Stock Exchange. *Brokers* worked as agents for buyers and sellers, who could only trade in shares through a broker. The broker received a commission (which had a fixed minimum rate) for buying and selling shares. *Jobbers* were rather like wholesalers in shares, buying and selling on their own account, and making their living from profit (called *jobber's turn*) on their dealings.

The crucial feature of the system was '*single capacity*' which meant that a person could only be a broker or a jobber. Brokers were not allowed to deal in shares on their own behalf, and jobbers were not allowed to deal directly with the public. This was to prevent members of the Stock Exchange from advising their clients to buy shares in which the broker or jobber had a personal interest.

In October 1986 this system was completely changed by what is generally known as the 'Big Bang'. The aim of Big Bang was to make dealing in shares more competitive and efficient. The key changes were:

*(a)* All members were now allowed to operate in '*dual capacity*', trading in shares both for themselves and clients.
*(b)* Scales of minimum commission were abolished.
*(c)* 'Corporate membership' by banks and financial institutions was allowed (until then membership had been restricted to individuals who had unlimited liability).
*(d)* Protection for investors was increased, particularly through electronic recording of all transactions.

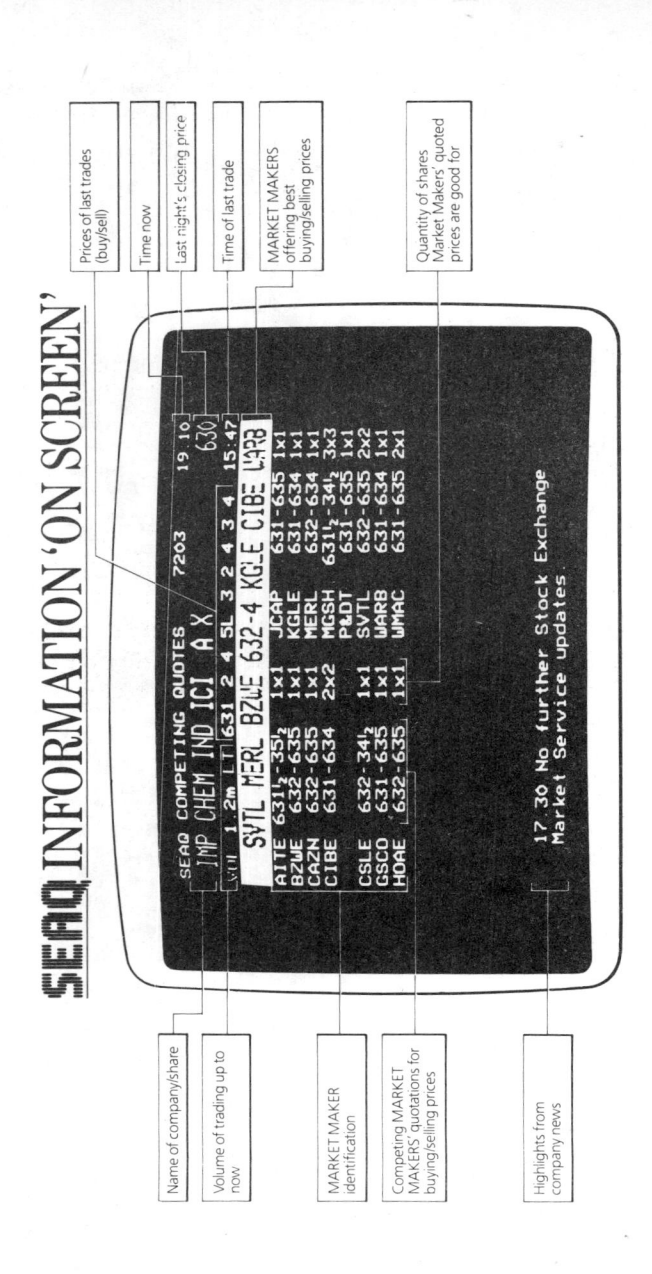

**Fig. 4.3** The SEAQ system

*(e)* A computerised dealing system called *Stock Exchange Automated Quotation* (SEAQ) system (Fig. 4.3) was introduced.

Instead of brokers and dealers, there is now only one type of Stock Exchange member – the broker/dealer. All members can deal with the public, but they must always tell the client whether they are buying or selling the shares themselves. As Figure 4.3 illustrates, the SEAQ system shows that the client has got the best price available at the time. The dealer cannot therefore sell shares to a client at a higher price than other dealers are prepared to pay.

Some members will act as *market-makers* in particular types of shares, such as oil or chemicals, rather as brokers did in the past. They are involved in buying and selling these shares on a regular basis and have a similar function to that performed by jobbers in the past.

All transactions will be recorded on SEAQ within five minutes of taking place. This means that all members have up-to-date information upon the latest prices at which a particular share is being traded. They can instantly see which market-maker is offering the best buying and selling prices (the best price is shown at the top of the screen). All deals are permanently recorded in case they need to be checked later.

## Factors affecting share prices

There are two ways of making money by buying shares. They can be sold at a higher price than is paid for them, resulting in a *capital gain* (if the price falls a *capital loss* will occur). The other way of making money is through the dividends which are paid annually or half-yearly to shareholders. The price paid depends upon a number of factors.

**The firm's profits**   The higher the firm's profit, the higher the dividend is likely to be. If a firm's profits are higher or lower than expected, the share price will also be affected. For example, one firm recently doubled its annual profits, but its share price fell because an even better performance had been expected.

**The dividend paid (or expected to be paid)**   This affects the earnings from the share and therefore the price.

# HOW SHARE BUYING WORKS:

## THE INDIVIDUAL INVESTOR

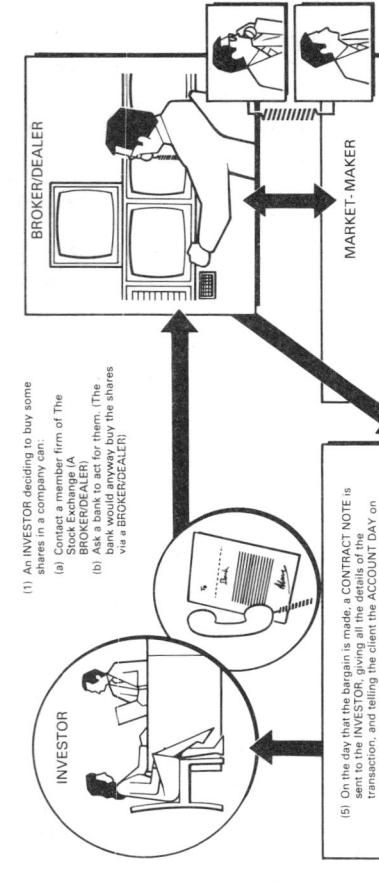

(1) An INVESTOR deciding to buy some shares in a company can:
  (a) Contact a member firm of The Stock Exchange (A BROKER/DEALER)
  (b) Ask a bank to act for them. (The bank would anyway buy the shares via a BROKER/DEALER)

(2) The BROKER/DEALER consults a SEAQ screen. SEAQ is the Stock Exchange Automated Quotation system, on which MARKET-MAKERS display their buying and selling prices to all the users of the system simultaneously. The prices are shown in pence per share.

**SEAQ**
SHARE PRICE INFORMATION CENTRE

(3) There are always at least two MARKET-MAKERS competing to quote prices for the shares of any company, and for the most active shares there can be as many as twenty competing for the business of the investing public.
The MARKET-MAKER quoting the highest price for buying the shares, or the lowest price for selling, is at the top of the SEAQ screen, so the broker can see which market-maker is offering the best price for the deal that the INVESTOR wants to make.

(4) As the INVESTOR wants to buy shares this time, the BROKER/DEALER contacts the MARKET-MAKER who is offering the cheapest price, either by telephone or on a Stock Exchange trading floor. The deal is agreed verbally, and is then reported via the SEAQ screen and recorded so that INVESTORS always know that deals have been done at the best price available at the time.

BROKER/DEALER

MARKET-MAKER

TRADING FLOOR

INVESTOR

(5) On the day that the bargain is made, a CONTRACT NOTE is sent to the INVESTOR, giving all the details of the transaction, and telling the client the ACCOUNT DAY on which payment will become due.

### COMPLETING THE PAPERWORK

- The Stock Exchange calendar divides the year into "ACCOUNTS", which are normally two weeks long. All deals done during an ACCOUNT PERIOD are put together, and paid for on the ACCOUNT DAY, which is usually six working days after the end of the Account.

- On or before the ACCOUNT DAY, the INVESTOR who has bought the shares must pay his broker for them, and the BROKER will arrange with the company involved for the change of ownership of the shares. The company then changes the name on its REGISTER OF SHAREHOLDERS, and issues a SHARE CERTIFICATE to the new owner.

- If an INVESTOR wants to sell shares instead of buy them, the process is much the same, except that by the ACCOUNT DAY the investor sends the SHARE CERTIFICATE to the BROKER, and receives the proceeds of the sale in return.

Fig. 4.4 How shares buying works

**The price of the firm's good or service**  For example, if the price of oil falls, oil companies will be expected to make lower profits, and their shares will tend to fall in value.

**Takeover bids or rumours**  If a firm is the target of a takeover bid, or is expected to be, its share price will rise because the buyer will be prepared to pay a higher price to gain control of sufficient shares. Even a rumour of a takeover can cause a rise in a share price.

**Government policies**  These affect share prices in many ways. If the Government puts up taxes on cigarettes, tobacco firms' profits and therefore their share prices will tend to fall. On the other hand Government plans to spend more on schools will push up the share prices of firms in building, school equipment and publishing.

**Wars and political events**  These may affect firms who produce in the affected countries. For example, a war in an oil-producing country would be expected to harm the profits of firms who produce or buy their oil from there. During the Falklands War, Lloyds Bank shares fell sharply because the bank had lent large sums to Argentinian borrowers.

**Expectations**  If people think that the price of shares in general, or of a particular company, is likely to fall, they will tend to sell shares, pushing the price down. Expectations of rising share prices will cause people to buy, therefore increasing the price.

## A typical share issue

Many new issues on the Stock Exchange are of companies with a successful trading record who wish to raise capital for expansion. Existing shareholders are often allocated shares in the company and given priority in purchasing extra shares up to a certain limit. Alternatively, as in the case described below, an existing public company may wish to raise capital by issuing additional shares.

Imagine that Oreco Equipment PLC, a successful office machinery manufacturer, has the following capital position (for simplicity the numbers involved are smaller than would actually be relevant to a public limited company);

|  | Nominal<br>£ | Issued<br>£ |
|---|---|---|
| 8% Cumulative Preference Shares | 400 000 | 300 000 |
| £1 Ordinary Shares | 2 000 000 | 1 200 000 |
|  |  | 1 500 000 |
| Reserves |  | 300 000 |
|  |  | £1 800 000 |

The reserves represent the portion of profits which has been 'ploughed back' into the business. The company is allowed to issue shares up to the value of £2 400 000 (*nominal* or *authorised* capital) but so far has only sold shares to the value of £1 500 000 (*issued* capital). It can therefore issue up to £900 000 worth of extra shares. A higher issue than this would require a meeting of shareholders and application to the Registrar of Companies. To avoid this eventuality, most companies submit a high share capital figure when drafting the Memorandum of Association (see Chapter 2).

Oreco wishes to raise £600 000 (£500 000 from ordinary and £100 000 from 8% preference shares). It will employ an *issuing house*, which is usually a department of a merchant or clearing bank. A prospectus is prepared which sets out details such as:

(a) The financial position of the company, e.g. profits, turnover, assets, authorised and issued capital
(b) The number and type of shares to be sold
(c) Future plans
(d) Date of share issue
(e) Application form to buy shares, with details of how shares are to be issued in the case of *oversubscription*.

It is very unlikely that the applications for shares will exactly match the amount available – the issue will either be *undersubscribed* (too few applications) or *oversubscribed* (too many). In the first case, the unsold shares will be paid for by the *underwriters*, usually a merchant bank which has agreed beforehand to take unsold shares at a particular price. If the issue is oversubscribed, shares will be allocated according to the formula described in the prospectus.

After the share issue, Oreco's capital position may be as follows:

|  | Nominal<br>£ | Issued<br>£ |
|---|---|---|
| 8% Cumulative Preference Shares | 400 000 | 400 000 |
| £1 Ordinary Shares | 2 000 000 | 1 700 000 |
|  |  | 2 100 000 |
| Reserves |  | 300 000 |
|  |  | £2 400 000 |

The company's assets have increased by £600 000, but it now has obligations to more shareholders. It will have to pay £8000 per year to new preference shareholders, and its new ordinary shareholders will also expect a dividend.

Suppose that Oreco makes a profit after tax of £267 000. The directors decide to put £65 000 back into the company and distribute the rest as dividends:

| Preference shares | 8% of £400 000 | 32 000 |
|---|---|---|
| Ordinary shares | 10% of £1 700 000 | 170 000 |
|  |  | 202 000 |
| Transferred to reserves |  | 65 000 |
|  |  | £267 000 |

The 10 percent dividend paid to ordinary shareholders is only an example – it could have been higher or lower, and in a bad year might have been nil.

A shareholder with 500 ordinary shares will therefore receive £50 (10 percent of £500). However, this does not mean that he or she has automatically received a return of 10 percent upon the investment. The 10 percent refers to the *nominal value* of the shares, i.e. the price at which they were originally sold. The shareholder might have bought the shares second-hand at a *market price* of £1.10, paying £550 in total. In this case the return would be:

$$\frac{\text{Dividend}}{\text{Price paid for shares}} \quad \frac{50}{550} \times 100 = 9\% \text{ (approx)}$$

The procedures for companies which are not already listed on the Exchange are broadly similar, but with extra checks by the Stock Exchange Council that the company is reputable and safe for the public to invest their money in.

# 5

# Public Sector Production

## The public sector

The *public sector* consists of central Government, local authorities, nationalised industries and other public authorities such as the Health and Safety Executive. It plays a very important part in the British economy, being responsible for a substantial proportion of both spending and production. As Figure 5.1 shows, Government spending has risen by three times in the last 40 years, even after allowing for inflation. However, it has not grown as rapidly as the economy as a whole.

The Government spends about 40 percent of the national income. Roughly half of this spending is upon *transfer payments* such as pensions, unemployment and child benefit, which switch spending

General government expenditure in real terms

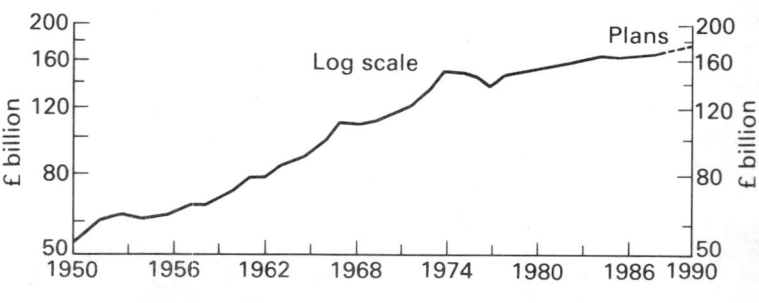

**Fig. 5.1** Government expenditure 1950–1990

## INCOME

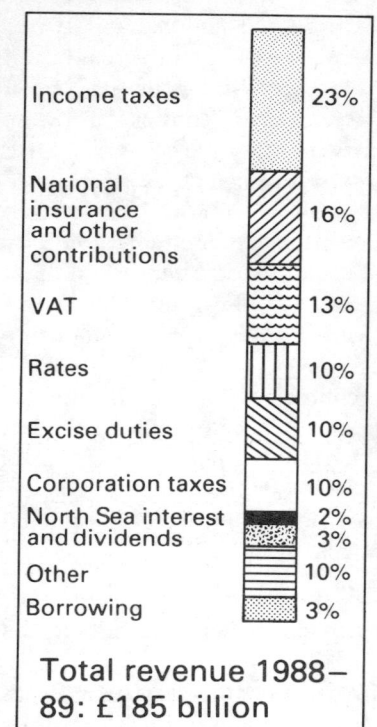

| | |
|---|---|
| Income taxes | 23% |
| National insurance and other contributions | 16% |
| VAT | 13% |
| Rates | 10% |
| Excise duties | 10% |
| Corporation taxes | 10% |
| North Sea interest and dividends | 2% / 3% |
| Other | 10% |
| Borrowing | 3% |

**Total revenue 1988–89: £185 billion**

## SPENDING

| | |
|---|---|
| DHSS: Social security | 27% |
| Defence | 11% |
| DHSS: Health and social services | 11% |
| Education and Science | 10% |
| Home Office | 4% |
| Employment | 2% |
| Other departments | 22% |
| Interest payments | 10% |
| Other | 3% |

**Total expenditure 1988–89: £185 billion**

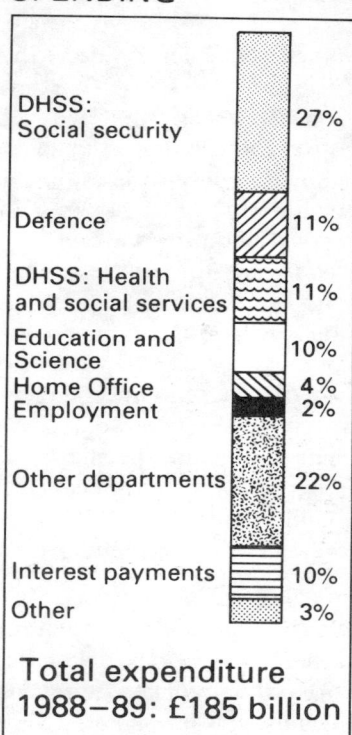

**Fig. 5.2** Government income and expenditure 1988–89

power from one group of people to another. The remainder is spent upon goods and services such as education, medical care and defence. Figure 5.2 shows the Government's planned income and expenditure for 1988–89.

As well as producing goods and services itself, the Government has considerable influence over the conduct of private sector firms. This intervention in the economy is described in Chapter 1.

## Local Government

Local Government in Britain has until recently been organised on a 'two-tier' system, with county and district councils (London and

Scotland had slightly different structures, but still used a two-tier scheme). However, in the *metropolitan counties* – Greater Manchester, Merseyside, Tyne and Wear, West Midlands, South Yorkshire and West Yorkshire – the county councils have been abolished, as has the Greater London Council. In these areas the district councils are the main authority, but in some cases they have retained county-wide authorities for services such as police, fire brigade and transport.

Local authorities are huge organisations. A medium-sized city such as Bradford or Newcastle will spend several hundred million pounds a year and employ thousands of staff. About half of this money will be spent on education, with social services and housing being the next biggest categories.

Unlike systems in some other countries, local authorities in Britain have few powers independent of the central Government. Their powers are specifically delegated by Parliament, and can be altered by central orders. During the 1980s the Government has steadily reduced the independence of local authorities by placing severe restrictions on their spending and authority.

Councils have two types of functions:

*(a) Mandatory* The council *must* provide certain services such as education and social services.
*(b) Permissive* The council *may* provide certain services such as museums, art galleries and family planning services if it wishes to do so.

Local authorities are also responsible for the implementation of much national legislation affecting business, such as consumer laws (see Chapter 15). Their activities are important to businesses, as Figure 5.3, listing the activities of just one council department, shows.

## Nationalised industries

*Nationalised industries* are firms owned wholly or mainly by the Government. Almost all are *public corporations* (see below). Before 1945 there were very few public corporations, and most of the nationalised industries were created by the Labour Governments of 1945–51, 1964–70 and 1974–79. Most *privatisation* has been carried out by Conservative Governments, mainly since 1979.

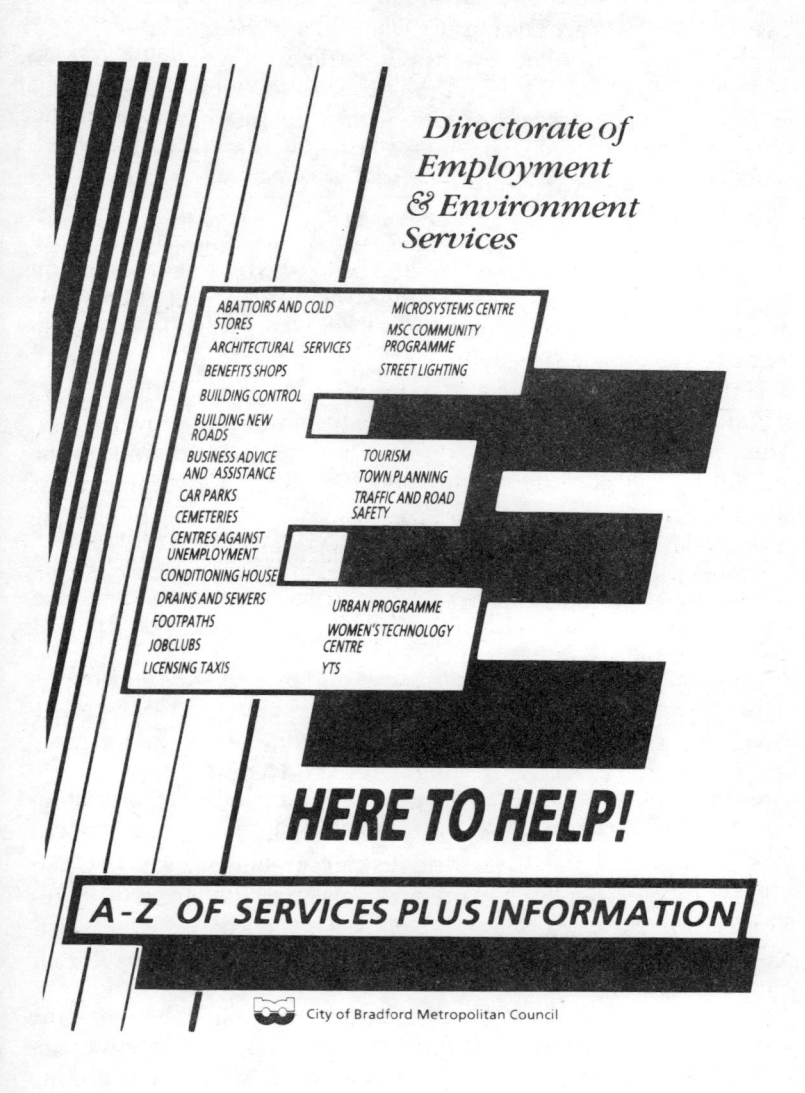

**Fig. 5.3** A council department's services

The first major round of nationalisation began just after the Second World War. During the war much of British industry had been strictly controlled by the Government. When the Labour Party won the 1945 election it took control of several major industries. The chief industries concerned are illustrated in Figure 5.4.

| Industry | Pre-1945 position |
| --- | --- |
| Coal | Privately owned collieries. |
| Railways | Four major privately owned companies, each with an area monopoly granted by Parliament |
| Electricity | Some undertakings owned privately, others run by local authorities. A national 'grid' fed them. |
| Gas | Some private, some local authority ownership. |
| Road Transport | Very large numbers of privately owned businesses. |
| Airlines (British Airways) | Civil aviation strictly controlled during 1939 to 1945 and immediately after the war; pre-1939 industry was comparatively small. |

**Fig. 5.4** Nationalisation 1945–51

In some cases, such as road transport, part of the industry remained in private ownership. Some industries have been de-nationalised since 1945. For example, the steel industry was nationalised in 1951, immediately de-nationalised by the newly-elected Conservative Government, partially re-nationalised by Labour in 1967, and was due for a second de-nationalisation in late 1988.

A list of the nationalised industries at the end of 1987–88, together with those already privatised, is given in Figure 5.5. Some of these industries, such as steel, electricity and water, were due to be privatised by 1990, and further sell-offs to the private sector are planned for the early 1990s.

Even after extensive privatisation, the nationalised industries were still important, producing over 5 percent of British output and employing 800 000 workers in 1987–88.

**Arguments for nationalisation**
*Nationalised industries don't have to make a profit*
Private firms are in business solely to make a profit, and will not

> The list of nationalised industries remaining in the public sector at the end of 1987–88 was as follows:–
>
> British Coal
> Electricity (England and Wales)
> North of Scotland Hydro-Electric Board
> South of Scotland Electricity Board
> British Steel Corporation
> Post Office
> Girobank
> British Railways Board
> British Waterways Board
> Scottish Transport Group
> British Shipbuilders (Merchant)
> Civil Aviation Authority
> Water (England and Wales)
> London Regional Transport
>
> The following industries have been privatised since 1979:–
>
> British Telecom
> British Gas Corporation
> British National Oil Corporation
> British Airways
> British Airports Authority
> British Aerospace
> British Shipbuilders (Warships)
> British Transport Docks Board
> National Freight Company
> Enterprise Oil
> National Bus Company

**Fig. 5.5** The nationalised industries 1987–88

supply goods or services unless they are profitable. For example, socially important services such as rural railway lines and postal services might not be supplied by a private firm because of the high costs. If they were supplied they might be too expensive for consumers. It is argued that a Government-owned firm will be prepared to provide these services as a public duty.

*Some industries are 'natural monopolies'*
For some industries such as gas or electricity, it would be economically impractical to provide a choice of services to the consumer because of the cost of laying mains and pipes. For example, a private

firm would be unwilling to invest in a gas main to a house unless it was sure that it would be able to sell its gas to the household. In these industries it is argued that it makes sense to have one producer, which should be owned by the Government to protect consumers.

The other advantage of a single producer owned by the Government is that having a guaranteed large market allows it to invest in expensive equipment and technology. For example an electricity power station costs billions of pounds, and a private firm might be unwilling to risk such a large sum. The experience of the Channel Tunnel Group shows the difficulty of raising capital for large-scale projects (although it did eventually succeed).

*Some industries are 'strategic'*
If an industry is vital to the economy or military strength of a country, it may be better for it to be provided by the Government, so as to ensure ample supply of vital goods and services. Most of the present and past nationalised industries are in major areas such as fuel and power, transport, communications and heavy industry. Their products are essential to people and firms throughout the economy, and would be vital in the case of war.

*The Government should control the economy on behalf of its citizens*
This is the major political argument for nationalisation, although it is heavily disputed. It is argued that a Government-owned industry will be run for the benefit of the people rather than for private profit. Nationalised industries may be prepared to provide socially important but unprofitable services, or to locate in depressed areas to create employment.

The political argument for nationalisation is included in Clause 4 of the Labour Party's Constitution, which declares that the state should take control of the 'commanding heights' of the economy (that is, the most important industries, upon which all of the others depend). However, even within the Labour Party there are many MPs who disagree with this clause, and it seems unlikely that even a future Labour Government will engage in large-scale nationalisation.

*It may be necessary to rescue private firms from bankruptcy*
Occasionally a private firm is nationalised to prevent it going out of business and causing unemployment or other economic problems.

British Leyland (now called Rover) was rescued in 1975 to prevent large job losses in the West Midlands. Rolls Royce Engines (not the car firm) was taken over in 1972 to ensure that Britain did not lose its capacity to make aircraft engines.

**Arguments against nationalisation**
*Nationalised industries don't have to make a profit*
It may seem strange that this is an argument both for and against nationalisation, but many people believe that nationalised industries have no incentive to make a profit because they can simply ask the Government to pay any losses made. (The world record loss of £1.8 billion was made by British Steel in 1980.) The taxpayer is therefore forced to support inefficient firms.

Nationalised industries are in an unfortunate position. Some have regularly made losses and been accused of inefficiency. Others regularly make large profits and are accused of exploiting consumers.

To encourage efficiency, nationalised industries have been given targets for performance, one of the most important of which is the *external financing limit*, which is the amount the corporation can raise from the Government. In 1988–89, for example, British Coal had an external financing limit of £670 million.

A negative limit is imposed upon some firms, which means that they are expected to pay money into the Treasury, and must therefore make a profit. In 1988–89 the Post Office was expected to pay the Government £97 million. The eventual aim of the Conservative Government was to make all remaining nationalised industries self-supporting.

*Nationalised industries often have a monopoly*
Most of the nationalised industries have enjoyed a *statutory monopoly*, which means that no other firm is allowed to compete with them. The Post Office's letter monopoly, an example of this, is discussed in Chapter 11.

Critics of nationalised industries argue that the lack of competition does little to encourage firms to provide good services, because they do not have to worry about consumers switching to another supplier. However, this is not always true – British Rail has a monopoly of rail travel, but has to compete against other forms of transport such as buses and private cars, and road haulage for heavy goods.

## 50   *Business and Commerce*

*State control of industry is politically undesirable*
It is often argued that a Government which controls industry has too much power over the way in which people make their living. A state monopoly also prevents new producers from setting up in competition.

Although they are meant to be largely independent of the Government, the nationalised industries are subject to political interference, often to benefit the party in power. Past examples include holding down commuter rail fares just before an election and being forced to locate factories in unsuitable areas to create employment.

## Control of public corporations

Virtually all of the nationalised industries are *public corporations*. A public corporation differs from a Government Department, such as the Ministry of Defence, in two main ways.

*(a)* It has an independent Board of Directors. Government Departments are controlled directly by a Minister, but the nationalised industries were set up to be 'at arm's length' from the Government. The Chairman and Board of Directors are appointed by the Minister, but are meant to have some independence and run the corporation as a commercial operation. The Chairman is usually recruited from business rather than being a politician, and is supposed to be largely free from political interference.

*(b)* It receives most of its revenue from selling a good or service. Government Departments such as Defence or Education provide most of their services free to the consumer, with their costs being paid from taxation. Public corporations also receive support from taxes, but are meant to obtain most of their income by selling their goods and services.

### The Minister responsible

Each nationalised industry chairman is directly responsible to a Government Minister, such as the Secretary of State for Energy or for Trade and Industry. The Minister appoints (and can dismiss) the Chairman and Board members.

In theory, the Minister decides upon general policies for the corporation, but is not meant to interfere in the day-to-day running of the industry. Policy decisions might include deciding whether the Post Office should charge the same price for all letters, but not matters such as the type of delivery vans used. In practice, however, politicians of both parties have constantly intervened for political reasons, sometimes making the industry more inefficient (and then complaining about it in public).

The Minister has considerable power over the industry, and will often appoint a Chairman to carry through a particularly important policy; Ian McGregor was chosen to reduce the size of the steel and coal industries and make them less unprofitable.

The Minister is a member of the Cabinet, and has to answer both to Cabinet colleagues and MPs who ask questions in Parliament; if a public corporation lays off workers, MPs from that area will demand to know why. The Minister is by far the most powerful outside influence upon the public corporation.

### Parliament
The Government is ultimately answerable to Parliament over any of its activities, and this applies to nationalised industries. The Minister may be asked questions by MPs at Minister's Question Time and may also be asked to appear before the Select Committee on Nationalised Industries (SCNI). This is a group of 20 to 30 MPs who specialise in investigating the running of the nationalised industries. The SCNI has slightly more power than individual MPs, but in practice only rarely manages to exert any real influence.

### Consumer Councils
These have been established to represent the interests of customers of the public corporations. Their role is discussed in Chapter 15.

## Privatisation
The Conservative Government elected in 1979 had as a major aim the *privatisation* of much of the public sector. Privatisation involves transferring the production of goods and services from the public to the private sector. It can be divided into three broad types of policy:

*(a) Denationalisation* – selling Government-owned enterprises to the private sector, e.g. British Telecom, Girobank

*(b) Deregulation* – removing statutory monopolies, e.g. abolition of restrictions upon bus services; allowing Mercury to set up an alternative telephone service

*(c) Contracting-out* – allowing private firms to bid for the supply of public services, e.g. hospital cleaning, refuse collection

## Arguments for privatisation
*It will lead to greater efficiency*
It is argued that by encouraging competition and moving production into the private sector, goods and services will be produced more cheaply and efficiently. Firms who are inefficient will not survive, whereas in the public sector the lack of competition makes management slack. Many local councils have cut their costs by contracting-out services such as refuse collection.

*Consumers will benefit*
Because of increased competition and efficiency, consumers should benefit from greater choice and better services. A good example of this is the deregulation of long-distance coach services in 1980, when the National Bus Company's monopoly of timetabled services was abolished. This deregulation led to increased services at lower prices, both for coach and other transport services such as rail travel.

*Taxpayers will benefit*
Government spending should fall because of cheaper services and lower payments to support nationalised industries. The sale of public corporations also brings in several billion pounds a year to the Government (more than enough to pay the cost of the police and fire services for the entire country).

In 1988–89 the Government was able to pay for all of its services without borrowing, for the first time since 1969. It has been estimated that by the year 2000, on present trends, the Government could eliminate income tax and repay the entire National Debt without having to cut public spending. Much of this is as a result of privatisation revenues.

*Privatisation increases share ownership*
The number of people owning shares in companies has tripled in recent years, largely because of denationalisation (most people only own shares in privatised companies such as British Telecom and British Gas). By increasing share ownership by consumers and workers, the Government hopes that people will have a stake in the success and efficiency of British industry.

## Arguments against privatisation
*Privatisation does not necessarily increase efficiency*
It can be argued that in many instances privatised production is not

necessarily cheaper or more efficient. In some cases, such as British Telecom and British Gas, privatisation has merely changed a public sector monopoly into a private sector one. In order to obtain the highest possible price from their sale, the Government has left these firms intact, and the customer still has little or no choice of suppliers.

Contracting-out of public services has also caused problems. There have been many complaints about the standard of work of private contractors in hospitals and Government offices, with several firms being sacked because of poor service. To keep costs low, these firms have also tended to offer their workers poor wages and working conditions.

*Consumers have not always benefited*
In some cases, such as gas and air travel, privatisation has brought little benefit to consumers. Generally, denationalisation has had little impact upon services to consumers, although it could be argued that nationalised industry service has been improved in preparation for privatisation. After criticism of its refusal to break up the gas and telephone services, the Government has made plans to introduce more competition when industries such as electricity are sold off.

*Privatisation costs the Government money*
Some people have complained that denationalisation is like selling off the family silver to pay the food bills. The profits from industries such as gas and electricity will be lost to future Governments and eventually the Government will run out of assets to sell.

In some cases the Government has sold public corporations at less than the value of their assets. For example, the electricity industry's assets are worth about £40 billion, but its price has been set at only half of this. The Government has also had to 'write off' the debts of some nationalised industries before they could be sold.

*The impact of increased share ownership has been minimal*
Although many people own shares in privatised industries, they have been reluctant to invest in other firms. Many sold their shares for a quick profit, and share issues with any risk are still not popular. For example, the Eurotunnel issue was undersubscribed in the UK because, unlike British Gas and British Telecom, there was no certainty of a rapid increase in the value of its shares.

# 6

# Business Documents

## A typical business transaction on credit

Buying goods or services is a form of contract under law, even if no documents are signed. For example, by getting into a taxi and asking to be taken to a particular place, a traveller 'contracts' to pay the agreed fare. Every day millions of such oral contracts are made.

For most business transactions, however, there is a need for recording the details in writing. Firms need records for their own use, and to show to people such as accountants, shareholders and tax officials. For these purposes a number of different documents are used at various stages of the transaction.

### 1 Enquiry

If goods are being ordered from a priced catalogue or from an existing supplier, the enquiry and quotation stages may be missed out. In other cases, a firm may write to enquire about a supplier's terms of sale. Names of suppliers are available from sources such as classified telephone directories (Yellow Pages), trade directories, Chambers of Commerce and business acquaintances.

The buyer will want details about prices, delivery times, discounts, etc. The enquiry may be an ordinary typed letter or a standard printed form.

### 2 Quotation

The supplier will send a quotation in reply to the enquiry. This will detail quantities, prices, delivery procedure and payment terms. Sometimes it will only be necessary to send a catalogue and price list, but in other cases a specially prepared quotation will be necessary. A typical example is illustrated in Figure 6.1.

(Note that details of Value Added Tax (VAT) are not included in

```
                        QUOTATION                        No. 931 X
          The Westbrook Manufacturing Company Limited
                            Whiteheath
                          LONDON SE3 0NP
Tel: 01-990 9999
Christopher and Susan Abbott & Co.                     17 March 199–
Chartered Architects
The Mound
LINCOLN

   In reply to your inquiry dated 8 March 199– under reference PG/ZP, we are
pleased to advise that we can supply goods as follows:

   Quantity       Ref. No.       Description              Gross Price
      6           ZC 164    Walnut Single Right-hand
                            Pedestal Desks 2.00 m ×
                            1.00 m                        £51.35 each
                            (as attached illustration)

   Delivery:  One month from receipt of your order.
   Terms:     Trade discount 25%,[1] carriage paid[2] to your works.
   Payment:   Cash discount 2%[3] for settlement within 10 days of invoice date or
              net monthly (payment due 15th of month following delivery date).

                                    (Signed) R. P. Nosraw, Sales Manager
```

*Notes*
[1] Trade discount – the price quoted is subject to a 25% discount. Many firms quote this way; it enables them to show a gross price in their printed advertising literature, and they can vary the discount according to quantity purchased. This practice is particularly common in transactions between wholesalers and retailers.
[2] Carriage paid – the seller will arrange transport for the goods and will bear the cost himself. Other common terms are:
Carriage forward – the buyer is charged an additional sum for transport costs.
Ex works or         – the buyer will have to arrange his own transport and collect the
Ex factory            goods from the seller's premises.
[3] The goods are being sold on *credit* terms. The buyer has the choice of paying the full sum on a monthly account basis or settling within ten days in return for a 2% discount. Some suppliers give limited credit to a new customer before making enquiries as to his credit standing. Others insist on cash-with-order terms for a first order (particularly if the buyer is not known to them). Many suppliers are subscribers to a firm of mercantile enquiry agents – for example, Dun & Bradstreet, who supply reports on the financial status of prospective buyers. Suppliers with a large number of credit accounts find it worthwhile to pay an annual subscription to one of these agencies, thus obtaining annually its credit ratings register – five volumes listing, geographically, brief details about the majority of businesses in the country (excluding small-scale retailers). Additionally, or alternatively, trade or bank references are requested from the potential buyer (note that, in the case of a banker's reference, application must be made by the creditor to his own bankers, who will pass the enquiry on to the buyer's banker).

**Fig. 6.1**  Quotation

this example, to make the form more simple, but a real quotation would allow for VAT. This tax is explained later in this chapter.)

**3  Order**

After considering quotations from various suppliers, the buyer will decide which is the best. The accepted quotation will not always be the cheapest. For example, a firm may have slightly higher prices than its competitors, but offer quicker delivery or more generous credit terms. The buyer will send an order such as that shown in Figure 6.2.

**4  Acknowledgement of order**

This is sent by the seller on receiving the order. It confirms the quantities, prices and other conditions of sale, as previously agreed. If delivery is to be made quickly from the supplier's stocks the acknowledgement may be omitted. Otherwise the supplier will inform the customer when delivery is expected to be made.

**5  Advice Note**

This tells the buyer that the goods are being sent, and to make enquiries if they are not delivered within a certain time. As with the acknowledgement, this stage may be missed out if delivery is to be made quickly.

---

ORDER                                     No. 83

Christopher and Susan Abbott & Co.
Chartered Architects
The Mound, Lincoln

Tel: Lincoln 9990
(STD code 0522)                           23 March 199–

The Westbrook Manufacturing Co. Ltd
Whiteheath
LONDON SE3 0NP

Your Quotation No. 931 X dated 17 March 199–

Please supply:

  6 Walnut Single Right-hand Pedestal Desks at £51.35 each less
  25% trade discount, carriage paid to our works.

                                          C. J. R. Abbott

---

**Fig. 6.2**  Order

```
                    DELIVERY NOTE                    No. A 734
         The Westbrook Manufacturing Company Limited
                         Whiteheath
                       LONDON SE3 0NP
  Tel: 01-990 9999

                                                    1 April 199–

  Christopher and Susan Abbott & Co.
  Chartered Architects
  The Mound
  LINCOLN

  Your Order 83 dated 23 March

  Please receive the following in good order:
  Description                    Quantity        Packages
  Walnut Single Right-hand
     Pedestal Desks                  6              6
```

Fig. 6.3   Delivery Note

## 6  Delivery Note

This is sent with the goods, and lists many of the details included on the order (usually prices are not shown on the delivery note). It often has a space for the customer to sign as proof that the goods have been received. If it is impossible to check the goods immediately upon delivery, the seller will allow a limited period for damaged or incorrect goods to be returned. An example of a delivery note is shown in Figure 6.3.

## 7  Invoice

The invoice (illustrated in Fig. 6.4) is a bill for the goods. It is usually sent separately by post.

If the seller does not wish to supply the goods on credit, a *pro-forma* invoice may be sent. This carries the same details as a normal invoice, but is sent to the buyer *before* the goods are sent. When payment is made the goods will be delivered.

On receiving the invoice, the buyer's accounts department will check that the details match those of the previous documents. If there is a discount for quick payment, the buyer may well ensure that the invoice is paid promptly. Sometimes the buyer may pay

58  *Business and Commerce*

```
                      INVOICE                    No. B 734[1]
         The Westbrook Manufacturing Company Limited
                        Whiteheath
                     LONDON SE3 0NP
    Tel: 01-990 9999
                                                  1 April 199–

    Christopher and Susan Abbott & Co.
    Chartered Architects
    The Mound
    LINCOLN

    Your Order 83 dated 23 March – our Delivery Note A 734 1 April

    Description                 Quantity    Unit Price   Amount
                                                £          £
    Walnut Single Right-hand
       Pedestal Desks              6          51.35      308.10
                       Less 25% Trade Discount             77.03
                              Net due                    231.07[2]

    Payment terms:

       2% cash discount for settlement by 11 April, or
       Net monthly (Payment due 15 May).[3]
```

**Notes**
[1] B 734 – Invoice bears same number as delivery note since it has been prepared as part of a preprinted set but bears a different prefix for easy identification.
[2] As already mentioned, VAT has not been included (see below).
[3] Monthly settlement does not normally mean payment to be received exactly one month after invoice date. In practice, some regular arrangement is made (in this case in the middle of the next month).

**Fig. 6.4** Invoice

several invoices with one payment (usually when a Statement of Account is received).

### 8 Credit Note
This will only be used if the goods are damaged or some are missing. When the supplier is notified, a credit note (see Fig. 6.5) will be sent and the amount owed by the buyer will be reduced.

### 9 Statement of Account
Regular customers will be paying in and receiving goods continually. In this case the supplier will send out monthly statements of

account, showing the customer's *debits* (charges for goods received) and *credits* (payments and allowances for damaged or incomplete deliveries). The *outstanding balance* shows the amount owed by the customer.

The statement of account will also contain information about when payment must be made, e.g. 'settlement due by . . .'.

## 10 Payment of Account

Business accounts are mostly settled by cheque or bank credit transfer (see Chapter 10) although occasionally cash or postal orders may be used. For international trade, payment may be made by bills of exchange or international money orders.

Receipts used to be sent for all payments, but many firms do not now send these unless asked to do so (except for cash payments). When payment is made through the banking system, proof of payment can be easily obtained. Some firms send *remittance advice notes* to inform the supplier that payment has been made.

---

CREDIT NOTE   No. X 16

6 April

Our Invoice B734 1 April
Your letter dated 4 April, reference 83/R/GKB[1]

We have credited your account as follows:

1 Walnut Single Right-hand Pedestal Desk returned as damaged   £38.51[2]

Replacement will be sent in 10 days and charged separately.[3]

---

**Notes**
[1] The buyer had used a reference comprising these elements (his letter is not illustrated):

 83 – his original order number.
 R – indicating 'returned'.
 GKB – initials of responsible member of staff.

[2] The seller did *not* charge £51.35 per desk but allowed 25% reduction.
[3] Most sellers follow this practice; it avoids the difficulties that arise if replacements have to be sent out free of charge.

**Fig. 6.5** Credit Note

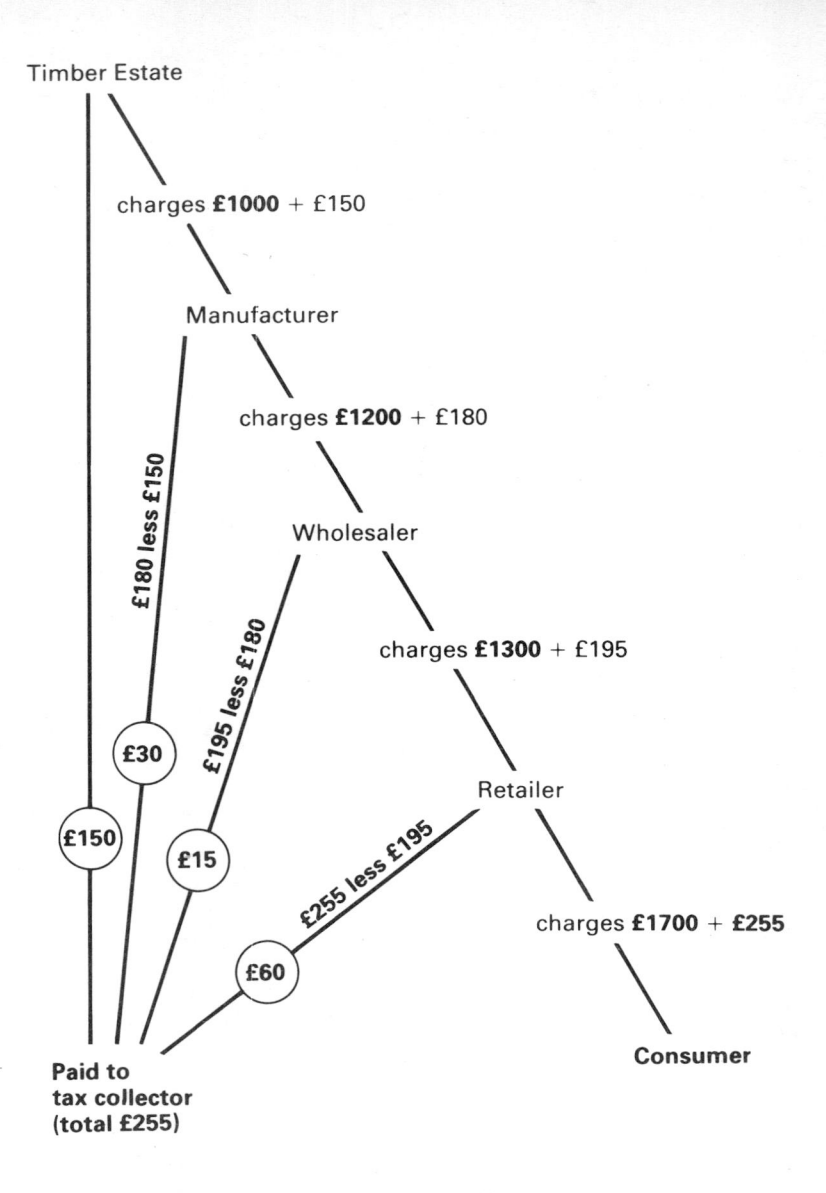

**VAT calculated at standard rate of 15%. The sums in bold type represent the basic selling prices required by each trader.**

Fig. 6.6   Calculation of VAT

# Value Added Tax (VAT)

Value Added Tax (VAT) was introduced into Britain on entry to the European Economic Community (EEC) in 1973. It is paid on most goods and services, but there are two important categories upon which it is not charged:

1 *Exempt*     For example, banking, insurance, education and health services
2 *Zero-rated*   Food, books and newspapers, children's clothing, transport services and exports

Neither category charges VAT on its sales. The main difference is that a zero-rated business can reclaim tax paid on its purchases (thus an exporter who pays tax on a calculator can claim it back, whereas a bank cannot).

Most of the exempt and zero-rated goods and services are not taxed because of one of two reasons – they are thought to be 'good' for people, e.g. education, newspapers, or they are 'necessities' which account for a large proportion of spending by people on low incomes, e.g. electricity, food. In recent years Britain has come under pressure from other Common Market countries to 'harmonise' tax rates by charging VAT upon such goods (food for example is taxable in most EEC countries).

## How VAT is calculated

As its name suggests, VAT is paid upon the 'value added' at each stage of the productive process. Value added is the difference between a firm's 'inputs', i.e. purchases of supplies, and its 'outputs', i.e. money received from customers.

For example, in Figure 6.6 the manufacturer pays £1000 plus 15% (£150). By turning the timber into goods worth £1200 it 'adds value' of £200. The Government is entitled to 15% of this, i.e. £30, which is paid by the manufacturer.

The manufacturer adds this £30, plus the £150 paid to the timber estate, to the amount paid by the wholesaler. The wholesaler will later pass this £180 on to the retailer, and so on until the final customer.

This is a very simplified summary, and the calculation of VAT is extremely complicated. The tax is collected by businesses on behalf of the Customs and Excise Department. Small businesses with an annual turnover of less than £23 600 in 1989–90 do not have to register for VAT or keep VAT records. This figure is updated every year to allow for inflation.

# 7

# Business Accounts

The aim of this chapter is not to describe book-keeping procedures in detail, but to show some of the basic figures and ratios used to measure a business's financial position. Accounting is vital as a tool of control for a business, serving several purposes:

*(a)* Recording debts owed to and by the firm.
*(b)* Showing the value of the business.
*(c)* Measuring the business's performance in sales, costs and profit.
*(d)* Providing information to shareholders, tax authorities and Companies House.

## The balance sheet

A *balance sheet* is a picture of the business at any particular time. It records its *assets* (property and possessions) and *liabilities* (amounts owed to creditors).

A simple balance sheet is illustrated opposite. There are several other ways of presenting a balance sheet; this is one particular style.

This balance sheet is a very simple one, but can be used to illustrate some important accounting terms. Although this is for a sole trader, who *is* the business, for accounting purposes the salon is regarded as a separate entity.

**Capital** This is the money that the owner has put into the business plus the net profit which has been retained in previous years. From the business's point of view it is a liability because the owner is entitled to withdraw her capital.

## Balance sheet of Anita's Hairdressing Salon at March 31, 1990

| LIABILITIES £ | | | ASSETS £ | | |
|---|---|---|---|---|---|
| Capital at 1.4.89 | 65 000 | | *Fixed assets* | | |
| Net profit for year | 10 000 | | Freehold premises | 63 000 | |
| *Less* Drawings | 5 000 | | Shop fittings | 3 000 | |
| | | 70 000 | | | 66 000 |
| *Current liabilities* | | | *Current assets* | | |
| Creditors | 400 | | Stock for sale | 800 | |
| | | 400 | Debtors | 200 | |
| | | | Bank account | 3 400 | |
| | | | | | 4 400 |
| | | 70 400 | | | 70 400 |

**Drawings** This is money that the owner has taken out of the business for personal use such as living expenses. In effect she has reclaimed part of her capital. £5000 of the net profit has been *retained* in the business.

**Net profit** The concept of net profit is explained later in the chapter. This is added to the capital of the business, as it belongs to the owner.

**Current liabilities** These are debts which have to be paid in the short term, usually defined as within a year. The *creditors* are people or firms who have supplied goods on credit.

**Fixed assets** These are assets which are likely to remain in the business for more than a year. This value tends to remain fairly steady, although fixed assets may increase in value (*appreciate*) or fall in value (*depreciate*). For example, the premises would probably appreciate, whereas the shop-fittings will fall in value as they become worn or out-of-date. In a more complex balance sheet, allowance would be made for changes in the value of fixed assets.

**Current assets** These change constantly during the year as the business buys and sells goods and services. *Debtors* are people and firms who owe the business money. *Stock for sale* is measured at its *cost price* (what the business paid for it) because until it is sold the anticipated profit cannot be included.

Note that both sides of the balance sheet are equal. This will always occur because, for example, every transaction which results in a profit is added to the capital (on the *liabilities* side). The payment received will be banked and therefore be included on the *assets* side.

The balance sheet can be used to calculate;

**Net worth of the business** This is also called the *owner's capital* and is measured by the equation:

$$\text{Net worth} = \text{Assets} - \text{Current liabilities}$$
$$= £70\,400 - £400$$
$$= £70\,000$$

The net worth will rise if the business makes a profit and fall if it makes a loss.

**Return on capital** This is measured by the formula:

$$\text{Return on capital} = \frac{\text{Net profit}}{\text{Capital}} \times 100$$

$$= \frac{£10\,000}{£65\,000} \times 100$$

$$= 15\% \text{ (approx)}$$

Whether this percentage is satisfactory depends upon the return which could be achieved elsewhere, for example by putting the money into a bank or another type of business. If a bank account pays 10 percent interest, an investment of £65 000 would earn £6500 a year. Anita might therefore consider a profit of £10 000 as satisfactory.

The views of the owner are also important. If she had put the money in the bank and worked for somebody else, she might have earned a salary of £5000 plus interest of £6500. This would have made her £1500 better off, without the long hours and risk involved in running her own business. Some people might regard running their own salon as not being worthwhile.

On the other hand, it could be argued that the satisfaction of running your own business is worth this financial sacrifice. Also, the business may well grow faster in the future.

**Working capital**  This is the money that is needed to pay expenses such as wages, stock and other day-to-day purchases. Fixed assets such as premises and fittings are not included because they must be left in the business for it to continue.

In this case:

> Working capital = Current assets − Current liabilities
> = £4400 − £400
> = £4000

**Liquid capital**  *Liquid capital* measures the assets of the business which can be quickly converted into cash. Stocks of goods are not included because they take time to sell, and could only be sold quickly at less than their true value.

> Liquid capital = Working capital − Stock
> = £4000 − £800
> = £3200

# Gross and net profit

### Gross profit

There are two commonly used measures of profit – *gross profit* and *net profit*. Gross profit measures the profit made from buying and selling goods or services before expenses involved in the sale are deducted. A business's gross profit is calculated from its Trading Account, an example of which is illustrated below;

### Littledeals Trading Account for year ending March 31, 1990

|  | £ |  | £ |
|---|---|---|---|
| Stock at 1.4.89 | 45 000 | Sales | 165 000 |
| Purchases | 60 000 |  |  |
|  | 105 000 |  |  |

*Less*

| | | |
|---|---|---|
| Stock at 31.3.90 | 40 000 | |
| Cost of sales | 65 000 | |
| Gross Profit | 100 000 | |
| | 165 000 | 165 000 |

*Sales* is the income received from selling goods before the cost of purchasing them is deducted.

*Stock* consists of the unsold goods held by Littledeals. The stock at the end of year (*closing stock*) is £5000 less than the stock at the beginning of the year (*opening stock*). The firm has used £5000 worth of stock and has spent £60 000 on *purchases* of goods for resale. The *cost of sales* is therefore £65 000.

These goods have been sold for £165 000, so:

$$\text{Gross profit} = \text{Sales} - \text{Cost of sales}$$
$$= £165\,000 - £65\,000$$
$$= £100\,000$$

Two important ratios can also be calculated from Littledeals' Trading Account.

*Mark-up* is the percentage which is added on to the cost of purchases to determine the price at which they are sold. In this case:

$$\text{Mark-up} = \frac{\text{Sales}}{\text{Cost of sales}} \times 100$$

$$= \frac{£165\,000}{£65\,000} \times 100$$

$$= 254\% \text{ (approx)}$$

*Gross profit margin* is measured by the formula:

$$\text{Gross profit margin} = \frac{\text{Gross profit}}{\text{Sales}} \times 100$$

$$= \frac{£100\,000}{£165\,000} \times 100$$

$$= 61\% \text{ (approx)}$$

The mark-up and gross profit margin will vary considerably from business to business. They depend upon factors such as the *rate of stock-turn* and *expenses* incurred.

For example, if the goods have to be stored for a long time, or expenses are high, the mark-up and profit margin will tend to be high. Storing goods ties up capital and expenses have to be paid for out of the gross profit.

If goods are sold quickly and expenses are low, the mark-up and margin are likely to be lower. For example, a tobacco wholesaler may work on a profit margin as low as 2% and still be profitable. This would be far too low for a car dealer, who has high capital outlay and selling costs.

**Net profit**

*Net profit* is a more important measure than gross profit because it measures the real profit made by a business after all expenses are paid. *Expenses* are the costs involved in selling goods and services, such as wages, transport, advertising and rent. Net profit is calculated from the Profit and Loss Account, of which an example is given below. (It is customary to present the Trading and Profit and Loss Accounts together, as shown in Figure 7.1.)

### Littledeals Profit and Loss Account
### for year ending March 31, 1990

|  | £ |  |
|---|---|---|
| Gross Profit |  | 65 000 |
| *Less* |  |  |
| Wages | 20 000 |  |
| Rent | 5 000 |  |
| Advertising | 5 000 |  |
| Transport | 12 000 |  |
| Heat & light | 2 000 |  |
| Other costs | 6 000 |  |
| Expenses |  | (50 000) |
| Net Profit |  | 15 000 |

This is a simplified example. Figure 7.1 gives a real example, with both the Trading and the Profit and Loss Account shown together.

It can be seen from Littledeals' Profit and Loss Account that:

$$\text{Net profit} = \text{Gross profit} - \text{Expenses}$$
$$= £65\,000 - £50\,000$$
$$= £15\,000$$

The *net profit margin* can also be calculated using the equation:

$$\text{Net profit margin} = \frac{\text{Net profit}}{\text{Sales}} \times 100$$

$$= \frac{£15\,000}{£165\,000} \times 100$$

$$= 9\% \text{ (approx)}$$

The net profit margin will tend to vary between industries. A high-risk industry with large capital investment (such as oil-drilling)

|  | 12 months to 31.1.88 £m |
|---|---|
| TURNOVER | 862.1 |
| Cost of sales | (684.1) |
| Gross profit | 178.0 |
| Distribution costs | (35.6) |
| Administrative expenses | (50.2) |
|  | 92.2 |
| Share of trading profit of associated companies | 0.3 |
|  | 92.5 |
| Profits of non-consolidated subsidiary, Club 24 Limited | 7.5 |
| OPERATING PROFIT | 100.0 |
| Employee profit share scheme | (1.0) |
| PROFIT ON ORDINARY ACTIVITIES BEFORE INTEREST | 99.0 |
| Net interest payable | (6.6) |
| PROFIT ON ORDINARY ACTIVITIES BEFORE TAXATION | 92.4 |
| Taxation on profit on ordinary activities | (31.1) |
| PROFIT ON ORDINARY ACTIVITIES AFTER TAXATION | 61.3 |
| Extraordinary items after taxation | — |
| PROFIT FOR THE FINANCIAL PERIOD | 61.3 |
| Dividends | (26.0) |
| RETAINED PROFIT FOR THE PERIOD | 35.3 |

**Fig. 7.1** *Next* profit and loss account

might expect a high margin. The margin would also tend to be lower when there is strong competition or falling sales in an industry.

In considering whether the net profit margin is high enough, a firm would have to consider questions such as:

(a) Is it comparable to that earned by similar firms in the same business?
(b) Is it rising or falling compared to past performance?
(c) Is it high enough to provide a reasonable return on the owners' capital?
(d) Is it high enough to allow profit to be put back into the business for expansion?

If the net profit is too low, there are a number of measures that the firm may take. Remembering the equation

$$\text{Net profit} = \text{Gross profit} - \text{Expenses}$$

it can be seen that the business must increase gross profit and/or reduce expenses.

To increase gross profit the firm could lower prices, hoping to increase sales by enough to make up for the lower profit on each item. Alternatively, it could raise prices and hope to keep enough custom to increase revenue from sales.

The firm could try to improve sales by other means such as more frequent advertising, offering better credit or delivery terms, or offering a wider range of goods and services. Gross profit would also rise if the firm could reduce the cost of purchases by changing suppliers or buying in bulk.

Some of the measures for increasing gross profit might also have the effect of increasing expenses. The business would have to ensure that any measures used to increase sales would not be cancelled out by higher expenses.

The firm might try to improve its profitability by reducing its expenses. This could be done by employing fewer workers, cutting advertising, holding less stock and reducing the quality of service offered. It would also be worth examining the profit obtained from different goods and services to discover whether any were making a loss.

In reducing expenses the firm would need to be careful that it did not lose too much custom through lower advertising or poorer service.

## Stock turnover

*Stock turnover* or *rate of stock-turn* measures the speed with which stock moves in or out of the business, i.e. the time taken from buying goods until they are sold. To calculate the rate of stock-turn, it is necessary to work out the *average stock* held during the year. This is the value of stocks normally held by the firm. It is calculated using the formula:

$$\text{Average stock} = \frac{\text{Stock at start of year} + \text{Stock at end of year}}{2}$$

For example, a business has £80 000 in stock at the beginning of the year and £120 000 at the end. Its cost of sales is £300 000:

$$\text{Average stock} = \frac{£80\,000 + £120\,000}{2}$$

$$= £100\,000$$

The rate of stock-turn is measured by the equation:

$$\text{Rate of stock-turn} = \frac{\text{Cost of sales}}{\text{Average stock}}$$

$$\text{Rate of stock-turn} = \frac{£300\,000}{£100\,000}$$

$$= 3$$

In this case goods are replaced on average three times a year; that is, goods are held in the business for an average of four months. A stock turnover of 365 would indicate that stock was being turned over every day – which might happen in the case of milk or newspapers.

The firm will try to achieve the highest possible rate of stock-turn, since keeping stock ties up capital and storage space. There is also the risk of deterioration or goods going out of fashion.

The ideal rate of stock-turn will depend upon the type of goods stocked. A rate of three might be acceptable for durable goods such as jewellery or furniture, which could be stored for four months. It would be unacceptable for perishable goods or goods which might go out of fashion.

# 8
# Retailing

## The organisation of retailing

Retailing is one of the most important and fastest growing industries in the United Kingdom. The average British household spent about £100 per week in British shops in 1988, and in recent years retailing has seen rapid increases in both sales and employment. Over 2 million people (a tenth of the UK workforce) now work in the industry.

Retailing is often defined as 'the sale of goods in small quantities to the public'. A more accurate definition would also include services, such as repairs or dry-cleaning. It does not include the sale of goods and services from one business to another – for example, a car manufacturer buying steel for car bodies (these are called *producer* or *capital* goods).

The retailer is the last link in the 'chain of distribution' between manufacturer and consumer. Goods may be bought from a wholesaler or direct from a manufacturer (see Chapter 9). The retailer's task is to provide consumers with the goods and services that they want *(a)* at the right time, *(b)* in the right form and quantities, *(c)* in the right place.

Thus, the consumer may wish to buy apples in December in 1 or 2lb quantities, suitably graded and with a choice of types. The consumer does not care that the apples may have been harvested in September – if the shop wishes to make a sale it must ensure that the goods are available.

In order to be successful any retailer, from a market trader to a multinational multiple chain, has to perform at least some of the following functions:

(a) Anticipate consumer demand by stocking appropriate quantities of goods that customers will wish to buy at different times.
(b) Open at times which suit the customers, e.g. most shops now open late on some nights because of the larger number of working women who cannot shop during the day.
(c) Stock a variety of types, brands, sizes and prices of goods.
(d) Choose goods which are suitable for the tastes of people in the area, e.g. people in Northern Ireland buy more dairy products than people in Yorkshire.
(e) Provide information about the goods and services on sale.
(f) Pack, sort and display goods attractively.
(g) Provide a pleasant atmosphere for customers to make their choices. For some products, such as clothes, an element of 'glamour' is vital.
(h) Accept the most common methods of payment, such as cheques and credit cards.
(i) Provide or arrange credit for more expensive goods and services.
(j) Arrange delivery and fitting where necessary, e.g. for carpets or electrical equipment.
(k) Provide after-sales services such as repairs and accessories.
(l) Make special orders for goods not in stock such as books or motorcycle parts.

Obviously, not all of these requirements will apply to every retailer, but a business which ignores the essentials for its particular products will lose possible sales.

The retailer has to have considerable business skills. As well as satisfying the customers' requirements, retailers have to:

(a) Raise sufficient finance to obtain suitable premises and stock.
(b) Select an appropriate location and premises, bearing in mind factors such as local competition, amount of 'passing trade' and room for expansion.
(c) Understand the market for the product – what type of people buy it, where supplies can be bought, what the 'trend' of the market is.

(d) Control the business's financial and tax affairs, e.g. bookkeeping, credit, cash-flow, pricing and profit margins, income tax and VAT.
(e) Select and train staff.
(f) Insure against risks such as theft, fire and accidents to customers and workers.
(g) Arrange publicity and advertising to get customers into the store.

As can be seen, retailing is a complicated business. Many shops fail because their owners do not cope with its demands, or fail to adapt to changes and competition.

## Types of shop

According to Government statistics, there are over 350 000 shops in Britain. These are owned by about 230 000 different firms, so the vast majority are single outlets or 'unit' shops. Shops can be divided into a number of categories, although with changes in retailing the distinctions are becoming very blurred.

### Unit shops

These are also called *independent shops* or *single outlets*. They are usually sole traders or partnerships (see Chapter 2).

An estimated 200 000 of Britain's shops are unit shops. Most are fairly small – although they are 80 percent of the total number, they account for only about one-third of total sales. This is about half the share of retail trade that they enjoyed 40 years ago. In recent years they have faced intense competition from the large chains of shops.

Compared to large-scale retailers, unit shops have considerable disadvantages:

(a) They have less capital to pay for premises and stock.
(b) They buy in smaller quantities and therefore pay more for stock than larger retailers. This means that their prices are often (though not always) higher.
(c) It is difficult to stock a wide range of goods.
(d) Small shops can't afford the extensive advertising carried out by chain stores.
(e) Many people start shops without the essential business skills.

Running a shop looks deceptively easy, but a large number fail because of their owner's inexperience.

Despite these disadvantages, small retailers continue to thrive and provide their owners with a good living. They are able to compete against larger firms in various ways:

(a) They are very successful in businesses where specialist knowledge and/or personal service is important, e.g. hairdressing, photography, DIY, floristry.
(b) Some trades can be established with a small amount of capital. Small shops are particularly successful where a 'labour-intensive' service is involved, i.e. labour is a high proportion of costs. Examples include carpets and picture-framing.
(c) The market for a product may be too small for large firms to get involved, but large enough for a small shop to make a profit, e.g. stamp-collecting.
(d) Small shops often have a monopoly position in a suburb or small village. They may be used for small purchases, or by people who are not mobile enough to travel into town.
(e) Many customers enjoy the friendly service offered in local shops (although the importance of this is often exaggerated).
(f) Small shops can benefit by opening later at night or at weekends, when their larger competitors are often closed. People who do their weekly shopping at Sainsbury's may need a bag of sugar at nine o'clock at night.
(g) Small shops may be part of a *voluntary chain* or be based upon a *franchise* (see Figure 8.1).
(h) Many people want to be their own boss, and a shop is a fairly cheap and easy way of setting up a business. Despite the fact that many such shops fail within two years, there is always a steady supply of people willing to take the risk.

**Supermarkets**

Self-service supermarkets started in the USA seventy years ago, but did not appear in Britain until just after the Second World War. Since then they have taken an ever-increasing share of the retail market, especially in the sales of food.

A supermarket is generally defined as a shop of over 2000 square feet, selling mainly food and household goods such as soap and

## VOLUNTARY CHAINS

Some independent stores are members of *voluntary chains* such as Spar, Mace and VG. They are still privately owned but get the advantages of bulk-buying by joining together.

## FRANCHISES

Some small shops are run as *franchises*, e.g. Kentucky Fried Chicken, Pizzaland, Prontaprint. Franchising is an American idea which is becoming more common in Britain. Franchises are run by individuals, who are given the 'franchise' or 'sole rights' for an area. They have to buy all their goods from the 'parent' organisation. In return the parent company pays for advertising and other services such as training.

**FAST FOOD FRANCHISE**
### SPUD U LIKE

With over 50 Baked Potato Restaurants now open or planned, SPUD U LIKE is growing fast and right now there are opportunities for people to join the franchise and share in our success. With a minimum investment of £15,000 attractive finance schemes are available to enable you to open a franchised unit. As a franchisee you benefit from initial training, on-going support, centralised marketing and purchasing, whilst still enjoying the rewards and satisfaction of running your own business.

Find out more by calling Jill Krebs on 01-965 0181. Spud U Like, 34 Standard Road, London NW10.

**A NEW CAR OR YOUR OWN BUSINESS?**

Today £7,000 isn't a lot of money, it's the cost of a medium car, and not a very fancy one at that. But for the same amount of money you can be your own boss.

You can join a well respected Group of Companies in your own proven, well established business which will typically earn you a pre-tax profit of over £1,500 each month all the year round.

**WHAT BUSINESS?**

Your own Home-cleaning business. If you have an aptitude for business and want to know more about our innovative speed team approach, contact Kevin Weam:

*The* Maids
Global House, Lind Road,
Sutton, Surrey SM1 4PJ
01-642-0054

**FASTFRAME**

Fastframe is one of the most exciting new retail Franchises to be launched in recent years. It combines an expert picture framing service with an attractive shop layout. Fastframe provides a total package including site selection, training, launch and ongoing group purchasing and marketing support.

Min. capital investment £10,000
Total capital investment £30,000

*Details available from*
John L. Scott, Managing Director,
Fastframe Franchises Ltd.
Percy St, Newcastle upon Tyne
NE1 4PX Tel: (0632) 615941

**Fig. 8.1** Voluntary chains and franchises

crockery. As the average size has become larger, the distinction between a supermarket and *superstore* has become less distinct.

Supermarkets generally sell a wide variety of packaged and branded goods. Many, particularly the larger shops, also sell a variety of *non-food* items such as clothes, stationery and toys. The range of goods stocked will vary considerably throughout the year, e.g. toys before Christmas, garden furniture in the summer.

Supermarkets are usually part of a large multiple chain such as Tesco or Sainsbury's and can therefore buy cheaply in bulk. Jack Cohen, who started Tesco in 1932, said that the company's policy should be 'pile it high and sell it cheap'. Supermarkets concentrated upon selling at lower prices than those of unit shops. They became able to do this after Resale Price Maintenance was abolished in 1964.

Until 1964, manufacturers could force all shops to sell their products at fixed prices. The supermarket buying millions of cans of beans a year had to charge the same price as the corner store buying a few hundred. Large supermarket chains could not use their buying power to cut prices. Resale Price Maintenance was made illegal in 1964 (except for books and brand-name medicines) and supermarkets were able to reduce prices and drive many small shops out of business.

In recent years this policy has been modified by Tesco and other supermarket chains. Although they still aim to sell staple goods such as bread and baked beans cheaply, they have started to concentrate upon better quality goods such as fresh fruit and vegetables, stocking a wider range of products. As people's incomes have risen they have been prepared to pay extra for these goods, which are therefore more profitable.

It is not always cheaper to shop at supermarkets than unit shops. 'Shopping-basket' surveys often show that they may have lower prices for the more common goods, but if people only bought the type of goods illustrated in such surveys many supermarkets would lose much of their sales. They rely upon people buying goods 'on impulse', and the layout of the shop is designed to encourage this. Common 'tricks of the trade' include:

(a) Blocking off the aisle by the door so that people have to walk to the back of the shop.

*(b)* Spreading the most commonly-bought items such as bread, milk, sugar and tea around the shop so that people are forced to pass other goods.
*(c)* Putting non-food items next to the door to ensure that people look at them.
*(d)* Stacking high-profit goods in 'hot-spots', e.g. at eye-level or the end of aisles, where people are more likely to see them.
*(e)* Placing sweets at checkouts to tempt children whose parents are waiting to be served.

Supermarket chains have many advantages over unit shops – larger capital, bulk-buying, more specialist staff, more spending on advertising, etc. However, they do have certain disadvantages which have prevented them from eliminating small shops altogether – they are impersonal and often inconvenient for the less mobile and their opening hours may be shorter or less flexible. As Figure 8.2 shows, they sometimes annoy their customers by using the methods described above.

Recent social and economic trends in Britain have helped the growth of supermarkets. These include monthly pay, more women workers and increased car ownership, all of which encourage less frequent shopping, but bigger shopping trips.

### Multiple stores

Multiple stores consist of large numbers of shops (at least ten) owned by one firm. Some specialise in one particular product, e.g. electrical goods (Dixons, Currys) or clothes (Burton, Next). Others such as Boots and Woolworths sell a wide variety of goods and are usually called *variety chain stores*.

Multiples of both types have several distinguishing features:

*(a)* Prices are usually very competitive.
*(b)* Each branch sells the same range of goods.
*(c)* They are usually located in the most popular sites in town centres and important suburbs. Usually, branches of the well-known chains will be close together. Even where three or four shops of the same type, e.g. Dixons, Currys, Lasky's, are close together, they will all benefit from the number of customers who will flock to the area.
*(d)* Layout and display within the stores is based upon standards set down by the head office.

# Shoppers blast big stores

SHOPPERS are fed up with rude assistants and endless queues in big stores and supermarkets, according to a report published today.

Four out of 10 shoppers interviewed for a magazine survey were upset by bad service and long waits.

Shoppers were particularly annoyed by psychological tricks like having sweets at checkouts, changing layouts, children's clothes on top floors, unmanageable trolleys, over-heating, paying for carrier bags and the lack of facilities for bored children and husbands.

Nearly half would prefer to

Argos — attacked

**Bradford Telegraph & Argus**

**Fig. 8.2** Supermarket service survey

*(e)* Buying of stock is centralised at head office. Computer records provide almost instant evidence of which lines are selling well and should be re-ordered, and which should be dropped or reduced in price.
*(f)* There is extensive advertising on television and in newspapers.
*(g)* Most run their own national training schemes for staff.

Most multiples aim to have common policies for all their branches, so that any branch, whether it is in Cardiff or Glasgow, will be immediately recognisable to the customer. In effect, the shop is 'branded' in the same way as Heinz Baked Beans or Kellogg's Cornflakes.

The specialist multiples tend to rely upon well-known brands, and 'own brands' are comparatively rare (although a store may turn an unknown manufacturer into a well-known name). Variety chain stores are more likely to use their own brand names, such as St Michael at Marks and Spencer.

Whether they use their own brand name or simply buy a large proportion of a firm's output, multiple chains tend to exert strict control over their suppliers, specifying exactly what they want in terms of quality, size and price. The most famous example of this is Marks and Spencer, which sends its own staff into suppliers to supervise their production.

## Superstores

A superstore is a shop with over 50 000 square feet of selling space. Like multiple stores, some superstores concentrate upon one particular product (e.g. MFI, B & Q) whilst others sell a variety of goods (e.g. Carrefour). The latter are sometimes called *hypermarkets*. Superstores selling one particular good are also called *discount stores* or *discount warehouses*.

Superstores are usually built on the edge of large towns, or on derelict main-road sites in inner-city areas. (The latter type of site has become more popular because of political pressure and concern about the effects upon city-centre trade.)

The main reason for choosing such locations is that superstores need large amounts of land for selling space, storage and parking. Some goods such as carpets, furniture and DIY goods are very bulky and require a lot of space to display effectively. Space in town

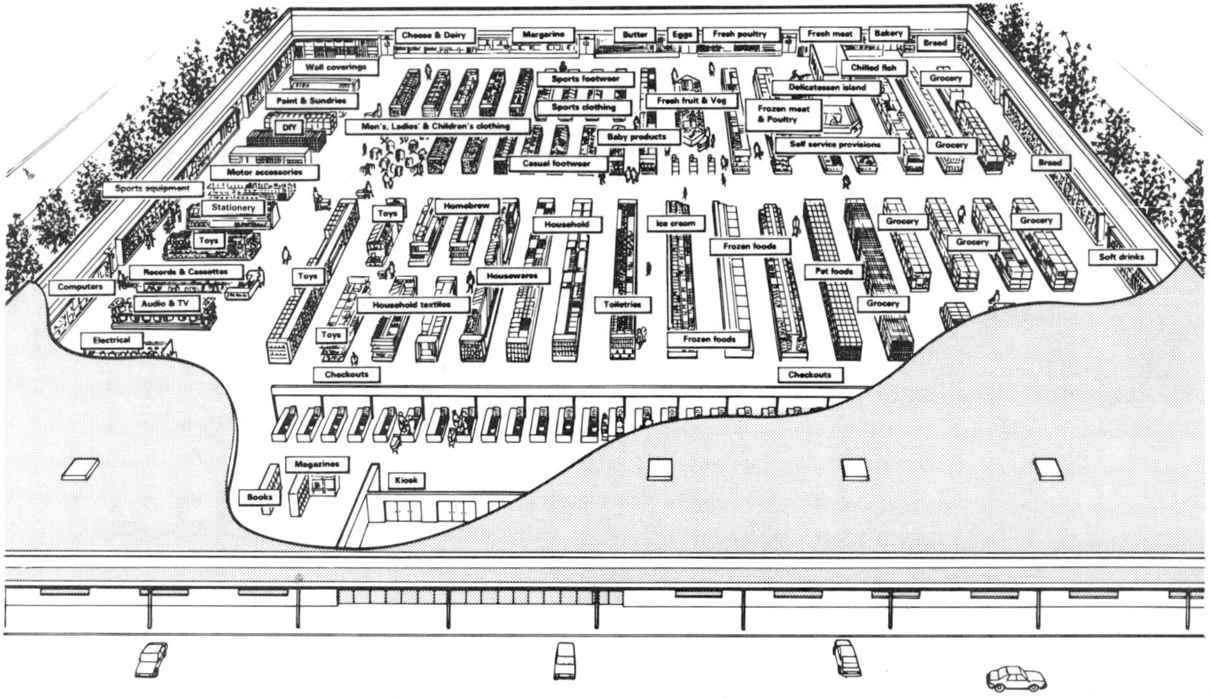

Fig. 8.3 Layout of a typical superstore

and city centres is usually restricted, and the competition for space means that land rents and purchase prices are very high.

Superstores do have some disadvantages for customers:

(a) They are difficult to reach for people without cars.
(b) They are sometimes unwilling to deliver, although this attitude is becoming less common.
(c) Service is often poor, with the minimum of staff available to advise customers. This is a disadvantage for some products such as DIY or electrical goods.
(d) Despite their size, the range of goods may be very limited. For example, most superstores selling computers do not sell accessories such as disks or printer ribbons, or offer services such as repairs.
(e) Because most goods are prepackaged, it is sometimes difficult to buy small quantities such as a single light-bulb or cassette.
(f) Prices are often higher than is generally realised, especially for more unusual items.

**Department stores**

Department stores are sometimes described as being several shops under one roof. The most famous example is Harrods in London – national chains include Debenhams, Rackhams and Lewis's.

The distinguishing features of a department store are:

(a) A large building with several floors, sited in the centre of a large town or city.
(b) Several distinct departments, under the control of departmental managers.
(c) A wide variety of goods (one famous department store boasts that it can supply 'anything from a pin to an elephant'). Department stores often supply goods which are not easily available elsewhere, such as unusual brands of tea and quality clothing material.
(d) A concentration upon good service, with specialist sales staff in each department.
(e) Luxurious surroundings.
(f) A range of services such as credit facilities, restrooms, restaurants and delivery.

In recent years, department stores have been very uncompetitive, and their share of the retail trade has failed to grow since the Second

World War. There are a number of reasons for this:

*(a)* Department store prices are high.
*(b)* Their buildings are old-fashioned and expensive to maintain. Many are now sited away from the focal point of city centres, which has shifted as new shopping centres have been built.
*(c)* Most multiple chains now offer the 'extras' which used to distinguish department stores, such as stylish surroundings and credit.
*(d)* Some people think of department stores as 'snooty' places.

**Co-operative retail societies**

Although the term 'Co-op' is seen on shops throughout the country, there are actually 90 separate locally-based organisations. The number has been reduced rapidly in recent years because of amalgamations. The retail co-operatives operate upon the principles of the co-operative movement as a whole (see Chapter 2) – democratic control, with profits being distributed to the members after allowance for future investment.

Many people think of the Co-op as being a large organisation run centrally from Manchester, but its control actually rests ultimately with the locally-based societies.

The modern co-operative movement is usually regarded as starting with the 'Rochdale Pioneers' in 1844, although there were some co-operatives before this, particularly in Yorkshire. The Pioneers were textile workers who put their money together to start a small shop in Toad Lane, Rochdale to provide good quality food for workers who were often exploited by shopkeepers.

The number of co-operatives grew rapidly. In 1863 the Co-operative Wholesale Society (CWS) was established because of the reluctance of many traders to supply co-operatives. Manufacturing of goods by the CWS began in 1873 with shoes and biscuits. It has steadily increased its range of activities, and now produces 60 percent of the goods sold in Co-op stores.

The CWS is involved in many industries (see Figure 8.4). It is Britain's largest farmer, undertaker and milkman. It is owned by the retail societies, from whose members the CWS Board is elected. The CWS also owns some 320 shops of its own.

The Co-op is unique amongst retailers in that most of its customers receive a dividend on their purchases (some societies do not

# UK CO-OPERATIVE MOVEMENT FACTS AND FIGURES

**CO-OPERATIVE RETAIL SOCIETIES**

| | |
|---|---|
| Turnover | £5350 Million |
| Trading surplus | £99 Million |
| Staff | 82 000 |
| Number of societies | 90 |
| Members' Benefits/dividend | £19 Million |
| Number of shops | 5000 (65 Superstores) |
| Number of members | 8 345 000 |

**THE CO-OPERATIVE WHOLESALE SOCIETY**

| | |
|---|---|
| Turnover | £2.4 Billion |
| Staff | 22 386 |
| Factories | 33 |
| Farms | 37 000 acres |
| Distribution centres | 18 |
| Co-op brand lines | 2000 |
| Number of shops | 320 |

**THE CO-OPERATIVE BANK GROUP**

| | |
|---|---|
| Assets | £1.64 Billion |
| Staff | 4409 |
| Branches | 100 |
| Handybanks | 586 |
| ChequePost (with cash-a-cheque support) | 370 |
| Cash-a-cheque points | 2370 |
| Customer accounts | 1.5 Million |
| Financial Centres | 49 |

**THE CO-OPERATIVE INSURANCE SOCIETY**

| | |
|---|---|
| Premium income | £768 Million |
| Assets | Over £5 Billion (market value) |
| Number of policies in force | 12 Million |
| Number of families insured | 3.9 Million |
| Staff | 11 200 |
| District Offices | 220 |
| Surplus on Life business for 1987 | £234 Million |

| | |
|---|---|
| CO-OPERATIVE TRAVEL (all societies) | 160 Branches |
| SHOEFAYRE | 180 Branches |
| CO-OPERATIVE OPTICIANS | 93 Practices |
| NATIONAL CO-OPERATIVE CHEMISTS | 150 Branches |
| WORKER CO-OPERATIVES (UK) | 2000 |

May 1988

Fig. 8.4 The Co-operative movement – facts and figures

pay a dividend as such, but keep prices low). Dividends are often paid by giving customers stamps which can be exchanged for cash, goods or shares in the society.

The retail societies have faced stiff competition because of the growth of multiple chains. They have reacted to this by merging from 200 societies in 1981 to less than half that number in 1988. Uneconomic factories and shops have been closed, and there have been extensive marketing campaigns to improve the Co-op's down-market image with many customers.

## Other types of retailer

### Mail order
Mail order, as its name suggests, involves buying goods and services by post. There are three main methods of obtaining mail order custom (most firms combine two or three of these).

**a) Direct advertising**  This involves selling goods and services through advertisements, usually in newspapers and magazines. Some publications such as the *Exchange and Mart* consist completely of such advertisements, with no editorial content at all.

A key feature of such advertising is 'targeting', i.e. reaching the right type of customer. It is often better to reach a few thousand of the 'right' people than millions who are not interested. For example, although four times as many people read the *Sun* as the *Times*, the *Times* is able to charge more for advertisements because its readers are generally better off than those of the *Sun*.

Many of the magazines we read are specifically aimed at a 'target group' so that particular products can be advertised to their readers with a high chance of success. For example, EMAP publishes titles such as *Your Horse*, *Q*, *Smash Hits*, *Trout Fisherman*, *Practical Gardening* and *Money Week*. Its aim is to have a publication for each interest and age group, e.g. *Smash Hits* for teenagers, *Q* for the over-25s. This policy is sometimes called *segmented marketing*.

Another method of reaching customers is through television advertising combined with 'phoning-in' of orders. This has been used very successfully with records. The advertisement is sold cheaply and can therefore be longer. The television company recovers the lost revenue by taking a percentage of the profits.

**b) Direct mail** This involves posting or delivering advertisements directly to people's homes or place of work. With the development of cheap and sophisticated computer technology, it is increasingly common for direct mail to be 'personalised' by having each individual's name already printed on the letter. This is thought to double the likelihood of people buying the product, because people are more inclined to read a letter with their name on it.

Direct mail can be very expensive. An 'unnamed' advertisement sent to homes or places of work at random is likely to achieve no more than one percent success. Allowing for postage and printing costs, this means that each order obtained will cost over £10. Because of this mail order firms try to 'target' their customers by various means:

*(a)* Concentrating upon existing customers. Some people absolutely refuse to buy anything by mail, so a list of people who are prepared to do so is very useful.

*(b)* Mailing to selected groups of people, for instance, a maths textbook publisher would be more successful with a list of named Heads of Departments than by sending adverts to schools at random.

*(c)* Using 'list' brokers who sell names of prospective customers for different products.

*(d)* Buying lists of names from other firms, for example, Readers Digest, department stores (account holders), magazines (subscribers) and Water Boards (ratepayers).

*(e)* Using information in publications such as *Acorn* or *Pinpoint*, which divide addresses into categories such as 'poor quality older terraced housing' and 'better-off retirement areas'. Adverts aimed at senior citizens, for example, could be sent only to addresses in the latter category.

By using methods such as these the proportion of successful mailings can be increased to ten percent or even higher. As Figure 8.5 shows, direct mail is a rapidly expanding form of marketing.

**c) Catalogues** Mail order catalogues started in the USA during the early 1900s. They were aimed mainly at farming families who lived a long way from the nearest town. Examples in Britain include Littlewoods, Kays and Peter Craig. They sell a variety of goods, although much of their business is in clothing.

## Direct mail: who sends it?

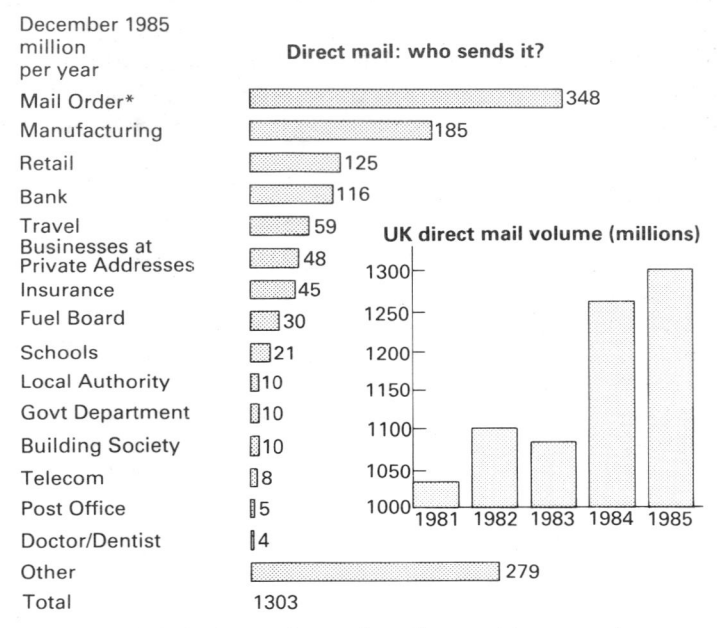

December 1985 million per year

| | |
|---|---|
| Mail Order* | 348 |
| Manufacturing | 185 |
| Retail | 125 |
| Bank | 116 |
| Travel | 59 |
| Businesses at Private Addresses | 48 |
| Insurance | 45 |
| Fuel Board | 30 |
| Schools | 21 |
| Local Authority | 10 |
| Govt Department | 10 |
| Building Society | 10 |
| Telecom | 8 |
| Post Office | 5 |
| Doctor/Dentist | 4 |
| Other | 279 |
| Total | 1303 |

UK direct mail volume (millions): 1981, 1982, 1983, 1984, 1985

\* Does not include the goods sent (usually parcels) as a result of mail order offers.

**Fig. 8.5** Direct mail in Britain

Originally, catalogues operated mainly through agents, generally women who sold to their friends and family. In recent years there has been a move towards people ordering mainly for themselves. The advantages of catalogues included 'free' credit, commission on goods sold and the ability to send back unwanted goods. These were offset by the disadvantages of having to wait for delivery and the high prices necessary to cover the costs of commission, postage and credit.

In the 1970s the mail order catalogues suffered badly from competition by the multiple chains. Shops began to offer their own credit cards, which removed one of the main benefits of catalogue purchases. Mail order catalogues have always had a 'downmarket' image, regarded by the better-off purchaser as being for people who can't afford to go to 'real' shops. Firms such as Next and Harrods have recently launched catalogues designed to overcome this image.

The mail order firms have begun to fight back, particularly by using their computerised records of customers. A typical mail order company will have information such as the following about its customers;

*(a)* Where they live, and in what type of house.
*(b)* The type of goods they tend to buy.
*(c)* Whether they have young children.
*(d)* If they have a garden.
*(e)* The size of clothes they wear, e.g. a person who consistently orders large-size clothes will tend to receive an 'outsize' catalogue such as Grattan's 'Fashion Plus'.
*(f)* Whether they have credit cards with shops.
*(g)* If they have any 'bad debts'.

By using this information the catalogue firms can aim their mailings more precisely at people who are likely to buy their products. Many now run 'specialogues' which concentrate upon one type of good, for instance, gardening or sporting equipment, or expensive 'gimmicky' goods such as a machine for stamping initials on golf balls. These will only be sent to people whose previous purchases indicate an interest in the particular type of good.

**Door-to-door sales**
Door-to-door sales are used to sell a variety of goods and services. The goods are usually small household items such as brushes and cleaning materials. Because of the expense of sending people round houses, at many of which they will be unsuccessful, selling goods by 'cold-calling' is not as common as it used to be.

The main growth area in door-to-door selling is in services, particularly home improvements such as double-glazing and porch extensions. The high cost of the product justifies the time and expense of sending sales staff.

**Auctions**
Auctions have always been popular for selling certain types of goods such as cars, antiques and 'bankrupt stock' from firms who have gone out of business. They are also popular for house sales when prices are rising rapidly.

88  *Business and Commerce*

**Fig. 8.6**  One view of auctions

Generally, goods sold at auctions are cheaper than elsewhere (cars can be bought for up to 50 percent less than dealers' prices). However, the legal rights of buyers are weaker and it is often difficult to inspect or try out the goods. Many auction firms make up for this by providing 'warranties' for certain classes of goods.

## Automatic vending

This means using machines to sell goods, mainly small items such as chocolate or cigarettes. Some also sell services such as railway tickets and entry to car parks. There are probably about half a million vending machines in the UK. Their growth has been hampered in the past by their proneness to breakdown and vandalism, but modern electronic machines are more resistant to these problems. (The latest 'pay and display' machines for car-parks will even resist a truck being driven over them.)

## Party-plan selling

Party-plan selling is used to sell many different products, usually small goods such as clothes, handbags and Tupperware. People invite friends and family to their home. The party organiser, who is employed by the firm, gives a short talk or demonstration and then takes orders for goods.

Party-plan selling can be fun and there are sometimes bargains. However, prices are often high, people may feel obliged to buy and there is usually a delay before the goods are received.

# 9

# Wholesaling

Wholesaling is the link between the manufacturer of goods and the retailer. It is part of the *chain of distribution*:

MANUFACTURER → WHOLESALER → RETAILER → CONSUMER

As explained below, this pattern does not occur for all goods, but the wholesaler's fundamental role is to act as a 'middleman', buying in large quantities from manufacturers and then 'breaking bulk' by selling smaller quantities.

A large proportion of wholesale custom is not actually with retailers. Many large organisations such as schools and hospitals buy direct from wholesalers. In some areas health and education authorities combine to run their own wholesale operation.

## Types of wholesaler

### Consumer goods wholesalers
There are many different types of wholesaler of consumer goods, as Figure 9.1 shows. Some, such as Booker and Linfood, are national organisations, but many supply a small area or region. They may be general stockists or concentrate upon a particular item such as clothes or electrical goods. A large number are *cash-and-carry* warehouses which, as their name suggests, do not offer delivery or credit. Cutting out the costs of these services allows them to offer very competitive prices.

### Industrial wholesalers
As well as consumer goods, a considerable part of the wholesaling

**Fig. 9.1** Examples of consumer goods wholesalers

industry is involved in distributing *producer goods* such as raw materials, components and machinery. These involve sales to firms rather than retailers, and are very important to the economy. For example, about 15 percent of wholesale businesses deal in industrial materials.

One example of this is the steel stockholding industry. Steel is manufactured on a large scale, but thousands of small engineering firms require a wide range of metal supplies, often in small quantities. Steel stockholders buy and store steel in vast amounts, whilst allowing small purchases to be made by their customers.

**Agricultural wholesalers**
The traditional system for distributing agricultural produce depended upon an involved network of local markets. Additionally, in a number of large towns, wholesale produce markets like Covent Garden were established for vegetables, fruit, poultry and flowers. This was ideal for the thousands of small farmers remote from towns, because wholesalers collected, graded and packed produce.

Since 1931, attempts have been made to assist farmers financially and to encourage higher production of food in Britain. Marketing Boards were set up to organise distribution, give guaranteed prices to farmers and set quality standards for products such as milk, eggs and potatoes. Although they are still important, the influence of the Marketing Boards has declined because of factors such as increased foreign competition and direct buying by retailers, some of whom actually own their own farms.

# Services provided by the wholesaler

The goods which are eventually bought by the public must firstly be distributed from the manufacturer to the retailer, and then presented in a form and quantity acceptable to the consumer. The wholesaler performs several functions during this process.

**1 'Breaks bulk'** The wholesaler buys large quantities from the manufacturer and sells in smaller amounts to the retailer. This is called *breaking bulk*.

For example, a soap manufacturer might sell bars of soap in hundreds or thousands to a wholesaler who would then sell the soap to retailers in boxes of a few dozen. The retailer would then sell single bars to the public.

**2 Provides services for the manufacturer** By breaking bulk the wholesaler saves the manufacturer a lot of money and trouble. It would be difficult and expensive for the manufacturer to sell small quantities of goods to thousands of different retailers. This would mean processing millions of orders every year, each of which would involve sorting, packing and delivery. There would also be extensive documentation for each of the individual customers (see Chapter 6) which would involve considerable costs.

Wholesalers save manufacturers this time and trouble. Instead of sending small orders to thousands of retailers, large orders can be dispatched to a small number of wholesalers, who take responsibility for distribution within their area.

The wholesaler also takes responsibility for storing goods, and may help the manufacturer's cash-flow by holding reserve stocks of goods. This is especially helpful in industries where there is *seasonal demand* such as toy manufacture, where goods have to be made several months in advance of the main buying period.

**3 Provides services for the retailer** The wholesaler enables the retailer to buy in small amounts, for example a few dozen bars of soap at once. Retailers have limited storage space and capital. The wholesaler holds easily available stocks and may provide credit terms.

Wholesalers also save retailers time and money by stocking goods from a variety of manufacturers. Even a small shop is likely to sell serveral hundred different items manufactured by many different firms. Corresponding with each of these suppliers would be expensive and time-consuming. By dealing with one or two wholesalers, the retailer can cut costs.

With some goods such as tea and other food products, the wholesaler may take responsibility for grading and packaging produce. Large wholesalers may sell under their own brand name.

**4 Provides market information** Through contact with retailers and manufacturers, the wholesaler learns a great deal about the demand for different products. The retailer learns of new products and suppliers from the wholesaler's displays and sales literature.

The wholesaler also helps manufacturers to decide how much of their goods to produce. For example, if consumers buy less of a product, retailers will order smaller quantities from the wholesalers. When wholesale orders drop, manufacturers will cut production. Large manufacturers often have their own market research programmes but for smaller firms their main information will come from wholesalers of their products.

## Is the wholesaler necessary?

It is sometimes suggested that wholesalers are unnecessary, and that if manufacturers sold direct to retailers the wholesaler's profit would be eliminated. This would result in lower prices for the consumer. However, as explained above, the wholesaler saves both manufacturers and retailers expense by cutting down on paperwork and transport costs.

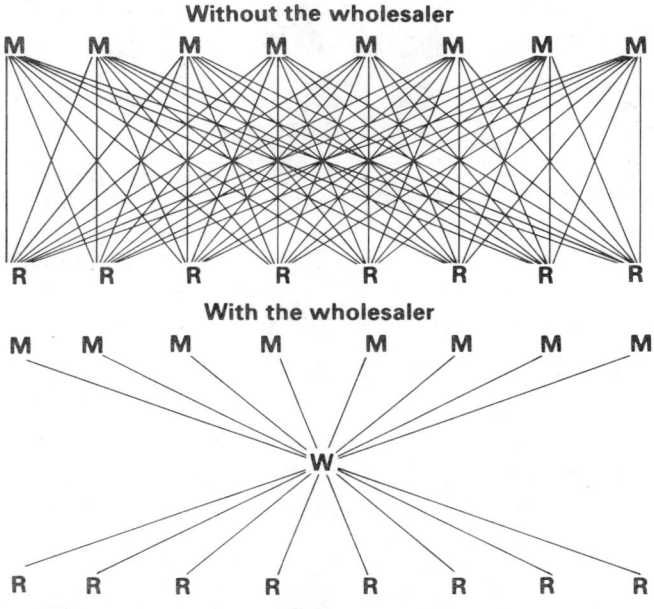

**Fig. 9.2** How the wholesaler saves time and money

This can be seen by taking a very simple example of a good for which there are eight manufacturers and eight retailers. Even with this extremely small and unrealistic number, the wholesaler can simplify the process of distribution considerably. As shown in Figure 9.2, without the wholesaler there are 64 lines of communication; with the wholesaler there are only 16. With a more realistic number of retailers, the saving would be even greater.

Although the chain of distribution need not include the wholesaler, the functions of the wholesaler such as storage, packing and distribution still have to be performed. There are many cases where the independent wholesaler can do this cheaply and efficiently.

## Bypassing the wholesaler

In some instances, the independent wholesaler (but not the wholesaling function) has been eliminated from the chain of distribution. There are several reasons for this:

(a) Large multiple stores often buy direct from the manufacturer, because they can afford to buy in bulk.
(b) Many large multiple chains sell 'own brand' goods which are made to their own specification.
(c) Some manufacturers own their own retail outlets.
(d) In some industries there are *tied outlets* which sell only or mainly one firm's products, e.g. petrol stations, pubs.
(e) Expensive and/or technical goods such as cars or machinery are often sold direct to the retailer or customer through special order. These may also require specialist advice from the manufacturer.
(f) The manufacturer may sell direct to the consumer, usually by mail order or in factory shops.

# 10
# Money and Finance

## The importance of money

In a modern economy a well-developed and efficient financial system is essential to allow for payments for goods and services, and for borrowing to finance investment and consumption. For example, the high level of house and car ownership is only possible because firms and consumers are able to borrow large sums of money in order to finance production and purchase of these commodities.

In primitive societies, goods and services were exchanged through *barter* – direct exchange of one good or service for another without the use of money. However, this meant that people had to find somebody willing to make a direct exchange, which could be difficult. Gradually, certain items began to be accepted as payment by all buyers and sellers.

This earliest type of money was called *commodity money* and its exact form varied in different societies. Cowrie shells, axe-heads, beads, cattle and tobacco have all been used as commodity money. During the Second World War cigarettes were used as a common medium of exchange in prisoner-of-war camps, since even a non-smoker could always find somebody to accept them.

With a few exceptions such as this, commodity money is non-existent in industrial countries in the twentieth century. This is because commodities generally lack the desirable characteristics of money.

Commodities are not *durable* – animals age and die, metals rust and so on. They are therefore a poor *store of value* because their value tends to fall. Some forms such as cattle are not *convenient* to use, and are not *divisible* into small quantities. They are not *standardised* because their size, weight and quality varies considerably. Most commodities were acceptable as money because they were *scarce*, in the sense that there was a natural limit upon their supply. However, in some cases such as tobacco in Virginia, the supply increased so much that it eventually became unacceptable as money.

Historically, commodity money was gradually replaced by the use of precious metals such as gold and silver. These had several advantages over most commodities – they were scarce, attractive-looking, durable, easily divisible into small quantities and easy to melt and work with primitive equipment.

Later, gold and silver came to be shaped into coins of recognisable weight and value. The first *standardised coinage* was issued by King Croesus of Lydia, a part of modern Turkey, in the 6th century BC. All coins had to be of the same shape, weight and value. Croesus had his picture put on the coins so that people would have faith in them, and nobody else was allowed to mint coins. Not surprisingly, given this monopoly, Croesus became very wealthy; hence the saying 'as rich as Croesus'.

The first paper money is thought to have been issued by goldsmiths in 13th century Italy (the word 'bank' comes from the Italian *banco* meaning bench). Goldsmiths kept strong boxes or rooms to store the valuable metals with which they worked. They would also allow people to deposit their money and valuables in their vaults, for which they paid a storage fee. The goldsmith would issue a receipt for the valuables.

These receipts were as good as money, and people began to sign them over to each other rather than go to the goldsmith to retrieve their money. Goldsmiths began to issue notes for fixed amounts and make them 'payable to the bearer' rather than to a named person. This is how the modern banknote began.

The use of notes meant that there was far less physical movement of gold. The goldsmiths found that people tended to actually withdraw only a small proportion of their money at any one time leaving the rest in the vaults. So the goldsmiths started to lend this surplus money to merchants, generally by issuing notes, and thus became the first lending banks.

The important feature of these new notes was that they were not totally backed by gold. The goldsmith was issuing more notes than he could actually give gold for and if more than a certain proportion of the gold was requested at one time, he would be unable to provide it. (When a goldsmith was unable to pay his debts, his bench was symbolically broken up, hence the word 'bankrupt'.)

Modern banks work in exactly the same way, depending upon people only wanting a certain amount of their money at any one time. A bank may typically only have enough cash or liquid assets to repay about ten percent of its deposits. As long as people have faith in it, this will not matter. If, however, people think that the bank is unsafe, there will be a 'run' on the bank as people try to take their money out. If this happens the bank will eventually run out of money and collapse.

It can therefore be seen that the use of paper money depends completely upon people having faith in the system. There are many regulations about who is allowed to run a bank, and the proportion of the deposits that must be kept for 'prudential' reasons. In most countries control over the banking system is the responsibility of a *central bank* such as the Bank of England or the Federal Reserve Bank in the USA.

Since 1921 the Bank of England has had the sole right to issue notes in England and Wales, with other banks being given permission to issue their own notes in Scotland and Northern Ireland. Notes are no longer backed by gold; the note issue is now *fiduciary* (based upon faith) and is backed by sales of Government securities.

In a modern economy, notes and coins are only a very small proportion (less than ten percent) of the total supply of money. Most money now consists of deposits in banks and other financial institutions such as building societies. Almost all large payments are made by transferring these deposits through means such as cheques and giro credits. Cheques are not actually money in themselves – they are merely a means of transferring money.

## The Bank of England

The Bank of England was founded in 1694 to raise money for foreign wars. Because of financial crises at the beginning of the nineteenth century, it gradually acquired special powers and

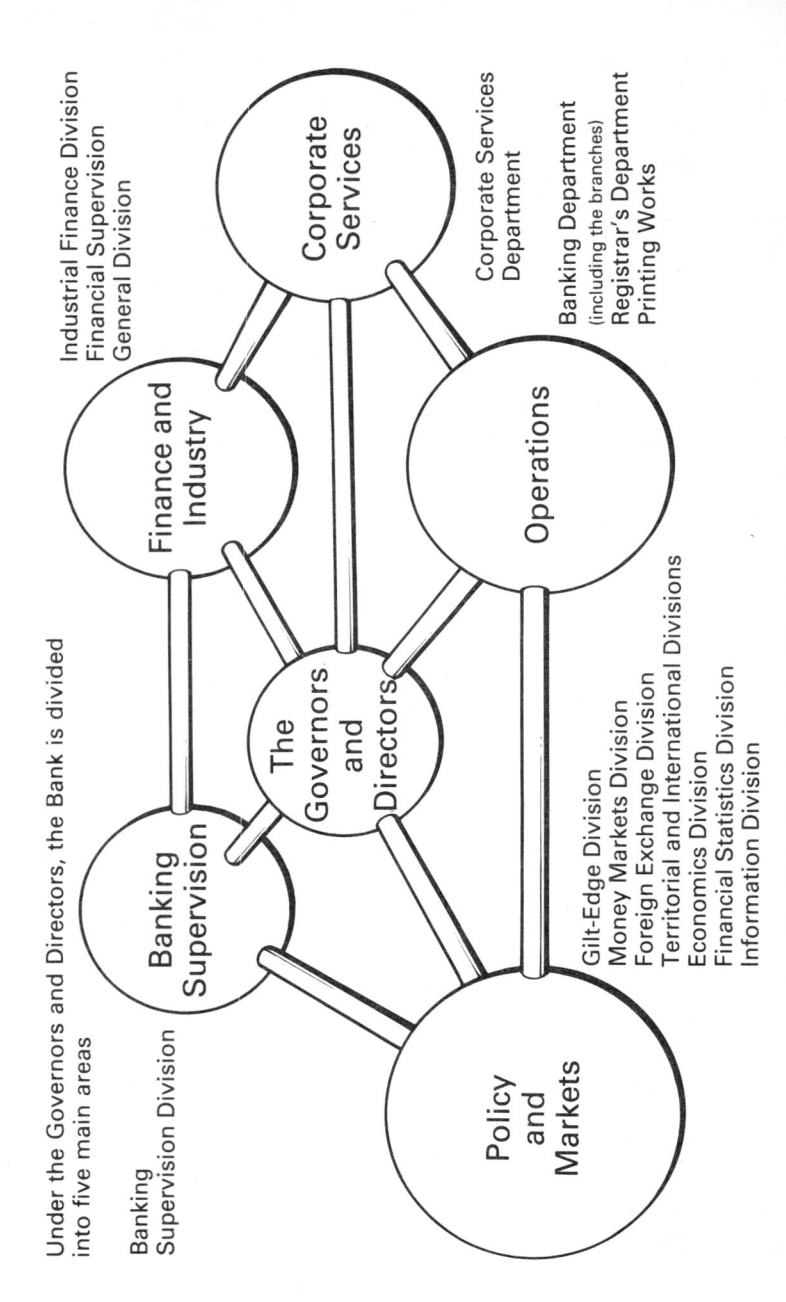

Under the Governors and Directors, the Bank is divided into five main areas

**Banking Supervision**
Banking Supervision Division

**Finance and Industry**
Industrial Finance Division
Financial Supervision
General Division

**Corporate Services**
Corporate Services Department

**Operations**
Banking Department (including the branches)
Registrar's Department
Printing Works

**Policy and Markets**
Gilt-Edge Division
Money Markets Division
Foreign Exchange Division
Territorial and International Divisions
Economics Division
Financial Statistics Division
Information Division

**Fig. 10.1** How the Bank of England is organised

responsibilities and became Britain's *central bank*. Although still a privately-owned joint-stock company, it was given the Government's authority to carry out monetary policy and supervise the banking system.

In 1946 the Bank was nationalised and its directors are now appointed by the Government. Its duties and responsibilities are as follows:

1 *Note issue*. Banknotes are issued on demand to the clearing banks, who can draw as many as they wish. The notes are paid for from the clearing bank's accounts at the Bank of England. The amount of cash in circulation varies throughout the year, with more being issued at peak times such as Christmas.

2 *The banker's bank*. The commercial banks keep accounts at the Bank. These *balances at the Bank of England*, as they are called, are used by the banks to make payments to each other, especially through the *clearing system*.

3 *The Government's bank*. The Bank is responsible for implementing the Government's monetary policy. It advises upon matters such as the level of interest rates, manages the Government's borrowing, and repays the National Debt (the money owed because of Government borrowing in the past).

4 *Lender of last resort*. The Bank of England ensures that there are always sufficient funds in the banking system by agreeing to lend to *discount houses* (see below) if they cannot obtain funds from the commercial banks.

5 *Exchange rate management*. The Bank of England operates the *Exchange Equalisation Account* which consists of reserves of foreign currency and other assets. If the value of sterling is falling on the foreign exchange markets, the Bank may use its reserves to buy sterling and maintain its exchange rate. If the Government wishes the exchange rate to fall, the Bank will sell sterling.

## Specialist financial institutions

### Discount houses

Discount houses are *market-makers*, specialising in buying and selling Government securities. They guarantee to buy any unsold Treasury Bills in the weekly issue, paying for these with money borrowed from the commercial banks. They make a profit by buying these securities and selling them on at a higher price.

**Accepting houses**
Accepting houses, which are often well-established merchant bankers, guarantee or *accept* commercial *bills of exchange* (see Chapter 16). They have agents throughout the world, and will investigate the credit-worthiness of any firm issuing a commercial bill.

**Merchant banks**
These include many well-known names such as Rothschild, Baring and Lazard. They undertake a wide range of activities. Some are discounting and accepting houses, and many specialise in arranging large loans for governments and large firms (see Chapter 2 for examples). They are also often used to arrange a new issue of shares.

**Finance houses**
These businesses originally specialised in providing finance for hire-purchase loans. In recent years many have extended their activities to include services such as personal loans, second mortgages and credit accounts.

Many of these finance houses are owned by commercial banks and some, such as HFC, have become banks themselves. Although many of their services are similar to those of the banks, finance houses are actually *licensed deposit-takers* and are not allowed to use the term 'bank' in their title.

## Commercial banks

The commercial banks are the large High Street institutions such as Barclays, Midland and Lloyds. They have four main functions:

1  To accept deposits.
2  To make loans.
3  To provide services for the payment of money (a *money transmission service*).
4  To undertake the physical distribution of notes and coins throughout the country.

The bulk of the banks' profits come from lending money, but they also provide a wide range of other services which are referred to later in this chapter. An increasing proportion of their total business and profits comes from extra services such as the sales of insurance and shares.

## Types of bank account

There are three main types of bank account – *current*, *deposit* and *budget*. Although there are always new types of account being created, most would fall into one of these three categories.

### Current accounts

Current accounts are intended mainly for making and receiving payments from other accounts, rather than saving. Generally, no interest is payable, as this type of account is expensive for a bank to run.

The main service offered to holders of current accounts is money transmission – cash withdrawals and deposits and payments to and from other accounts. The latter can be made through various means such as cheques, giro credits and standing orders. These are discussed in greater detail later in this chapter.

Opening a current account is a fairly simple process. A reference may be required from an employer or another bank. The customer will be asked to provide specimen signatures so that if a cheque book is lost or stolen, forged cheques can be identified easily.

The administration costs of current accounts are high – cheques have to be handled and statements prepared – so there are often charges to be paid by the customer. These are usually based upon the number of payments made out of the account, with payments in not usually charged for on personal accounts. Nowadays, most banks do not charge at all if the customer is in credit, hoping to recover their costs by not paying interest and selling other services.

Business accounts are usually charged for both paying in and withdrawing money, as the number of transactions is likely to be much higher than for personal accounts. However the extent of charges can be negotiated, and concessions may be made where salaries are paid through the bank.

## Cash

The most widely used way of making payments. Almost 90% of all payments are still settled with cash

## Cheque

Can be used to purchase goods and services or to obtain cash from a bank account

## Credit Cards

Card holders can obtain goods and services from those shops, garages and other organisations which accept the cards. Can also be used to obtain cash from banks at home and abroad

## Regular Payments

### Standing Order

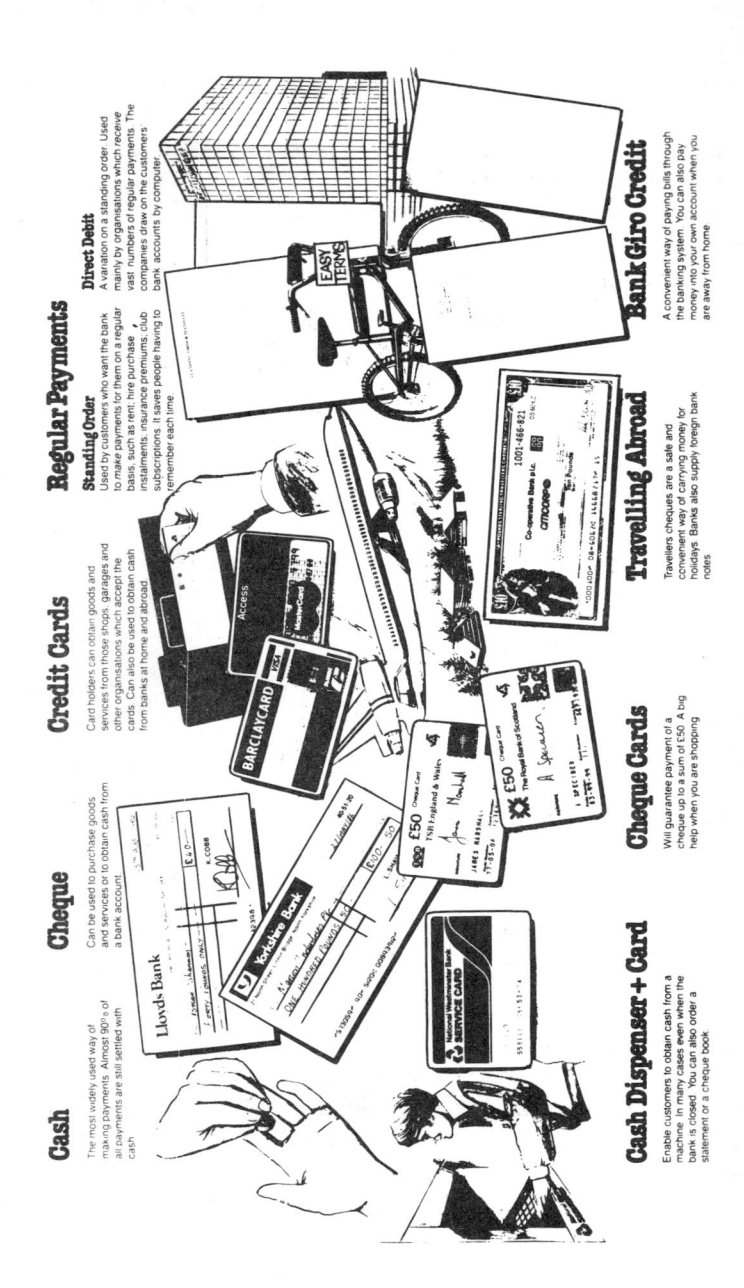

Used by customers who want the bank to make payments for them on a regular basis, such as rent, hire purchase instalments, insurance premiums, club subscriptions. It saves people having to remember each time

### Direct Debit

A variation on a standing order. Used mainly by organisations which receive vast numbers of regular payments. The companies draw on the customers' bank accounts by computer

## Cash Dispenser + Card

Enable customers to obtain cash from a machine in many cases even when the bank is closed. You can also order a statement or a cheque book

## Cheque Cards

Will guarantee payment of a cheque up to a sum of £50. A big help when you are shopping

## Travelling Abroad

Travellers cheques are a safe and convenient way of carrying money for holidays. Banks also supply foreign bank notes

## Bank Giro Credit

A convenient way of paying bills through the banking system. You can also pay money into your own account when you are away from home

**Fig. 10.2** Banks and payments

## Deposit accounts

Deposit accounts are designed for saving, and pay interest upon money deposited. The account cannot be overdrawn, and services such as chequebooks and standing orders are not provided; a current account must be opened to obtain these. The customer has to give seven days notice before withdrawing money, although this rule is normally waived for small amounts.

## Budget accounts

These are designed to allow customers to pay large bills which occur at awkward times, such as the gas, electricity and telephone bills all arriving at the same time. The customer makes regular payments, usually monthly, into a special account. He or she is then permitted to withdraw from this account to pay bills.

Budget accounts work in one of two basic ways. In one, the customer adds up all the expected bills for the next year. The total is divided by twelve and this amount is paid in monthly. The account will be in credit at some times and overdrawn at others, but has to be balanced at the end of the year, with a new arrangement then being made.

The other method is a *revolving credit* account. A minimum fixed sum is paid in every month, and the account can be overdrawn by a multiple of the monthly payment. One bank currently operates upon a credit limit of 30 times the monthly payment. A customer with a minimum payment of £20 per month would therefore be allowed to overdraw by up to 30 × £20, i.e. £600.

# Cheques

A cheque is a written instruction to a bank to pay a certain sum of money to a named person or organisation – the *payee*. A specimen cheque is illustrated in Figure 10.3, with explanatory notes.

## Cashing of cheques

A cheque that is *open* (i.e. does not have the two parallel lines drawn across the cheque as shown in Figure 10.3 or has the crossing cancelled by the account holder as shown in Figure 10.5) can be exchanged for cash at the bank branch on which it is drawn. Unless special arrangements are made it cannot be cashed at any other branch.

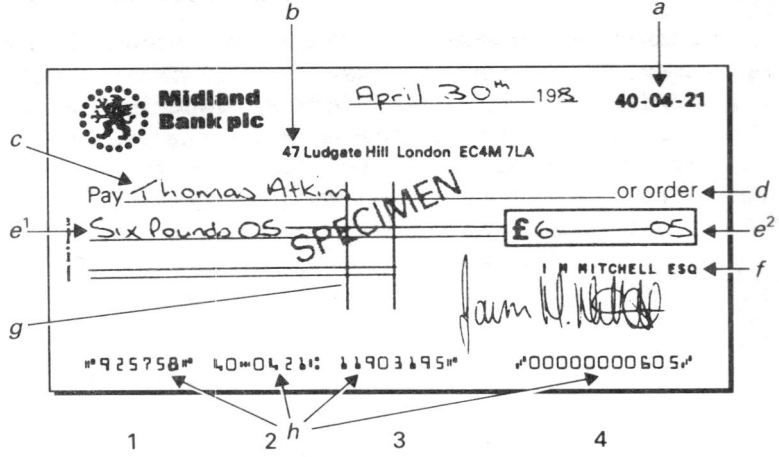

**Notes**

(*a*) The branch/bank identification code number – all cheques drawn on this particular branch office bear this number.
(*b*) The drawee – the branch where the account holder maintains his account.
(*c*) The payee – if the account holder is withdrawing cash, it is usual to insert the one word 'Cash'.
(*d*) Virtually all cheques are made payable 'or order' (see explanation below under negotiation of cheques). A cheque could be made payable 'or bearer', which means that whoever presents it for payment is entitled to the amount stated, but in view of the risks involved this style is rare.
($e^1$) and ($e^2$). If the cheque is hand-written a hyphen is used; if typed or printed a decimal point is made. Note that if a cheque is for an amount under £1 it should be made out thus:

*Words*: Sixty eight pence ─────────────────────
*Figures*: £0-68

Care should always be taken to ensure, by using dashes and not leaving spaces, that alterations cannot be made. For example, £6 has been easily altered in the following case:

Six   pounds        £6
Sixty pounds        £60-00

(*f*) The drawer – the account holder.
(*g*) The crossing – see notes below.
(*h*) Magnetic ink character recognition (MICR) – this gets information relating to the branch book-keeping into the computer. (1), (2) and (3) represent the cheque number, the bank/branch number referred to in (*a*) and the customer's account number respectively; these are already printed on the cheque when the customer receives his cheque book. (4) is a transaction code, identifying the type of voucher being processed, and the amount of the cheque; this is printed on during the clearing process.

**Fig. 10.3**   A specimen cheque

An account holder can draw cash up to a certain maximum (£50 for most people) at any commercial bank if a *cheque card* is used. A cheque card can also be used to pay for goods and services up to a value of £50. In these cases the retailer or other payee is guaranteed payment even if the account holder has no funds in his or her account, provided that the conditions of use are observed.

These conditions are fairly simple. There is a limit of £50 per transaction, the cheque must be signed in the presence of the payee and the number of the cheque card must be written on the back of the cheque by the payee.

In recent years most banks have installed electronic *cash dispensers* at their branches. These allow customers to withdraw money without having to be served by a cashier, and most provide 24-hour cashing facilities. Some also allow customers to order statements and chequebooks, check their balance and pay money in.

As well as being convenient for customers, cash dispensers save the bank money. For example, if a customer cashes a cheque, the bank has to pay costs such as the cashier's wages and the physical handling of the cheque (which may have to go through the clearing system). The same withdrawal made at a cash dispenser only costs computer time, which is far cheaper.

**Crossed cheques**

Most cheques issued are *crossed* to make them more secure if stolen. A crossed cheque has to be paid through an account at a bank, building society or other financial institution. Most cheques have two lines drawn on them to indicate that they are crossed. There are two types of crossing, *general* and *special*, as illustrated in Figure 10.4.

Most cheques have a general crossing, which is sufficient for most normal purposes. However, account holders sometimes add the words 'non-negotiable' which means that a cheque can only be paid into the account of the payee. If these words are not added the payee may transfer the cheque to somebody else by signing the back of the cheque or writing 'Pay A. Brown' or some other name and adding a signature.

A crossing can be cancelled by the account holder. For example, if it is intended to allow the payee to draw cash the words 'pay cash'

1 *General crossing.* This is the one commonly used. Often the words '& Co.' are added, but this has no particular significance, merely being a relic of early banking practice. A cheque with a general crossing can be paid into any bank and normally can be paid into another person's account.

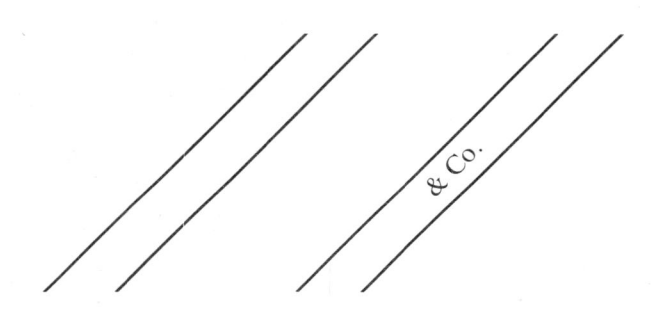

2 *Special crossing.* This is an added precaution, because it ensures that the cheque can be paid only into a particular bank and sometimes to a named account only. A few examples are:

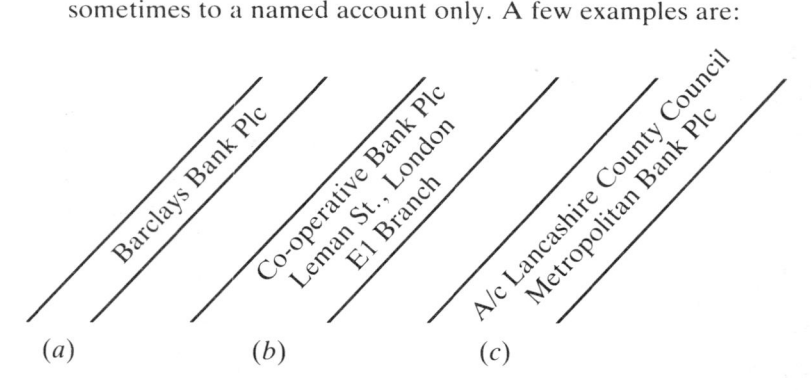

(a)  (b)  (c)

(a) Cheque can be paid into any Barclays branch.
(b) Although the drawer has named a particular branch, the cheque can nevertheless be paid in to any branch of the Co-operative Bank.
(c) Cheque can only be paid into the named account at the bank referred to.

**Fig. 10.4** Types of cheque crossing

can be written across the printed lines, followed by the signature of the account holder, as in Figure 10.5. The bank will usually cash cheques for small amounts presented in this way.

### Precautions in the use of cheques

The commercial banks issue the following recommendations to their customers:

1. Use the printed order form in the chequebook when requesting new cheques.
2. Write in ink, leaving no spaces for other words or figures to be inserted. Businesses often print the information by computer.
3. Sign your name (not just initials) against any alteration – in practice it is best not to alter cheques at all.
4. Take care of your chequebook and do not keep it together with your cheque card.

### Postdated cheques

This is a cheque dated for some time in the future, which cannot be paid until that date. The bank may therefore refuse to accept it until the stipulated date.

### Stopping a cheque

If the drawer does not wish a cheque to be paid (if it is lost or stolen for example) an instruction can be issued to the bank to *stop* it, i.e. refuse to pay it. However, a person who pays for goods at a shop using a cheque card cannot subsequently stop the cheque if the conditions of use have been followed.

**Fig. 10.5** Cancelling a cheque crossing

### Banker's draft
This is a special cheque drawn up by the bank itself. The payee is guaranteed payment. Banker's drafts are used for urgent or large payments such as those made for house purchases.

### Bills of exchange
These were the original form of cheque, but they have largely been replaced for most payments. They are now mainly used in international trade, and are discussed in Chapter 16.

### The clearing system
A cheque can be used to draw money at any branch of any bank. Because the banks accept cheques from each other's customers, the *clearing system* has been set up to arrange for the exchange of cheques and the adjustment of accounts. If a bank branch receives a cheque from another bank, it will send the cheque through the clearing system, which is illustrated in Figure 10.6.

Cheques received from a different branch of the same bank are dealt with by the bank's Head Office and do not go through the clearing system. Clearing a cheque generally takes about three working days, although quicker clearing can be arranged for a small fee if payment is required urgently.

At the end of each day's clearing, each bank prepares a *settlement sheet* showing the amounts owed to or by other banks. The difference between the two amounts is added to or deducted from each bank's *balances at the Bank of England.*

Sometimes a cheque may be returned to the payee because the person or firm who wrote it does not have enough in their account. Banks are usually reluctant to do this, but if it is necessary the cheque is marked 'refer to drawer' or 'R/D' and the payee has to ask the drawer to provide payment. This is known as 'bouncing' a cheque.

## The credit transfer (giro credit) system

Many payments are made between bank accounts using the credit transfer system. Examples include:

1 A customer paying money into his or her account from a different branch.

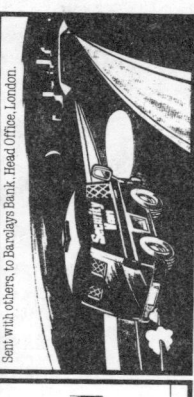

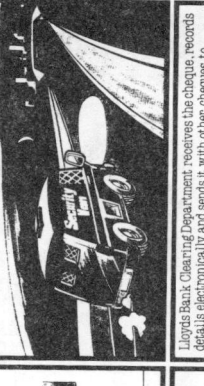

**Fig. 10.6** Life story of a cheque

2   Regular payments made by *standing order*. A standing order is an instruction to a bank to pay fixed amounts to another bank account at specified times. For example, a person might tell a bank to pay £300 from his or her account on the first of every month to a building society for a mortgage.
3   A business paying its employees by issuing a single cheque payable to its own bank. The business will supply a list of the names, branches and amounts to be paid to each person. The bank then arranges credits for each of the relevant accounts.

In 1960 these credit transfer activities were extended to include the following:

4   A customer or non-customer could pay in money at one branch for the credit of a customer at a different branch or bank. Institutions such as local authorities, gas and electricity boards began to include a credit-transfer slip in their bills. The customer could thus pay easily either by cash or cheque, instead of having to visit the organisation's offices. Mail order companies also use this system extensively.

Since 1960, the items paid under 1 to 4 have been settled through the bankers' clearing house under a credit clearing. This operates in a similar way to the cheque clearing described above. The number of credit vouchers is increasing rapidly every year, amounting to several million every week.

## Direct debiting

This is another system for settling debts which has been introduced in recent years. As far as the ordinary customer is concerned, the working of the system is similar to that of standing orders. However, there are two significant differences.

A standing order is an instruction by the customer to make a payment. When a direct debit is issued, however, the account holder gives a creditor permission to claim direct from his or her bank. For example, a customer may give an electricity company permission to deduct the quarterly bill from an account. When the bill becomes due the electricity board will ask the customer's bank for the money, and this will be paid.

The other main difference is that a standing order is for a fixed amount specified in advance, whereas a direct debit is for any sum claimed by the payee. This makes it suitable for payments for electricity and insurance, where the amount payable cannot be known in advance, or to save the bother of changing standing orders every year. There are safeguards to ensure that this freedom is not abused – a bill is usually sent some time before the deduction is made.

The direct debit system is very convenient for businesses, saving time and money on making and receiving payments. Sometimes part of this saving is passed on to the customer through lower prices or interest rates for credit card holders.

## Other banking services

Banks offer many services to both individuals and firms, and the range offered grows every year. They include the following.

### Advice
Personal and commercial customers can obtain advice and assistance from the bank's specialists upon matters such as taxation, finance and business. The bank may also provide a personal or trade reference for a customer seeking to obtain credit or rent a flat.

### Safeguarding of valuables
Valuable items and documents such as house deeds can be deposited in banks' strongrooms. Some branches have special safe-deposit facilities which enable customers to have access to their own secure private compartments. Businesses such as shops also make great use of *night safes*. These are secure metal boxes set into the wall of the bank into which keyholders can deposit money after the bank has closed. The money is placed in a special pouch which is opened the next day by a cashier and credited to the account.

### Securities and shares
Banks will buy and sell shares and Government securities on their customers' behalf. Since the 'Big Bang' on the Stock Exchange (see Chapter 4) this service has expanded rapidly. Many large branches now allow instant trading in securities by computer link. Banks' special investment departments will also manage a portfolio of shares on their customers' behalf.

**Services for foreign travel and trade**
These are dealt with in detail in Chapter 16.

**Executor and trustee departments**
People often ask a bank to act as their *executor* after their death. The bank will undertake the work involved in making payments specified in a will. If money is to be left to a person under 18 or invested for a particular period, the bank may act as *trustees*, managing the money for the agreed length of time.

**House purchase**
Since the late 1970s banks have become increasingly important mortgage lenders in competition with the building societies. They also give *bridging loans* when a person buys a new house before their old one is sold.

**Insurance and pensions**
Most banks own their own insurance and pension companies or act as agents for independent companies. They have to make a choice between these two alternatives. Commission from sales of these policies is a fast-growing proportion of banks' income.

**Credit cards**
These allow the cardholder to obtain credit at a large number of establishments such as shops, garages, restaurants and hotels. They can also be used to draw cash from banks. The two largest schemes in Britain are operated by Barclaycard and Access, both run by commercial banks (Access is run by a consortium of banks).

The customer receives a monthly statement showing the amounts spent using the card, and has to make a minimum payment (usually about 5–6 percent of the amount outstanding). If full payment is made within a time limit, there is no interest charge (except for cash withdrawals). The firms accepting the card pay a commission of about 2–4 percent to the credit card company, and hope to benefit from increased sales as a result of accepting the cards.

# Building societies

The building society movement in Britain is unique, with no other country having such a large system of housing finance separate from

| Year | Number of Societies | Number of Share Investors 000s | Number of Borrowers 000s | Amount Advanced £m | Total Assets £m |
|---|---|---|---|---|---|
| 1900 | 2286 | 585 | | | 60 |
| 1920 | 1271 | 748 | | 25 | 87 |
| 1940 | 952 | 2088 | 1503 | 21 | 756 |
| 1960 | 726 | 3910 | 2349 | 560 | 3166 |
| 1980 | 273 | 30 636 | 5383 | 9503 | 53 793 |
| 1985 | 167 | 39 997 | 6659 | 26 508 | 120 764 |
| 1986 | 151 | 40 563 | 7025 | 36 619 | 140 603 |

**Fig. 10.7** Growth of the building society movement

the commercial banks and established on a non-profit-making basis.

The first building society of which records remain was formed in Birmingham in 1775. The early societies consisted of twenty or so workers who made a weekly contribution to the society. In their spare time the members built houses, which were allocated by ballot or sometimes by auction. These were 'terminating' societies, being disbanded when all of the members were housed.

In 1840 the first 'permanent' societies developed. These took deposits from people who did not want to buy houses. Interest was paid to savers and therefore had to be paid by borrowers.

In 1986 there were 151 societies, with total assets of £140 billion. The number of societies has fallen steadily through amalgamations, but the volume of saving and borrowing has grown rapidly (see Figure 10.7).

Building societies have now replaced banks as the largest holder of public savings in the UK. During the last 20 years they have been much more successful in attracting savings, for several reasons:

(a) They have offered competitive interest rates to savers.
(b) They have been more aggressive in marketing their savings schemes than banks. Until the 1980s banks did very little to capture personal accounts. The societies offered longer opening hours and a more friendly atmosphere in their branches. They have been particularly successful in attracting savers who have no account at banks or other financial institutions.
(c) Until recently almost all mortgages for house purchase were taken out through building societies, with banks paying little

**1970**

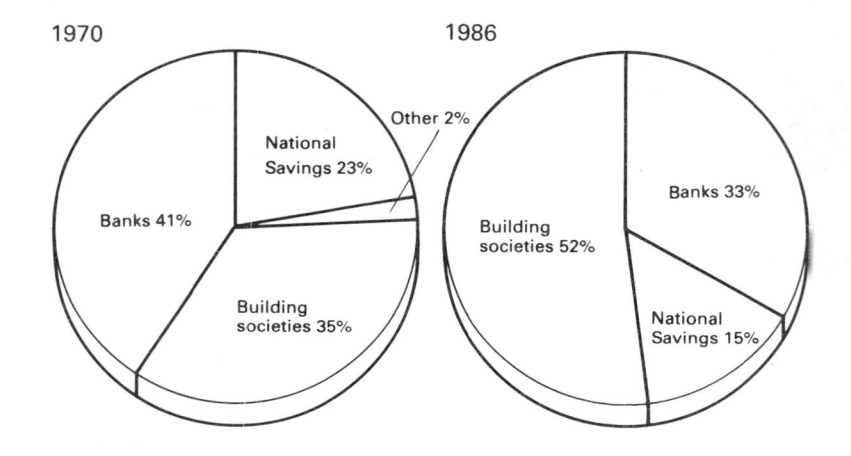

- Banks 41%
- National Savings 23%
- Other 2%
- Building societies 35%

**1986**

- Banks 33%
- Building societies 52%
- National Savings 15%

**Fig. 10.8** Personal savings in the UK

attention to house-buyers. People tended to save with building societies, who were more likely to give a mortgage to existing savers.

There have been major changes in the activities of the building societies since the Building Societies Act 1986. They have always been run on a 'mutual' or 'friendly society' basis, being owned by their depositors, who actually purchase shares in the society when they put money in. The Board of Directors is elected by members, and the societies are technically 'non-profit-making' bodies.

The 1986 Act changed this system, and societies are now allowed to become joint-stock companies if they wish to do so. Abbey National became a public limited company in 1989, and other societies may do the same.

The Act also removed restrictions upon the societies, which until 1986 were only allowed to make loans secured on property, and for the purpose of home loans or improvements. They now provide services such as credit cards, overdrafts and personal loans. It is likely that the differences between banks and building societies will become less obvious in the 1990s.

# 11
# Communications

## The importance of communications

Communications are vital to people and firms in a modern economy. They can be divided into three categories – transmission of money, transport of people and goods, and communication of information. Money transmission and transport are dealt with in Chapter 10 and 12 respectively, and are only mentioned incidentally in this chapter, which is concerned principally with the transfer of information.

Communications can be subdivided into two main types, although some forms of communication such as telex and fax combine both methods:

*(a)* Traditional written information on paper, e.g. letters, invoices, advertising leaflets.
*(b)* Electronically transmitted information, e.g. telephone calls, teletext.

Because of their importance in the economy, communications in the UK were provided and controlled by the Government until the 1980s, being mainly supplied by the Post Office. In the last few years, changes in technology and new legislation have led to increased competition, and this trend is likely to continue in future years. There are now many firms providing communication services, of which the three most important are the Post Office, British Telecommunications and Mercury Communications.

## The Post Office

The Post Office was established by Charles 1 in 1635. In 1969 its status was changed from a Civil Service Department to a public corporation. It was responsible for both post and telecommunications until the British Telecommunications Act 1981 split the latter service off to the newly established British Telecommunications. The Post Office still remains one of the UK's largest employers, with over 200 000 staff in 1988.

Until 1989, the Post Office was organised into four separate businesses – Letters, Parcels, Post Office Counters Ltd and Girobank PLC. Girobank was taken over by the Alliance & Leicester Building Society in late 1989.

### The letter service

The Post Office delivers 50 million letters a day to over 23 million addresses. Two basic letter services are offered – first class and second class. In theory a first class letter should arrive on the first working day after posting and a second class letter should take three working days. The Post Office admits that these targets are not always met, but claims about 90 percent success.

The prices for ordinary first and second class stamps allow for inland letters up to 60 grams. The Post Office has always operated a policy of charging the same for any destination in Britain, despite the fact that it costs over twice as much to deliver to country as to town addresses. The reason for this policy is to keep the pricing system as simple as possible.

The Post Office has a 'statutory monopoly' for its letter service. No other company is allowed to offer a letter service, except for special mail services costing over £1. It has been suggested that this monopoly should be abolished to allow competition and give consumers more choice. However, there are strong arguments for the statutory monopoly:

(a) The cost of a first class letter is lower than in most other European countries. The Post Office also provides more frequent deliveries than are normal abroad.
(b) There are large savings to be made by having a single provider. It costs very little more to deliver two letters rather than one, or

empty a full postbox rather than a half-empty one. If the business was divided between firms, costs might rise.
(c) The letter service faces increasing competition from other forms of communication such as telephones, motorcycle despatch services, telex and fax machines. These services are widely available to business users who send 80 percent of letters.
(d) At present, the Post Office has a duty to accept letters from all users, and to deliver to all UK addresses. New competitors would be mainly interested in the most profitable parts of the letter service, such as business and big-city users. They might refuse to deliver to remote areas.
(e) If the Post Office lost its most profitable business it would be forced to make higher charges for some mail, e.g. letters to the Outer Hebrides would cost more than those to London. This would destroy the single-price structure which is easily understandable to users.

Despite criticism, the letter service is expanding rapidly, with a 25 percent increase between 1980 and 1987. The Post Office is continually trying to improve the service, concentrating on increasing the speed and efficiency of letter-sorting, mainly through mechanisation. The letter service is very labour-intensive, with wages accounting for over 75 percent of costs. It collects from 100 000 postboxes and uses 150 000 workers to collect, sort and deliver letters.

A crucial part of the policy of mechanisation is encouraging the use of postcodes (see Figure 11.1). Although these have been available since 1974, almost one-third of letters are still not postcoded. Mechanised sorting can only occur if the postcode is included. It is retyped on a special machine, using special phosphor dots. Letters marked in this way can be sorted at the rate of 16 000 letters per hour. The latest Optical Character Recognition (OCR) machines can sort 35 000 letters an hour if the postcode is typed by the sender.

A letter without a postcode has to be sorted manually. Even the most efficient human sorter can only sort 2000 letters an hour. This is actually very fast (two letters per second put into one of 144 boxes) but is obviously far more expensive than mechanised sorting.

## Pass on your postcode

## Are you making the postcode work for you?

Postcodes make up a unique reference map of the UK. Businesses and other organisations can use them to:

- pinpoint target zones for advertising or market research
- plan retail or wholesale distribution systems
- compile customer records
- identify sales areas for particular goods and for many other practical purposes.

In addition, Royal Mail offers businesses advice, help and, under certain conditions, financial assistance with postcoding their mailing lists. Customers using first or second class post discount services can save an extra two per cent if all the addresses are postcoded.

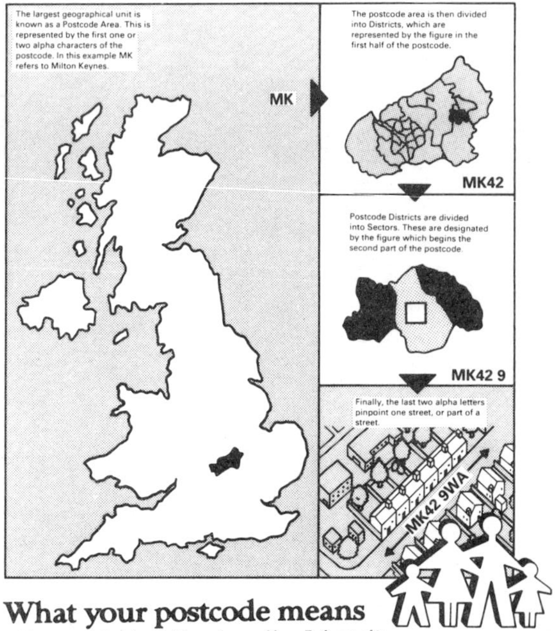

## What your postcode means

Your postcode is a simplified form of your address. Each part of it focuses on a progressively smaller geographical area, coming closer to home. The diagram above illustrates what the various parts mean. The code is in two halves. The first is used at the outgoing sorting office to sort mail automatically to the correct town and district. The second is used on arrival to sort it right down to an individual postman's walk – again by machine. UK postcodes form the basis of one of the world's most sophisticated mechanised sorting systems.

Fig. 11.1 Postcodes

## Specialised letter services

The Post Office provides a wide range of specialised letter services, the most important of which are described below. Services and conditions of use are likely to change periodically. Increasingly, these special services are being offered for international letters.

**Certificate of posting**  This provides proof of posting and can be obtained when a letter is posted at a Post Office.

**Registered letters**  Registered letters are used for sending money or valuable items through the post. They can only be used for first class post. The registered letter service provides evidence of posting and special secure handling. The letter is signed for upon delivery. Compensation for loss or damage is payable up to a limit which depends upon the fee paid.

**Recorded delivery**  Recorded delivery is used for sending letters which do not contain valuables, but for which evidence of posting and delivery is needed, e.g. legal documents and contracts. No special security is provided, as the letter is sent through the ordinary post. It can be used with either first or second class post.

**Special delivery**  This is used with first class letters, and provides delivery by special messenger for a letter arriving at a local delivery office. If the letter does not arrive on time the sender's fee is refunded.

**Express delivery**  This is similar to Special Delivery, but applies to letters to the Isle of Man, Channel Islands and Irish Republic.

**Business reply service**  This allows the sender of a letter to enclose a special pre-printed Business Reply card, label or envelope for first or second class post. It is widely used by mail order sellers. The firm obtains a licence, and pays slightly above the normal charge for all letters returned.

**Freepost**  Freepost allows the sender to write the word 'freepost' on a letter, which does not then need a stamp. Alternatively, the envelope may be pre-printed. The postage is paid by the recipient, with a small commission charge.

**Cash on delivery (COD)**   Firms can arrange for the Post Office to collect payment for goods when they arrive at their destination.

**Post Restante**   A letter can be sent to a Post Office and held there until the recipient comes to collect it. This service might be used to contact a person such as a sales representative who is moving around the country.

**Mailsort discounts**   If a company is prepared to sort its mail into postcoded areas before posting, large discounts are available (up to 32 percent for 1 million or more letters). The size of the discount depends upon the amount of work that the company is prepared to do before posting. Special software packages are available to sort mail based upon a computerised list.

**Franking machines**   These allow the user to use the postal service without the necessity of purchasing stamps. Machines can be bought or rented from approved outlets.

**Printed postage impression**   This service is an alternative to using stamps or a franking machine. The firm has special envelopes or packets imprinted with its name and address.

**Intelpost**   This is a *facsimile* service, i.e. it transmits copies of documents by electronic means. This type of service is often called *fax* (as in Bureaufax or Nefax). Companies can send copies of documents such as letters and drawings along a telephone line. If the sender or recipient does not have their own fax machine, the message can be sent from or to one of the Intelpost centres found in most large towns.

**Household delivery service**   This enables a company to send un-addressed mail – usually advertising circulars – to a particular area. They are delivered with the normal post, which the Post Office claims makes them more likely to be read. One common example of their use is by retailers opening a new supermarket or superstore.

**Private boxes**   It is possible to have letters retained at a main Post Office to be collected by the recipient. A fee is charged for this service.

**Collection for large users**  Firms who guarantee to post more than a certain number of letters can have their mail collected from their premises.

### The Parcels Service

The Post Office delivered 187 million parcels in 1986–87 – about 600 000 every working day. Unlike the letter service, the Post Office has no legal monopoly, and there is fierce competition from other carriers. However, the Post Office is the largest parcel carrier in the UK, with a rapidly expanding custom (see Figure 11.2). As with letter services, facilities for international parcel delivery are being improved constantly.

| Year | Inland Parcels (millions) |
|---|---|
| 1980–81 | 163.6 |
| 81–82 | 174.6 |
| 82–83 | 184.6 |
| 83–84 | 189.5 |
| 84–85 | 195.8 |
| 85–86 | 181.2 |
| 86–87 | 187.3 |

**Fig. 11.2**  The growth of the Parcel Post

Packages up to 25 kilograms can be posted anywhere in the country, and should normally be delivered within three days. Customers posting 20 or more parcels a week can obtain credit and collection from their premises.

**County parcels**  Reduced rates are available for parcel post within certain areas, usually one or more counties, e.g. Devon/Cornwall or Staffordshire/Warwickshire/West Midlands/Worcestershire.

**Rider services**  These guarantee overnight delivery within a particular area, e.g. London, North East, Thames Valley.

**Trakback**  Trakback gives the sender confirmation of parcel delivery, with a customer's signature if required.

**SuperService**  This is designed for large users (over £10 000 per year) and offers guaranteed delivery within 48 hours to most UK destinations. Free insurance for up to £1000 per parcel is included.

**Datapost**  Datapost guarantees next-day delivery, usually before 10 a.m., but slightly later for some areas. If delivery is not achieved on time the fee is refunded. This service is used mainly for urgent documents and computer programmes.

Datapost International offers guaranteed times to other countries, e.g. Hong Kong 48 hours, Tokyo 72 hours.

### Post Office Counters Ltd

Post Office Counters Ltd was established in 1987 as a separate business within the Post Office. With approximately 21 000 different premises, it is by far the biggest chain of retail outlets in Britain (almost as large as the banks and building societies combined).

Only about 1500 of these are Crown offices owned by the Post Office itself. The remainder are sub-offices run as agencies by sub-postmasters, usually as part of a shop such as a newsagents.

Over 25 million people a week visit Post Offices. Apart from the post, the offices provide many different services, including:

*(a)* Postal orders.
*(b)* Payment of social security benefits.
*(c)* Transactions for National Savings and Girobank.
*(d)* Payment of accounts for gas, electricity and water boards.
*(e)* Licences for everything from televisions to cars.
*(f)* Passports.
*(g)* Travel passes and railcards.
*(h)* Stationery
*(i)* Special editions of stamps and coins.

This is only a small sample of the services offered. In recent years the Post Office has lost some of this business, for example as more people have social security payments paid direct to banks or building societies. The National Savings Bank and Girobank may also start to open their own outlets in the next few years.

Going to a Post Office is sometimes regarded as a 'distress visit' –

rather like a petrol station, people only go there because they have to. The popular image is of a drab place where you have to queue. One of the aims of Post Office Counters is to change this image, making the Post Office a place that people make a positive decision to visit. Millions of pounds have been spent on automation and refurbishment in order to speed up the service and make surroundings more appealing.

There have also been moves to increase the range of products to include stationery, building society agencies, buying and selling of shares and other financial services. However, some of these efforts have been hampered because of the delay in obtaining Government approval. This is one of the classic problems of nationalised industries (see Chapter 5).

**Girobank**
Girobank was founded in 1968 as a basic money transmission service. Its original purpose was to provide a method of paying bills for people without bank accounts. Over the years it has developed into a fully fledged clearing bank.

Girobank uses Post Offices as its branches, paying the full cost for these facilities. After its privatisation in 1989, it may start to develop its own branch network. Apart from depositing and withdrawing money, all personal customer transactions are handled by post or telephone.

Girobank has attracted many people who did not previously hold bank accounts, partly because of its connection with the Post Office and its longer opening hours. It is also used for wage and other payments by many firms.

Apart from the usual banking facilities Girobank offers two distinctive services:

**Transcash**  Transcash allows people without bank accounts to make payments to Girobank account holders such as gas and electricity boards, local authorities and mail order firms.

**Freepay**  This gives advertisers the facility of collecting orders and payments at Post Offices. For example, some mail order catalogues use this system to collect money from their customers.

## British Telecommunications PLC

British Telecommunications PLC (usually referred to as British Telecom or BT) was formed as a result of the British Telecommunications Act 1981. This transferred the telephone service, previously run by the Post Office, to a newly formed public corporation. In 1984 it became a public limited company as a result of privatisation.

At the time, the sale of BT to the public was the largest share issue ever made in Britain. Many of the original shareholders sold their stake, but BT still had over 1.3 million shareholders in 1988. It is one of the world's largest telecommunications companies, with an annual turnover of over £10 billion and 220 000 employees.

### The telephone service

There are approximately 18 million private and 4 million business telephones in the UK, and BT handles 70 million calls a day. The telephone service has changed rapidly in recent years. Only 30 years ago most long-distance calls had to go through an operator, and international calls usually had to be booked – sometimes several days in advance.

With the development of the Subscriber Trunk Dialling (STD) and International Direct Dialling (IDD) systems, it is now possible to dial direct to over 600 million phones worldwide.

### Specialised telephone services

**Transferred charge calls**  The person who is receiving the call agrees to pay the charges.

**Telephone credit cards**  A card-holder can have calls from any telephone charged to a personal account.

**Personal calls**  In return for the payment of a fee, the timing of a call does not start until the required person is available. With the introduction of STD this service is much less used than formerly.

**Telephone answering service**  A variety of telephone answering machines are available, which answer calls automatically and can record messages.

## Communications

**Private telephone lines**  Direct lines can be installed to allow communication between two or more points without using the public system. These circuits can also be used for the transmission of data, alarm signals and pictures.

**Freefone**  This allows anyone to call the Freefone subscriber without charge. The subscriber pays the bill. It is often used by advertisers and mail order firms.

**Telex**  This system enables a copy of a message to be produced on teleprinters by both sender and receiver. Most international calls can be made directly. The advantage of telex is that a written message can be sent very quickly. The message can also be received automatically even if the receiving office is unattended.

The minimum rental for telex is expensive, but with the use of a skilled typist a message can be sent more clearly and cheaply than by a normal telephone conversation. Most of the 90 000 subscribers in the UK are business users.

**Information services**  These provide a recorded message on subjects as diverse as share prices and the latest news from football clubs. Some are run by BT itself but many are organised by private concerns, with BT taking a proportion of the revenue.

**Prestel**  Prestel is a two-way service which a subscriber with a special terminal can use either to obtain information such as weather forecasts or share prices, or to place orders for goods and services such as holidays and theatre tickets. It is even possible to place a bet through Prestel. The service is also used by many businesses such as travel agencies and shops.

One multiple chain uses it to transmit information about goods and prices to its branches. The Head Office can pass information to all its stores at much greater speed than would be possible by telephone and letter.

**Radiopaging**  This allows a firm to contact employees on the move by 'bleeping' them as a warning to telephone their office. More sophisticated versions can send a written message.

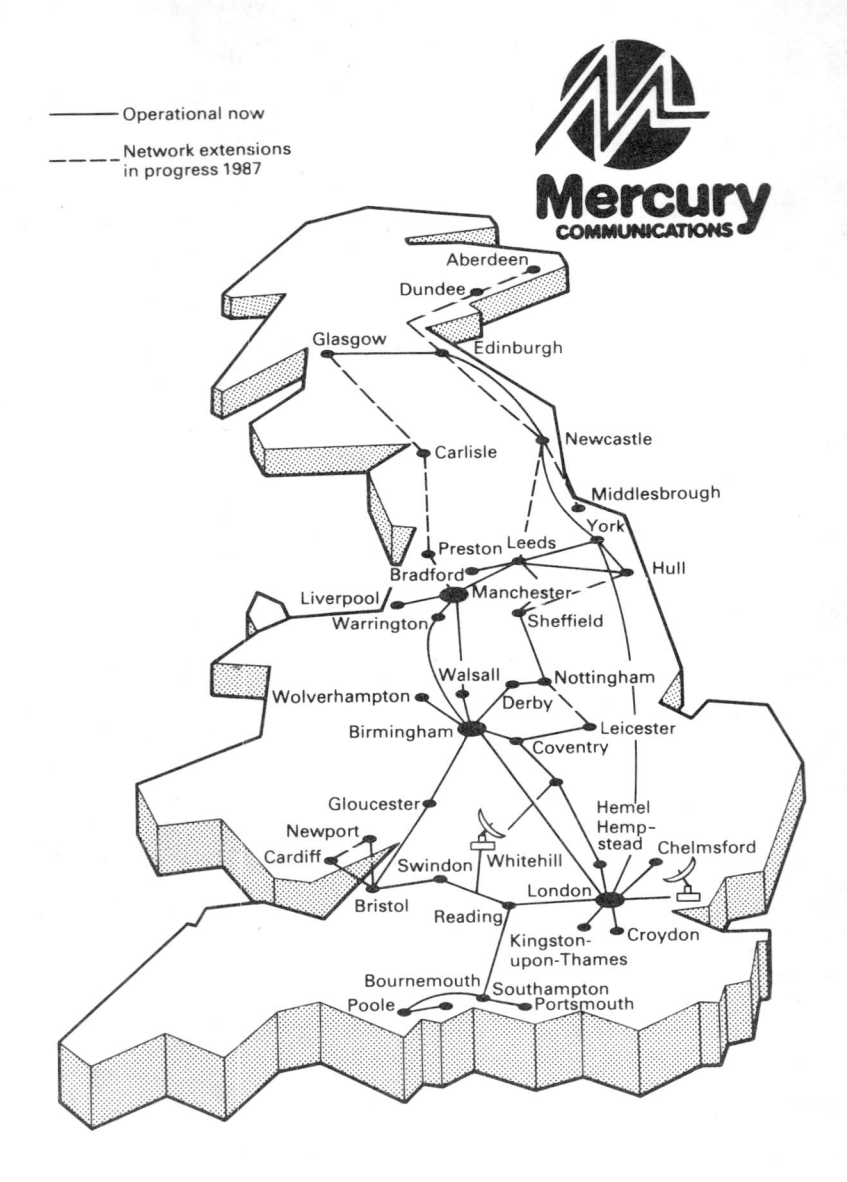

**Fig. 11.3** Mercury network October 1987

**Cellnet** Cellnet is a mobile telephone service covering most of the UK. It allows full telephone services to cars and mobile phones.

**Bureaufax** Bureaufax is British Telecom's facsimile service. Documents can be sent and received electronically by means of a customer's own terminal, or via local bureaux.

The services described above are only a small proportion of those offered by BT. The company's publication *Products and Services* lists nearly 400 services available to its customers.

## Mercury Communications Ltd

Mercury Communications Ltd is a subsidiary of Cable and Wireless PLC, itself one of Britain's most successful international telecommunications companies. Mercury was established in 1981 to offer competition to British Telecom.

Mercury uses British Telecom lines for some of its business (permission to do this was one of the conditions attached to the privatisation of BT). It has also invested over £300 million in laying its own network (see Figure 11.3), which reaches about 70 percent of the UK population.

Originally Mercury concentrated upon business users, mainly large firms and City institutions such as the Stock Exchange. As its network has grown it has established services for residential users and launched a public callbox service.

# 12

# Transport

## The importance of transport

Good transport links are vital for a modern economy. They allow people more freedom of travel, provide a wider market for firms' products and make possible the vast choice of goods and services enjoyed by consumers in Britain and other industrial countries.

Many early industries were built around seaports and inland waterways. Later, the development of the road and railway networks fostered the growth of many industrial areas. Even today, the existence of an airport or motorway can be vital to an area's prosperity, as in the growth areas around the M4 'corridor' west of London and the towns around Gatwick airport.

## Factors affecting the choice of transport

Choosing a method of transport for people, goods or documents involves considering several factors. These are interlinked, and decisions about transport involve weighing up all of these factors.

### Nature of goods
All goods (including people) have different characteristics which may restrict or determine the type of transport chosen. The goods may need refrigeration, may be gases, liquid, or need special handling because of safety (e.g. chemicals, nuclear waste).

### Speed
Faster forms of transport such as air are often more expensive, and a decision has to be made as to whether the cost is justified. People

## GOODS

| Method | tonne kilometres (bn) |
|---|---|
| Road | 104.1 |
| Rail | 16.5 |
| Water | 51.4 |
| Pipelines | 10.4 |
| TOTAL | 182.4 |

## PASSENGERS

| Method | passenger kilometres (bn) | |
|---|---|---|
| Air | | 4 |
| Rail | | 37 |
| Road; | | |
| Bus & Coach | 41 | |
| Car & Taxi | 424 | |
| Motorcycle | 6 | |
| Bicycle | 4 | |
| | | 475 |
| TOTAL | | 516 |

**Fig. 12.1** Transport in Britain 1986

may wish for faster transport to save leisure or working time. Perishable products such as fruit, flowers and daily newspapers have to be delivered quickly. Similarly there may be an urgent need for documents or spares for machinery which will mean that the fastest form of transport must be used.

### Convenience and flexibility

Nearness to a railway station or airport may make a particular form of transport more convenient. For example, the City of London Airport is attractive to people who want to get in and out of London quickly. Businesses often deliberately locate close to a particular form of transport, e.g. offices near railway stations, haulage firms and warehouses near motorways.

People and firms who are far from a railway station or airport may choose road transport for its convenience and speed. Most forms of transport apart from road involve people or goods being switched from one type of transport to another. They also tend to travel according to a fixed timetable. On the other hand, some people like travelling by rail or air because they can work during the journey.

**Cost**
People and firms may wish to keep transport costs as low as possible, particularly if their time or goods are not valuable enough to justify expensive travel.

**Size and weight**
Bulky low-value goods such as coal and sand will usually be sent by the cheapest form of transport; for example, neither would be sent by air because the cost of transport would make them too expensive for the buyer. On the other hand, for a valuable low-bulk item such as diamonds, the cost of air-freight would be a small fraction of the price charged.

# Road

Road transport is by far the most commonly used form of transport in Britain (see Figure 12.1). There are over 21 million vehicles on British roads, of which about three-quarters are private cars. An increasing proportion of passenger transport is by private car, with buses and motorcycles becoming less popular every year.

The rapidly increasing volume of road traffic is causing severe environmental problems. It is estimated that traffic congestion in the UK costs some £3 billion a year in wasted time, wages, extra fuel and other costs.

About half of this cost occurs in London alone, where the average motorist spends three hours a week in traffic jams. The problem has become so severe that London traffic now moves at an average speed of 8 mph, slower than horses and carts travelled in Victorian times.

Outside London, traffic congestion is not as severe, but the increase in road traffic has destroyed road surfaces, created dangerous levels of lead pollution and damaged historic buildings such as York Minster. These problems are likely to get worse as 2 million new vehicles are registered each year. Building new roads usually makes the problems worse, as it simply encourages more people to use cars.

Advantages of road transport:

1. It is usually faster than other forms of transport over short distances (up to about 200 miles). Over half of all journeys are for less than 25 miles.
2. It is very convenient, allowing door-to-door delivery and passenger journeys. Other forms of transport usually require switching to or from road transport.
3. It is very flexible. There is no fixed timetable and it is easy to visit or deliver to several different destinations in the same journey or delivery round.
4. Unlike rail, water or air transport there is no fixed network, and all inland destinations are connected to the road system.
5. The amount of handling is minimised, reducing the risk of breakage or theft.

Disadvantages of road transport:

1. It is often slower and more expensive than rail for distances over 200 miles, although motorway journeys cut time and costs.
2. There are restrictions upon the weight of goods which can be carried.
3. It is expensive if return loads cannot be arranged.
4. Road transport causes congestion and other environmental problems.
5. It is by far the most dangerous form of transport for both travellers and pedestrians.

# Rail

Rail transport in Britain started during the early 1800s, largely as a means for transporting coal from mines to the nearest canal. However, it grew very quickly to replace canals as the major form of transport, until the spread of motor transport took its place.

The railways were privately owned until 1947, when they were taken over by the Government and amalgamated into a single company now known as British Rail. During its early years the newly nationalised firm had to pay interest on the money borrowed to compensate the former owners. Prices were often held too low to make enough profits to reinvest in the network.

As a result of these problems and the increasing number of cars and lorries, the railways have faced a steady decline in their share of transport of passengers and freight. Over the last ten years, freight mileage has fallen by a quarter and passenger travel has remained virtually static. As the volume of all forms of transport has risen by over 20 percent during this time, the railways' performance is even worse than these figures suggest. It has also lost much of its traditional business of mail and newspaper distribution.

Despite these problems, British Rail is starting to reverse this trend. Its policies include closure of uneconomic stations and freight-yards (and opening of new ones where profitable, e.g. in some city suburbs). It has invested in new and better trains which are more comfortable and require less maintenance. More lines are being electrified, which cuts travelling time and costs considerably.

There has also been increased emphasis upon the 'leisure market', e.g. day and weekend trips, through new products such as Family Railcards. This helps to fill seats on 'off-peak' trains. Higher quality services such as luxury carriages and better catering have also been introduced.

Freight services now include:

*Night Star* This guarantees next-day delivery to the receiver's address.
*Red Star* This guarantees same-day delivery for parcels taken to and collected from main railway stations.
*Freightliner* This is British Rail's own container service.

British Rail now makes a substantial income by exploiting its property assets. It owns valuable buildings and land in all major cities. These can generate revenue in various ways, for instance through land sales, shops on stations, and office developments such as that planned for Kings Cross which reduce commuters' travelling time.

Advantages of rail transport:

1. It is usually quicker than road transport for distances over 200 miles, particularly on mainline services. Electrification has made it more competitive as a form of travel.

2  It is less wasteful of resources such as labour and fuel than other forms of transport. For example, a train with two staff can carry hundreds of times more passengers or goods than a single road vehicle.
3  Bulky goods such as coal can be transported more economically by rail, particularly where private sidings and containerisation are used.
4  Rail travel is far safer than road.

Disadvantages of rail transport:

1  Rail transport is usually slower over short distances, although there are exceptions such as peak hours in some large cities.
2  It is less convenient than some forms of transport. People and goods usually have to transfer to and from road travel.
3  Large parts of Britain, especially in Scotland and Wales, have poor access to railway lines.
4  Trains have to run to a fixed timetable, which may be inconvenient for people and firms.
5  The capital costs of maintaining the rail network are very high. About 60 percent of British Rail's costs are on signalling and track maintenance.
6  Because goods usually have to be transferred to other forms of transport, there is a danger of theft or breakage.

## Sea

Sea transport has long been a major source of Britain's prosperity, which depends heavily upon foreign trade. Despite competition from air travel, sea transport is still vital to the UK economy. By far the greatest proportion of international freight, and over a third of all passengers, are still carried by ships. Sea transport is likely to remain important in the future, especially for European destinations.

**Types of sea transport**

**Passenger ships**  These include ocean-going liners such as the QE2, roll-on roll-off (ro-ro) ferries and hovercraft. All of these travel to a fixed timetable.

**Cargo liners**  These are ocean-going ships travelling to a fixed timetable. They usually carry mixed goods and mail.

**Tramps**  These carry goods all over the world, but have no fixed schedules. They are chartered for different loads, with the captain often receiving details of the next destination on arrival at a port or in mid-ocean. They are commonly used for bulky goods such as iron ore, timber and grain.

**Coasters**  As their name suggests, these travel mainly around the British coast, although they may make short cross-channel trips. Within these restrictions, they operate on a similar basis to tramp ships.

**Bulk carriers**  These are very large ships which usually specialise in a particular type of cargo such as oil. Most of the world's largest ships are bulk carriers (sometimes called *supertankers* or *very large crude carriers*).

Britain used to have one of the world's largest merchant shipping fleets, but the number is less than a third of its 1975 level and is declining every year. This is due to factors such as the world recession, foreign competition and 'flags of convenience' (ships are registered in countries where safety standards and wage levels are lower than for UK-registered ships). Traditionally, shipping provided a surplus in foreign trade, but this is no longer true. Some people are also worried that in the event of another war such as that over the Falklands, Britain would have very few merchant ships to rely upon for essential supplies.

# Inland waterways

Until the advent of the railways in the early 1800s, inland waterways were the major form of transport within Britain. Poor roads offered little competition. Since then the canal system has declined steadily because of competition from the railways, and later road transport. It now accounts for about a thousandth of goods traffic, and the heaviest usage is in leisure boating.

However, there has been a small revival during the 1980s. Canals in relatively flat areas such as South Yorkshire have been dredged and widened. Although canal transport is slow, it can still be economic for bulky cargo such as coal.

## Air

This is one of the fastest growing forms of transport. Both passenger and cargo mileage have doubled in the last ten years, and they are still increasing annually. Eighty million people fly in and out of British airports every year. Air traffic in the UK is controlled by the Civil Aviation Authority (CAA), an independent statutory body. The CAA is responsible for licensing, safety and navigation.

Two-thirds of passenger traffic in the UK is provided by British Airways PLC, which was privatised in 1986. It carries more passengers than any other airline in the world.

Advantages of air transport:

1. It is normally the quickest form of transport, especially for international or cross-country journeys.
2. It is usually more secure than other methods (although Britain's largest robbery was from a warehouse at Heathrow airport).
3. It is one of the safest ways to travel.

Disadvantages of air travel:

1. Air transport is usually the most expensive type (although for some journeys within Britain this is no longer true).
2. It is not suitable for bulky goods, especially those with low value.
3. Air transport relies upon people and goods switching to other forms of transport. It is also often subject to delay by bad weather, technical problems and strikes by air traffic controllers. All of these factors reduce the time-saving over other forms of transport.
4. Airports cause noise pollution to the immediate area, and often face opposition when extending runways or increasing the number of flights.

## Pipelines

These are used only for certain types of goods such as oil and gas, but can be very economical for such commodities. Most North Sea oil and gas is transported through undersea and overland pipelines – there are over 3500 miles of pipeline for natural gas. However, pipelines are very expensive to lay and are inflexible because they are immobile.

## Containerisation

Containerisation has been one of the most important post-war developments in transport. Containers are large metal boxes built to standard sizes to fit different lorries, rail transporters (*freightliners*), ships and even wide-bodied planes. The container is packed and sealed by the sender. It can then be transferred intact from one form of transport to another, using special straddle cranes designed for this purpose.

Using containers cuts out much of the handling of goods, reducing the danger of theft and breakage. It requires large-scale investment in specialised vehicles and equipment, but this is repaid by the tremendous saving of time. Because containers are of standard sizes, it is easy to plan storage within the restricted space of container ships and planes.

The *Transport Internationale Routier* (TIR) system increases the benefits of containerisation by cutting out customs delays. Customs officers in the country of origin inspect and seal the container. It is then allowed to travel through other countries without being inspected. When it arrives at its country of destination the local customs officers break the seal, inspect the container and charge any relevant duties.

## The Channel Tunnel

In January 1986 the governments of Britain and France announced that they had approved plans for a consortium of firms to build a tunnel under the English Channel. One of the conditions was that there would be no Government funding. After some difficulty the finance was found privately and work began on the tunnel, which was due to open in 1993.

The tunnel is the biggest civil engineering project ever undertaken in Britain; the estimated cost before allowing for inflation was £2.6 billion. The actual cost will, of course, be a lot more than this.

Initially it will be run with ordinary trains and special car transporters. The builders have undertaken to provide a 'drive-through' tunnel by 2000, although as yet the technology for extracting exhaust fumes does not exist.

Supporters of the tunnel have claimed that it will provide many benefits to the British economy, including

*(a)* Extra jobs for construction and engineering workers, both on the site and in other parts of Britain, where there will be contracts for materials and equipment such as the car-carriers.
*(b)* Faster and direct rail travel, e.g. London–Brussels in 3 hours, Leeds–Paris in 5 hours.
*(c)* Easier and cheaper foreign trade for firms.

Opponents of the tunnel argue that it is unlikely to be a commercial success, and will have to be bailed out by the French and British governments. Their arguments include

*(a)* Jobs will be lost in ferry travel and at ports such as Dover and Ramsgate.
*(b)* Ferries are still likely to be competitive because some people will not want to travel through a 20-mile tunnel. Ferries are getting faster, and the tunnel won't save very much time.
*(c)* There will be congestion and environmental damage in Kent.
*(d)* The high cost of construction will leave the tunnel with massive interest repayments which will push up the tolls charged. This has proved a problem in the past for projects such as the Humber Bridge and Dartford Tunnel, which have not recovered the full construction cost.

Obviously, until it is built and operating, nobody knows which of the arguments for and against will come true, but the tunnel is likely to have a great effect upon the British economy.

# 13

# Insurance

## The statistical basis of insurance

Insurance is one of the aids to trade, allowing risks to be taken without fear of disastrous loss. People and firms can protect themselves financially against events such as fire or burglary. Without adequate insurance many enterprises would be too risky to undertake.

Insurance works by pooling risks. Risk is the chance of a disaster happening, together with the loss to be borne if it occurs. Everybody contributes to a common fund, which is used to pay out to those who do suffer a loss.

To take a very simplified example, suppose that 100 people each have a horse worth £1000, and wish to insure against the possibility of their horse's death. If past experience shows that on average this will happen to 2 of the horses every year, the total yearly loss will be £2000. By paying £20 a year each, the owners can ensure that both of the unfortunate owners will receive compensation for their loss. (A death rate of 5% would require an annual premium of £50, and so on.)

In effect, this is how insurance works. Using statistical records of past events such as accidents, fires or burglaries, insurers calculate the risk of an event happening and set premiums accordingly. The setting of premiums is undertaken by *actuaries*.

For example, motor insurance premiums depend upon factors such as:

*Age of driver* The younger the driver, the higher the likelihood of an accident. A 17-year-old will pay at least three times as much as a 50-year-old.

*Type of car*  The larger or more expensive the car, the higher the premium. Sports cars or cars for which parts are expensive also cost more.

*Area where owner lives*  Accidents and thefts are more likely in large cities than rural areas. A driver in London will usually pay at least twice as much as one living in Doncaster, for example.

*Insured's occupation*  Some types of workers, such as teachers and civil servants, are known to be less likely than the average motorist to have accidents. Other occupations, such as journalists, entertainers and pub landlords, are notoriously bad risks.

*Past driving record*  Motorists who go for a year or more without claiming are given discounts. Those with bad records, e.g. accidents, speeding convictions and disqualifications, pay more.

These are just some of the factors affecting motor insurance premiums. They are based upon statistical analysis of past claims, and the weighting given to different factors is periodically changed. For example, drivers over 60 used to be charged more, on the grounds that their eyesight and reactions were likely to be slower. However, research has proved that they drive less than most motorists, cover lower mileages, and tend not to be on the road at the peak accident times such as late at night. Most companies now charge much lower premiums for senior citizens.

The statistical measurement of risk goes back several centuries. For example, after the Great Fire of London in 1666, fire insurance became more popular, and insurers wisely charged more for wooden than brick buildings.

Although most events can be insured against, there are some *uninsurable risks* which cannot be covered. These may include eventualities such as

(a) Risks which are not measurable, e.g. risk of war or nuclear explosion.
(b) Normal business risks such as goods left unsold because of changes in fashion.
(c) Depreciation of vehicles or equipment through wear and tear.
(d) Contracts with an illegal purpose, e.g. risk of being imprisoned for a crime.

# Principles of insurance

All insurance is governed by certain principles:

### Insurable interest
A person can only insure against an event which will cause them a personal or monetary loss. For example, it is possible to insure your own car against accident, but not your next-door neighbour's, because in the latter case there would be no financial loss. Similarly, it is no longer possible to insure against the death of the Prince of Wales or a famous general (which was actually common practice before it was banned in 1774). Life assurance can now only be taken out on a close relative such as a husband or wife.

### Utmost good faith
A person taking out insurance must not tell lies or omit to mention relevant facts which might affect the insurer's decisions about whether to issue a policy or what premium to charge. For example, a person who installs a larger engine or changes jobs after a motor policy is issued would not be telling lies at the time of filling out the form. However, if he or she did not inform the insurers of the changes, it is possible that any claim made might be disallowed, as the change may have increased the risk insured and therefore the premium.

### Indemnity
This means that if a claim is made the insured person should be restored to the same position as he or she was in before the event, and should not make a profit from insurance. If this was allowed, it might result in people staging a fire or theft to make money.

For example, a car's value might be stated as £2000 when it is originally insured. If it has lost value since then the owner will only receive the current value in the case of an accident.

There are some exceptions to the rule of indemnity. Household contents policies are usually on a 'new-for-old' basis, which is allowed for in the premium. If a four-year-old lounge chair is destroyed by fire, a new-for-old policy will pay the full cost of a brand new replacement. In the case of death or injury, it is of course impossible to restore the previous position. Life and personal accident insurance therefore works on a 'benefit' basis, with a fixed amount being paid.

Two additional principles arise out of the basic one of indemnity. *Subrogation* occurs in a case where the insured has a legal right to recover from another person as well as claiming under their own insurance policy. A hotel guest who has insured personal possessions loses a suitcase through staff negligence. The insurance company takes over their customer's claim against the hotel, paying him or her for the loss. If the case against the hotel is admitted or proved the insurance company receives compensation.

*Contribution* occurs when the same risk is insured against with two separate companies. This is not illegal, but the person taking out the policies cannot normally receive payment from both insurance companies. This would be possible, however, in the case of life assurance.

**Proximate cause**

This can best be explained by a simple example. If a fire occurs in a building, damage may be caused by efforts to put the fire out – doors broken down to gain access or water damage to furniture. A valid claim could be made that this damage occurred as a direct result of the fire, and should therefore be paid for by fire insurance. However, indirect losses such as loss of trade or theft of stock might be regarded as not being covered by the policy unless specific allowance for such *consequential loss* is made in the policy.

# Personal insurance

Insurance for people can be divided into *insurance* and *assurance*. Although these terms are sometimes used interchangeably, there is a difference. Insurance covers an event that *might* happen, such as a fire, accident or theft. Assurance refers to events that *will* happen, basically a person dying or living a certain number of years.

**Life assurance**

Life assurance dates back at least as far as Roman times, when part of a soldier's wage was put into a fund to make payments if he died or retired from the army. Its mathematical basis was worked out by an eighteenth-century teacher, James Dodson. Dodson worked out that the older a person was, the higher the risk of their death, and the lower the number of years that they would be able to pay into the life fund.

Premiums for life assurance are based upon Dodson's principles, which have been refined and developed using statistical analysis. The older a person is, the higher the premium that they are required to pay. For example, a 40-year-old man might receive about a third less cover than a 30-year-old for the same premium.

People take out life assurance for two main reasons – protection for the insured's dependents and as a form of saving, e.g. for retirement. The main types of life assurance policy are

(a) *Whole life*  This insures only against death. The premium is paid every year until the insured person dies. Whole life policies are for protection only; they cannot be used for saving.

(b) *Term*  This is similar to a whole life assurance, but is for a fixed period. Common forms are *mortgage protection* which lasts until the mortgage is fully paid, travel insurance for air journeys and insurance for skiing or motor-racing, which are not covered by most normal life assurance policies.

(c) *Endowment*  Endowment assurance provides a fixed payment on death or after a specified period, e.g. £20 000 in 25 years' time (the *maturity date*). Premiums for endowment policies are much higher than those for whole life or term assurance, as there is a higher risk of the insurance company having to make a payout. This type of policy is a popular form of saving, although it is only worthwhile in the long-term, as the value of a policy is usually small if it is 'cashed in' before the maturity date.

(d) *Annuity*  With this type of policy, the customer pays into a fund, usually to provide an income after retirement. The payments may be made in instalments during a working life, or as a single lump-sum payment. In return the insurance company pays an agreed fixed sum until the policyholder's death.

These are only examples of the types of policies available, and there are many variations, e.g. 'with-profits' and 'unit-linked' policies, where the amount eventually paid out depends upon the success of the insurance fund's share purchases and other investments (see Figure 13.1).

### Household
There are two main types of household insurance. *Buildings* insurance covers damage to the building itself, such as storm damage to the roof, destruction by fire and damage to 'fixtures' such as fitted cupboards. *Contents* insurance covers theft or damage to moveable items such as carpets, electrical equipment and furniture.

### Motor
This is compulsory by law for all vehicles driven on public roads. The two most common types are *third party, fire and theft* and *comprehensive*. Third party, fire and theft covers damage to other people and their property, and damage to the insured's own vehicle through fire or theft only. Comprehensive insurance covers the insured's own vehicle for most other types of damage as well, and is approximately twice as expensive.

### Travel
This type of insurance covers eventualities such as medical expenses abroad, cancellation of holidays and accidents while travelling.

### Personal liability
This covers people against damage caused by their own fault such as a pedestrian causing a road accident by stepping into the road or personal injury caused by the insured's pet dog. Most *household* policies include some personal liability insurance.

### Health
People often insure against illness in order to be able to pay for private medical care. This is provided by many firms as a benefit for their staff.

## Insurance for business

Some of the types of personal insurance described above are also used by businesses, although premiums are usually higher because of the greater risk involved. (One exception is health insurance, which companies can buy for large numbers of employees at a substantial discount.) There are also special types of policy for firms. These include:

### Liability

Even the most safety-conscious firm's activities can cause danger to workers, customers and the general public. All employers are required by law to have *employers' liability insurance* which covers accidents or illnesses arising out of their employees' work. Firms usually insure against *public liability* claims such as those from explosions or airline accidents.

A growing area of insurance is *product liability*, which covers claims when a firm's activities or products cause injury or illness, such as a drug causing deformities in babies or a type of food causing illness.

### Money

This covers theft of cash, cheques and other *negotiable* documents. The firm is usually required to observe strict conditions about security.

### Goods in transit

This allows for theft or damage to goods which are being transported.

### Credit

This insures a business against creditors who do not pay their bills. It is commonly used in international trade, with the *Exports Credit Guarantee Department* (see Chapter 16) being a major insurer in this field.

### Fidelity guarantee

Fidelity guarantee insurance compensates a business for acts of dishonesty by its employees, such as embezzlement. It can be taken out for theft by any employee, or for particular individuals such as cashiers or accountants.

### Legal expenses

This covers legal costs for disputes about issues such as contracts or employment.

### Business interruption

This type of insurance (also called *consequential loss*) provides compensation if a business has to cease or reduce trading temporarily because of a fire or other accident. A firm whose factory was burnt down might receive payment for lost profit, temporary premises, rates and wages while the factory was being rebuilt or new premises were found.

## Organisation of British insurance

Insurance is sold both directly by branches of insurance companies, and through intermediaries who are either *agents* or *brokers*. The majority of insurance sellers are members of one of the trade associations – Association of British Insurers (ABI), Life Offices Association/Associated Scottish Life Offices (LOA/ASLO) and British Insurance Brokers Association (BIBA).

*Agents* are appointed by an insurance company to sell its particular products. They usually do so on a part-time basis through offices used for another purpose – solicitors and estate agents often act as agents. Generally, agents act only for one or two companies.

*Brokers* are full-time specialists who offer a wide range of policies from different companies, and usually handle customer claims on behalf of the insurance company. They are controlled by a registration council, and it is no longer permissible for a person to set up as a broker without registration.

### Re-insurance

Re-insurance is in effect an insurance policy taken out by an insurance company. If a company feels that it has too much risk in a particular type of business such as oil-drilling or air travel, it will pay part of the premiums received to a re-insurer such as a Lloyds underwriter. In return, the re-insurer agrees to pay part of the compensation if there is a claim. This allows insurers to avoid financial ruin in the case of a large disaster such as a major earthquake or city fire. The world's most important re-insurer is Lloyds of London, which earns half of its income in this way.

### The Insurance Ombudsman

A number of leading insurance companies have established the Insurance Ombudsman Bureau, an independent organisation, to deal with consumer complaints. The Bureau had about 200 members in 1988, accounting for two-thirds of personal insurance policies.

The Ombudsman Bureau investigates complaints by the public (7433 in 1987) and has the power to make awards of up to £100 000 against insurance companies, who are obliged to accept its decisions. Many claims are rejected, often because they are rather dubious, but over 300 people a year receive awards. If the Ombudsman agrees with the insurance company, the complainant can still take legal action, although such a case is unlikely to succeed.

## Lloyds of London

Lloyds of London is the major market for insurance in Britain. It is controlled by the Corporation of Lloyds. Like the Stock Exchange, it originally started in a coffee shop where people met to do business. Edward Lloyd had a reputation for obtaining up-to-date information about shipping movements. Merchants and shipowners used to meet at his coffee shop to arrange insurance for ships and their cargoes and in 1680, Lloyds of London was formed. It has since moved three times; the present building has been occupied since 1986.

Although marine insurance still accounts for over 40 percent of Lloyds' business (the Titanic was insured at Lloyds), it now covers many different risks. It was the first insurer of cover for burglary, cars and planes. It also covers more dramatic and unusual risks such as discovery of the Loch Ness monster (for a firm offering a £1 million prize), boycott of the Olympic Games reducing attendances (for television companies) and theft or damage to wooden 'pet slugs' (a recent craze in the USA). Its more conventional policies have insured against the 1906 San Francisco earthquake and the collapse of the Channel Tunnel.

Insurance at Lloyds is arranged through *brokers* who are approached by people, firms and other organisations to advise upon the exact type and amount of cover needed. The broker (usually a firm itself) will prepare a *slip* showing the type of cover and conditions required. This will be offered to *underwriters* who will be asked to quote the premium needed. Usually several underwriters will be asked to compete against each other.

For large risks, a number of underwriters will each accept part of

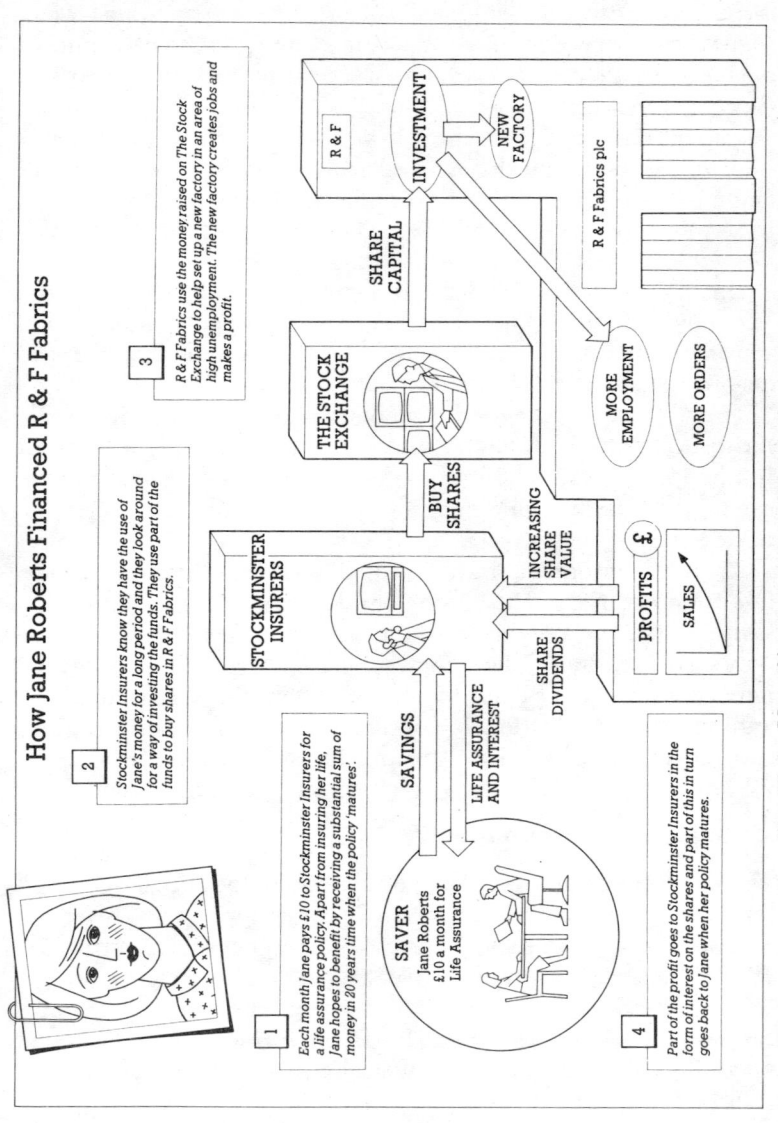

**Fig. 13.1** Use of insurance premiums in the economy

the contract. In these cases the first underwriter to accept the risk is called the *leader*. The leader will set a rate for the premium, which will then be followed by other underwriters. A typical motor policy might be covered by six underwriters, with the leader taking 75 percent of the risk.

Underwriters are professionals who usually represent a *syndicate*. The members of the syndicate have liability up to an agreed amount, and share a certain proportion of the risks and profits (typically between ½% and 2%). They do not usually take part in the actual business – many are sporting celebrities or entertainers.

Underwriters have unlimited liability, and have to have a minimum amount of personal wealth and deposit money with the Corporation of Lloyds before being allowed to underwrite insurance.

The reason for this unlimited liability is to maintain confidence in the insurance market. People must be certain that they will receive full compensation. As an extra safeguard, all underwriters pay into a central fund which guarantees payment if one of them cannot pay its debts.

As well as insurance, Lloyds provides a comprehensive shipping information service. The Shipping Index records the movements of ships throughout the world, showing where they are, which port they were at last and where they are going to. Lloyds List is a daily newspaper which supplies information about the world's transport and insurance industries. It also contains specialist articles about subjects such as offshore oil, aviation and freight.

## Insurance and the economy

The insurance industry is an important part of the British economy. Apart from providing a valuable service, it employs a quarter of a million workers and earned over £4 billion in overseas earnings in 1988. It is a major source of overseas earnings (see Chapter 16). Insurance companies invest billions of pounds in shares and other securities every year, and own a large proportion of shares in British firms. Figure 13.1 shows how a typical insurance premium is used.

# 14

# Advertising

## Types of advertising

Over £5 billion a year is spent on advertising in Britain. This ranges from people advertising second-hand bikes to car manufacturers spending £2 million on a television campaign.

*Informative* advertising is concerned with giving information, e.g. about timetables, changes in prices or new Government legislation.

*Persuasive* advertising aims to get people to buy a product in order to increase sales. Advertising of goods such as petrol is often included in this category because the competing products are virtually identical. Persuasive advertising is often used to establish and maintain *brand names*. The term *competitive* is sometimes used to describe advertising which aims to increase a particular firm's market share.

*Collective* or *generic* advertising involves publicising a type of product rather than a brand (for example, butter rather than Kerrygold). This is often undertaken by trade associations such as the Milk Marketing Board. The use of collective advertising often indicates a product for which demand has been falling (dairy products and meat are recent examples).

In practice, the distinction between informative and persuasive advertising is rather artificial, as most advertisements are a combination of both methods.

Arguments for advertising:

1 Advertising tells consumers about the products that are available, allowing them to make a wider and more informed choice.
2 It encourages competition between firms, who have to produce cheaper and better products. Until the 1980s, many professions such as solicitors were not allowed to advertise. When these regulations were abolished, prices for services such as house conveyancing and drawing up of wills were reduced.
3 By creating a wider market for products, advertising makes large-scale production and sales possible. Mass production also makes goods and services cheaper for consumers.
4 Without advertising, media such as newspapers and television would be more expensive. Many sporting clubs and other organisations also benefit from advertising revenue.

Arguments against advertising:

1 Advertising is expensive and may lead to prices being higher than necessary. High advertising costs may also prevent new firms from entering the market because they cannot afford the expense.
2 Advertising is often wasteful, sometimes involving the same firm advertising virtually identical products against each other (washing powder is a good example). Some writers claim that advertising has little or no effect upon the total demand for goods or even upon the demand for a particular type of good or service. This argument is supported by cigarette manufacturers, who claim that advertising only causes a shift from one brand to another.
3 Advertising can be misleading. However, there are substantial controls upon the industry (see 'Control of Advertising' below).
4 Advertisers can exert control over media such as the press and television, who often design their content specifically to reach target groups such as the young or better-off (see Chapter 8 for examples). It can be argued, however, that such 'targeting' only works by providing consumers with the reading or entertainment that they want.
5 Advertising can put pressure upon people to buy products that they don't really need or can't afford.

# Advertising media

TOTAL ADVERTISING EXPENDITURE
£ millions (at constant 1980 prices)

|  | 1961 | 1986 |
|---|---|---|
| National newspapers | 332 | 577 |
| Regional newspapers | 415 | 752 |
| Consumer magazines | 208 | 187 |
| Business and professional | 166 | 255 |
| Directories | 10 | 182 |
| Press production costs | 78 | 189 |
| TOTAL PRESS | 1209 | 2142 |
| Poster and Transport | 83 | 134 |
| Cinema | 26 | 13 |
| TOTAL MEDIA COVERED-ASA | 1318 | 2289 |
| Television | 431 | 1144 |
| Radio | 5 | 62 |
| TOTAL ALL MEDIA | 1753 | 3495 |

*Source: Advertising Statistics Yearbook*

**Fig. 14.1** Advertising expenditure 1961 and 1986

## Television

Commercial television is the most effective medium for reaching large numbers of people, and has been proven by research to be most noticed and remembered. It is also the most expensive, with peak-time adverts costing £30 000 or more per minute.

Television advertising can be very effective, but has several drawbacks. Because of the cost, TV adverts have to be very brief, most being for less than 30 seconds. They cannot be very informative, and display images rather than information. Car advertisements on television are noted for the fact that they say very little about the car itself.

The other major problem is that, although the potential audience for an advertisement is very large, many of the viewers will not even see it (at any one moment, less than half of the audience will actually be looking at the set).

Television advertising is not very selective – it is hard to reach a particular group of people, except for certain programmes. An exception to this was the programme 'The Equalizer' in the USA which was due to be dropped because of poor ratings. It was retained when advertisers discovered that it was one of the few programmes that men made a special effort to watch, and therefore ideal for advertising 'male' products.

**Radio**
At present there is no national commercial radio station in Britain, although this may change in the future. Local radio advertising is fairly cheap and can be effective in reaching certain types of people such as housewives.

**National press**
National press advertising is expensive, but much cheaper than television. It also has the advantage of allowing detailed information to be given, as people have time to consider it at their leisure. Reaching a particular audience is also fairly easy as the readership of newspapers is well-researched – for example, *Daily Express* readers are mostly over 30, *Times* readers are mostly well-educated.

**Magazines and trade press**
There are thousands of specialist magazines and trade papers which offer a moderately cheap and effective way of reaching a specialised group of customers. There are magazines for almost any interest from golf to stamp-collecting, and for every conceivable type of industry from construction to newsagents. Magazines have the advantages of a much longer life than TV or newspapers and of a readership who usually study the advertisements in considerable detail.

**Local press**
The local press is the main market for classified or 'small ads'. It varies tremendously – the *Leamington and District Morning News* sells 10 000 copies a day, the *Manchester Evening News* over 300 000. Apart from being cheap, press adverts are scanned thoroughly by people who want a new house, a second-hand car or

somewhere to go for a night out. Within its area, a local paper will also be read by far more people than even the most popular daily national.

**Posters and hoardings**
These are cheap and effective if good locations can be found. They have to be easy to read quickly, and are usually used together with other forms of advertising, particularly where a slogan or strong visual image is used. Guinness and Benson & Hedges advertisements are classic examples of this.

**Sales promotions**
These include free gifts, competitions, give-away samples and special offers. They are very common for products such as petrol, and food and drink.

**Direct mail**
This is often used by local firms such as supermarkets, but also by national advertisers such as the AA and Readers' Digest. Direct mail is discussed in more detail in Chapter 8.

**Sponsorship**
This is becoming increasingly common, especially for sporting events. Most leagues and competitions now have the name of a company or product in the title, and a famous show-jumper has even named his horses after a type of stereo system. The arts, such as theatre and opera, also attract sponsorship.

Sponsorship has the advantage of connecting the sponsor's name with a popular cause. If a sponsored event is televised the sponsor can obtain effective advertising very cheaply. In the past, cigarettes were indirectly 'advertised' on television through events such as the Embassy World Darts Championship, but this practice has now been discouraged.

**Advertising agencies**
These are professional companies whose purpose is to design advertising campaigns and book advertising slots for products. They will also conduct market research to find out the public attitude to existing or new products. The most famous agency in Britain is Saatchi and Saatchi.

**Fig. 14.2** Examples of sales promotions

## Control of advertising

There are very strict controls upon advertising in Britain. Advertisers have to obey laws such as the Trade Descriptions Act, which makes it illegal to make misleading claims about products. There are also voluntary 'codes of conduct' monitored by the Independent Broadcasting Authority (IBA) and the Advertising Standards Authority (ASA).

The IBA is responsible for controlling television advertising and has to approve all TV adverts before they can be broadcast. About a third are rejected outright or sent back for amendment.

The conditions for television advertising are very similar to those set by the Advertising Standards Authority (see below) but there are additional rules. For example, cigarettes and political causes cannot be advertised, some products can only be advertised after 9 o'clock, toy adverts must give prices, and a Volkswagen advertisement which put new words to a popular hymn was not allowed to be shown on Sundays.

### The Advertising Standards Authority (ASA)

The Advertising Standards Authority (ASA) is an independent body financed by the advertising industry. It is responsible for monitoring almost all advertising in the UK (except for television).

The ASA's slogan is that all advertising must be 'legal, decent, honest and truthful'. Its *British Code of Advertising Practice* sets rules for all advertisers to follow. There are special sections on certain products:

*(a)* Cars must not be advertised in a way which condones reckless driving. Amongst the slogans which have been banned are 'the trigger is under your right foot', 'flying lessons optional' and 'capable of 123 mph (sorry officer)'.

*(b)* Slimming products cannot make claims such as 'lose 10 pounds in 2 weeks', must show that diet plans will contain adequate amounts of essential proteins and vitamins and must stress that only a calorie-controlled diet can cause weight loss.

*(c)* Children must not be urged to buy a product unless they can reasonably afford it themselves, or made to feel that they will be inferior or unpopular with other children if they do not possess a particular product.

### What can you do?

If you see an advertisement you think is wrong, you can write to the Advertising Standards Authority, giving the following information:
- ☐ The name of the company advertising;
- ☐ The name of the paper or magazine that ran the advertisement, or where you saw the poster;
- ☐ The date of the advertisement;
- ☐ Exactly what you think is wrong with the advertisement;
- ☐ If possible, enclose a copy of the advertisement.

### How can misleading advertising be stopped?

When someone complains about an advertisement to the Advertising Standards Authority, the ASA will decide whether the advertisement is acceptable or not, using the British Code of Advertising Practice as a guide.

If the ASA decides an advertisement is unacceptable (because it is either misleading or in bad taste), they will tell the advertiser to stop running the advertisement.

**Fig. 14.3** How to complain to the ASA

The ASA receives thousands of complaints about advertisements every year. It also regularly scans a sample of advertising material and investigates a proportion in more detail. As there are an estimated 25 million advertisements a year in Britain, it relies heavily upon public complaints and the observance of its *British Code of Advertising Practice*.

If an advertisement is thought to break its rules, the ASA will contact the advertiser to ask for an explanation. If necessary, advertisers and advertising media will be asked to discontinue or amend an advert.

For example, in February 1988 the ASA received 716 complaints. 99 were investigated, of which 33 were related to slow or non-delivery of mail-order goods. 73 were rejected because there was no case to answer, and the remainder gave inadequate information or were outside the ASA's scope (e.g. TV adverts which were sent on to the IBA).

Complaints which were upheld included the following:

*(a)* A computer advert which promised technical facilities which were only available to users who bought additional equipment costing almost as much as the computer itself.

*(b)* A mail order advert promising 'immediate despatch' when a customer was told there would be a 30-day wait.

*(c)* Adverts for garage equipment containing a picture of a nude woman.

*(d)* Misleading statements about the performance of an electric heater.

*(e)* 'Reduced prices' holidays which were more expensive than the normal brochure price.

*(f)* A restaurant which claimed to be 'recommended by Egon Ronay' but which was not in the current edition.

*(g)* Adverts by chain stores for products which were never available at some branches.

# 15
# Consumer Protection

## Principles of consumer law

Every time a good or service is sold, the two parties enter into a contract and obtain both rights and duties. Until fairly recently most of these rights and duties came from the *common law*. Common law is 'unwritten' and is based upon the accepted practice and court judgements in the past. The other type of law is *statutory law*, which is based upon Acts of Parliament.

Where there is no statutory law, common law is the basis upon which judgements about particular legal disputes are made. The main principle of common law for consumers is *caveat emptor* (let the buyer beware). It is assumed that the buyer inspects the goods and knows what he or she is buying. However, the seller is supposed to provide a reasonable quality of goods and charge reasonable prices.

During the last hundred years many common law rights have been written into Acts of Parliament, and most cases are now based upon statutory law. This can be further divided into *civil* and *criminal law*.

*Criminal law* sets rules for sellers of goods to follow. If they break these rules they are guilty of a criminal offence, and can be prosecuted by the state and possibly fined or imprisoned. A person cannot sue for damages under the criminal law. However, the Powers of Criminal Courts Act 1973 does give courts the right to award compensation to anybody who has suffered loss or damage as the result of a criminal act (except for motoring offences).

*Civil law* is designed to allow one citizen or firm to sue another for damages. A seller cannot be prosecuted as a criminal under civil law, but can be made to pay compensation.

The difference between the two can be illustrated by the example of a trader selling plastic shoes but describing them as made of leather. This would be a criminal offence under the Trade Descriptions Act (part of the criminal law), but the buyer could not sue for compensation under this Act. This could be done, however, under the Sale of Goods Act, which is part of civil law.

## Consumer legislation

There are many Acts of Parliament which protect the consumer. Amongst the most important are:

### Sale of Goods Act 1979
This was based upon the Sale of Goods Act 1893 and the Supply of Goods (Implied Terms) Act 1973, combining and replacing them both. It sets out three particular rules about any goods sold. All goods must be:

1. 'Of merchantable quality'. They must be capable of doing what would be expected for normal use. For example, wellington boots must keep out water, but the consumer could not complain if slippers were ruined by walking in the rain.
2. 'As described'. The goods must be what they are said to be, e.g. a 'solid teak' table must not be made of some other wood. Deliberately misdescribing goods is also a criminal offence under the Trade Descriptions Act.
3. 'Fit for the purpose'. If a seller gives incorrect advice, he or she can be held responsible. If a shop assistant describes a rope as suitable for rock-climbing and it snaps under use, the shop can be sued for damages.

The provisions about 'implied terms' make it illegal for a seller to attempt to take away the consumer's legal rights. Before these provisions, some sellers tried to include clauses or notices such as 'no refunds' or 'no guarantee'. These were often referred to as 'exclusion clauses'. This type of exclusion is now illegal. Even where the buyer is given extra rights such as 'your money back if not satisfied', the trader must point out that 'statutory rights are not affected'.

There are some exceptions to these rules. They apply only to purchases from traders. In 'private sales' from one member of the public to another, only the 'as described' condition applies. (It is illegal for a trader to advertise or pose as a private seller.) If the goods are sold second-hand or as 'seconds', top quality cannot be expected. A seller may also point out a defect such as a mark or fault on clothing. In these cases, the buyer is regarded as having accepted the goods with the fault.

The Sale of Goods Act is a civil act, which means that it is up to the consumer to sue for damages. However, there are several organisations which exist to help consumers (see 'Consumer Organisations' below).

**Supply of Goods and Services Act**
This extended the provisions of the Sale of Goods Act to services such as car repairs and dry cleaning. The consumer is entitled to a reasonable standard of work, completed in a reasonable time and at a reasonable price (assuming that the time and price are not agreed in advance).

**Trade Descriptions Act 1968**
This law makes it a criminal offence to give a misleading description of goods or services – this includes size, weight, materials and methods used and so on.

It is also an offence to make false comparisons between the present and previous prices. If, for example, ties are advertised as 'pure silk, manufactured in UK, original price £20, sale price £9.50' then it is an offence if:

(a) the ties are not made of silk.
(b) they are made in another country.
(c) they have not been on sale at the old price for at least 28 consecutive days in the last six months (unless the seller clearly states that this is not so).

The Trade Descriptions Act is enforced by the Consumer Protection or Trading Standards departments of local authorities. It does not allow a consumer to sue the seller; this must be done under other Acts, although a court can award damages to the buyer if it wishes.

## Unfair Contract Terms Act 1977
This prevents sellers of services using exclusion clauses to take away statutory rights. For example, many ferry companies used to print on their tickets that they could not be sued for damage or injury to passengers or their property, even if the company was at fault. If a careless crew member damaged a car, the firm was not responsible.

The Unfair Contract Terms Act made this type of rule illegal, unless it was considered reasonable. For example, the typical car-park sign 'cars parked at own risk' would cover a business in the case of theft, but it would still be responsible if part of its building fell on top of the car.

## Unsolicited Goods and Services Act 1971
This protects consumers who are sent goods that they have not requested. In these cases the consumer can give the sender notice to collect the goods, and keep them if they are not collected within 30 days. Alternatively, if the consumer does not inform the company, the goods become his or her property if they are not collected within six months.

## The Weights and Measures Act 1979
This is one of a series of Weights and Measures Acts which make it an offence to give 'short weight' or 'short measure', even by accident. Associated laws such as the Prices Act 1974 also set rules about the way in which prices are marked and displayed – for example, pubs and restaurants must show their prices in a prominent place. Some goods such as butter and sugar can only be sold in metric quantities, and not by the pound. Equipment such as scales or petrol pumps must also be tested and approved by a trading standards officer.

## Consumer Credit Act 1974
This law gives protection to consumers buying goods and services on credit. A business which offers credit must be registered with the Office of Fair Trading, must not charge extortionate rates of interest, and must show the Annual Percentage Rate of interest (APR) on all advertisements and documents. The cash and credit prices must also be shown so that the buyer can see how much is being charged for credit.

Under this Act, the provider of credit is jointly responsible with the supplier for faulty goods or services for transactions between £50 and £30 000 (with some exceptions such as building society mortgages). Credit card companies often offer additional protection with free insurance against financial loss on purchases such as holidays.

**Consumer Protection Act 1987**
This Act included and extended the provisions of the Consumer Safety Act 1978 and the Consumer Safety (Amendment) Act 1986. It allows the Government to ban certain unsafe goods from sale, and to prosecute the sellers of dangerous goods such as toys with spikes or lead paint. The Government has the power to make compulsory rules about products.

Manufacturers are also responsible for damage or injury caused by defective products (not including food) unless they can prove that the danger could not have been seen beforehand.

**Fair Trading Act 1973**
This set up the Office of Fair Trading (OFT), a Government agency whose purpose is to protect consumers against unfair practices by firms. Some ways in which the OFT helps the public are:

*(a)* Publishing leaflets to help people to know their rights.
*(b)* Encouraging trade organisations such as the Motor Agents Association and the Footwear Distributors Association to prepare voluntary *codes of practice*. These are rules which their members agree to abide by.
*(c)* Proposing new laws and regulations to help consumers.
*(d)* Prosecuting traders who persistently break the law.
*(e)* Issuing licences to providers of credit under the Consumer Credit Act.
*(f)* Recommending to the Monopolies and Mergers Commission (another Government agency) that certain firms or markets should be investigated. For example, large mergers may be examined to see if they would be likely to reduce competition. Another investigation was concerned with deciding whether breweries should be allowed to retain control of public houses.

## CONTENTS

**Inside Story** **p491**
Credit cards; phone calls; safety warnings; car imports; the NHS; and a new instant picture camera

**Annual Report** **p537**
CA's successes and achievements: April 1985 to March 1986

## PUBLIC INTEREST

**Water** **p494**
Whether a meter might save you money. And why our water is below scratch

**Consumer safety** **p540**
Tightening up the law on unsafe products
– we campaign for changes

## ABOUT THE HOUSE

**Telephones** **p498**
Best Buy home phones

**Typing at home** **p524**
Electronic typewriters, word processors and printers

**Filter coffee makers** **p532**
Several recommended from our tests

## LEISURE

**Zoom lenses** **p503**
On test: wide-angle-to-semi-telephoto camera lenses

**House swapping for holidays** **p511**
California to Clapham – and very cheerful

**Stereo systems** **p534**
Sets worth buying for £300 or less, with or without CD

## MONEY

**Where to keep your savings** **p506**
Best Buy building society accounts, and other rewarding homes for your money

**Money facts** **p510**
Facts to help borrowers and investors

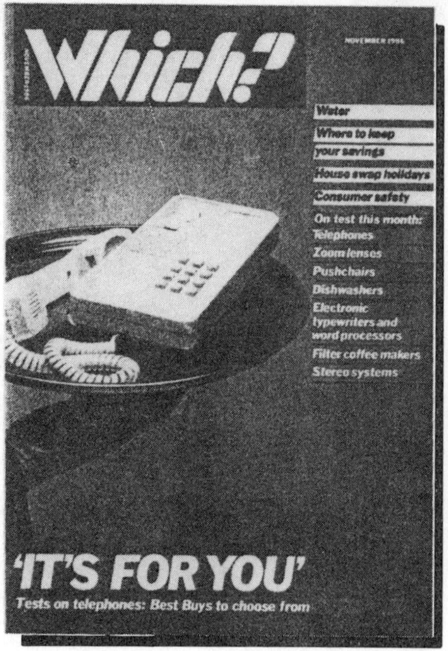

**Fig. 15.1** A typical issue of *Which?*

## Consumer organisations

There are many organisations which exist to protect consumers. Some of the most important include:

**Local authorities**
Councils help consumers in various ways. There are two especially important local authority departments.

**(a) Trading Standards or Consumer Protection** The Trading Standards Department enforces the major consumer legislation such as the Weights and Measures Act. Trading standards officers carry out tests and surveys such as checking that pubs are giving full measure. They investigate complaints from the public about local and national traders. Many councils also run Consumer Advice Centres for their area.

**(b) Environmental Health** Environmental health officers' duties include checking that food is sold and served in clean and hygienic conditions. They inspect shops, cafes and restaurants to see that they are not dirty or a health hazard, and prosecute traders who break the regulations.

**Citizens Advice Bureau (CAB)**
This is an independent organisation which receives some grants from the Government, but relies upon unpaid volunteers for much of its work. CABs can be found in most large towns and deal with consumer problems of all types.

**Consumers Association**
This is another independent organisation which campaigns for consumers. Its income comes almost entirely from selling books and other publications. The most famous of these is the magazine *Which?*, where readers can see the results of tests and surveys of many goods and services. The contents of a typical issue are shown in Figure 15.1.

**Nationalised Industry Consumer Councils**
Most of the major nationalised industries have a corresponding Users' Council. These are set up to represent the interests of

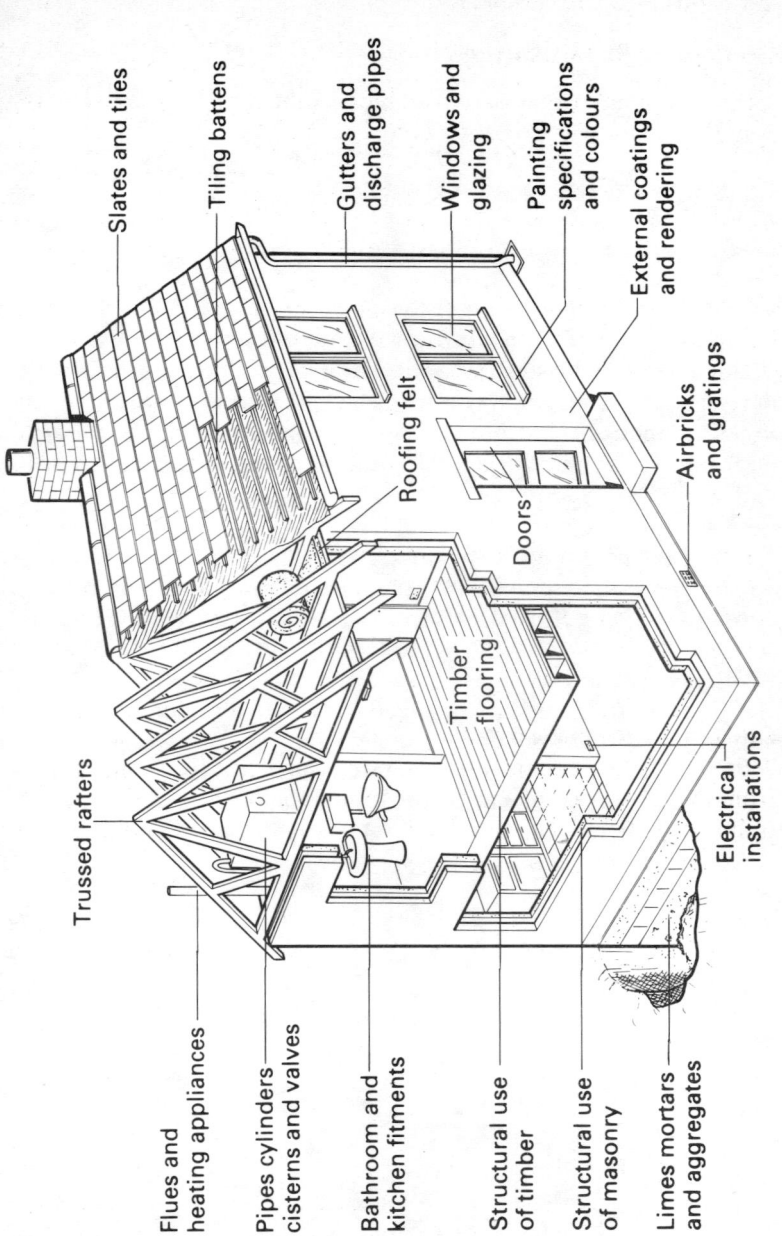

**Fig. 15.2** British Standards in construction

consumers. For example, the Electricity Consumers' Council has investigated issues such as

*(a)* The cost of electricity.
*(b)* The efficiency of the industry.
*(c)* Policy on disconnection of non-payers.
*(d)* Methods of paying bills.
*(e)* Plans for the privatisation of the industry.

**British Standards Institution (BSI)**

The British Standards Institution is financed jointly by industry and the Government. It sets standards for a very wide range of goods and services – everything from cricket balls to the way in which books are indexed. It is best known to the public for its 'Kitemark' and other safety markings, which show that a good is claimed to conform to British Standards. For example, fireguards must have mesh small enough to prevent a child putting its fingers through.

The kitemark is only a small part of the BSI's work. It also sets standards for many materials and industrial processes. Figure 15.2 shows how British Standards apply to the construction industry.

**National Consumer Council**

This body is appointed and financed by the Government to investigate and campaign on behalf of consumers. It regularly publishes reports on matters of consumer interest such as housing problems, hospital waiting lists and pension arrangements.

# 16

# Overseas Trade

## The advantages of foreign trade

The British economy is heavily dependent upon foreign trade for satisfying the needs of its population, and providing markets for its products. Many industries could not survive in their present form without imports of raw materials or customers in other countries. About a quarter of consumer spending in Britain is on imports (compared to 10 percent for the USA).

There are several advantages to allowing *free trade* between countries without restrictions on imports and exports such as *tariffs* and *quotas* (see 'Protectionism' below).

**Countries can obtain goods and services which they cannot produce themselves**  Because of a lack of natural resources, most countries are incapable of producing certain goods and services. Britain, for example, could not produce bananas or coffee (except at prohibitive expense) because of the unsuitable climate. Services such as foreign holidays and Australian soap operas would also be unavailable to British consumers without foreign trade.

**Countries can specialise in the goods and services that they produce most efficiently**  Through foreign trade, countries are able to obtain goods and services which they could produce themselves, but which other countries produce more cheaply and efficiently. Britain produces about half of the food needed to feed its population. This proportion could be increased, but more land, labour and capital would have to be switched from other industries into agriculture. It is cheaper to buy food from abroad and use

British resources for goods and services that Britain is more efficient at producing.

There are many goods and services which Britain both imports and exports. About half of all the new cars bought in the UK are made abroad, but Britain also exports cars. One of the reasons for this is that British car firms are more competitive in the luxury car market, and do not produce cheaper cars as efficiently as European or Japanese firms.

International trade therefore allows countries to specialise in the goods and services that they produce best, satisfying their other needs by importing commodities that they do not produce themselves.

**International trade makes mass production possible**  By providing a wider market than is present in a single country, international trade allows large-scale production, with all the benefits of *economies of scale* (see Chapter 3). Many products such as aircraft, chemicals and oil are produced more cheaply because they are sold on a world-wide basis. All countries receive the benefits of greater world output and cheaper products.

**Competition makes domestic producers more efficient**  If a firm faces competition from abroad it will be forced to become more efficient if it is to stay in business. One of the aims of the European Community is to increase competition across Europe to encourage firms to produce cheaper and better quality products.

**Consumers benefit from international trade**  Because of the reasons outlined above, consumers gain from international trade by getting a wider choice of goods and services because of the efficiency created by international competition.

**Trade between countries leads to international peace and co-operation**  It is often argued that international trade makes countries dependent on each other, and that if they are in contact through trade they will be less likely to go to war. One of the reasons for establishing the European Community was to encourage international co-operation in order to avoid another world war.

# Protectionism

## Methods of protectionism

Despite its benefits, there are many restrictions upon free trade between countries:

**Tariffs**  A tariff is a tax upon imports. It may be imposed in order to make them more expensive compared to the domestic product, to discourage imports of a particular product or simply to raise money for the Government.

**Quotas**  Quotas are physical limits upon the amount of a good or service which can be imported. They are often used to restrict imports where tariffs seem to make little difference because consumers are prepared to pay high prices for foreign commodities. The limit may be in various forms, e.g. 'x tons of coffee', '£x worth of steel', 'x percent of the clothing market'.

Quotas are often 'voluntary' or 'gentleman's agreements' made between a government and importers, such as the agreement by Japanese car manufacturers in the 1980s to sell not more than 11 percent of new cars in Britain.

**Embargoes**  An embargo is a complete ban upon trade with a particular country (sometimes only for certain goods such as scientific or military equipment). It is usually imposed for political reasons.

**Subsidies**  A government may give money to domestic producers to give them an advantage against foreign firms in the home and export markets. This practice is strongly discouraged by the European Community for sales within the Common Market.

**Exchange controls**  Importers need foreign currency to pay for imports, and governments sometimes limit the amount of currency which can be bought by their consumers and firms. Exchange controls were abolished by the British Government in 1980 but are commonly used elsewhere, particularly in Eastern Europe and the Third World.

**Government procurement**  Some governments insist upon domestic goods and services being bought wherever possible by public authorities. For example, many councils and police authorities would only permit the purchase of British vehicles. Britain now has international agreements which restrict its power to follow a 'buy British' policy. Despite these agreements, however, most governments favour their own country's firms, with less than 1 percent of contracts in EC countries going to foreign firms in 1986.

**Special rules and regulations**   All countries have regulations about standards for products. Occasionally these may be deliberately designed to prevent or hinder imports. Recent examples include a ban on European skis in Japan (on the grounds that Japanese snow is different) and time-wasting Customs procedures for imports of Japanese video-recorders into France.

**Reasons for protectionism**

**To cure a balance of payments deficit**   A balance of payments deficit occurs when more capital flows out of a country than comes in. This may be as a result of factors such as imports being greater than exports or of a country's residents investing abroad. Protectionist measures may be designed to reduce imports and investment in other countries.

**To protect domestic industry and employment**   A government may wish to help its own industries by restricting imports or helping to make exports more competitive. This policy is often used for *infant industries* which are newly established and find it difficult to compete with foreign firms. A country will often wish to broaden its range of industries if it is dependent upon a particular industry (for example, Mauritius has tried to develop industries which do not depend upon sugar production). The argument for protecting infant industries is that once they are established the restrictions on imports will be dropped.

Other industries which may be protected are declining industries, such as textiles in the UK, which have suffered as a result of cheap imports. It is sometimes argued that certain countries are *dumping* goods or services on the world market at less than their cost of production, usually to earn foreign exchange or ruin their competitors. Restrictions may be placed on imports from these countries, such as the EC's 'anti-dumping tax' on Japanese electrical equipment.

Other types of industry that are often protected are *strategic* industries such as steel or agriculture, which are thought to be vital to a country's economy or military strength. For example, the Common Agricultural Policy of the EC was intended to make Europe self-sufficient in basic foodstuffs.

**To protect the exchange rate**   If more capital flows out of a country than is coming in (for the reasons described above) its exchange rate will tend to fall. If the Government wishes to maintain the value of its currency it may impose exchange controls or restrictions upon imports.

**Disadvantages of protectionism**

The main argument against protectionism is that it removes the advantages of free trade between countries. If one country imposes restrictions others usually retaliate, and the volume of trade falls so that all lose potential customers. Free trade encourages countries to specialise in the types of production that they are best at.

Protectionism also hits the consumer, who generally gets less choice and higher prices as a result. It has been estimated that the restriction upon Japanese car imports into the UK adds about 15 percent to the cost of a small car, and that clothing prices would fall by 10 percent if import quotas were abolished.

Advocates of free trade also state that it is nonsensical to protect inefficient industry, as this costs both the Government and consumers money. They argue that these industries should be forced to become more efficient or switch production to products which they can sell profitably.

# The balance of payments

The balance of payments is a record of all transactions between Britain and other countries. It is made up of two parts. The *capital account* measures the flow of capital to and from other countries for purposes such as investment in foreign banks and industry. The *current account*, which is discussed in more detail below, records payments for goods and services to and by British residents. (The term *residents* is used to include people, firms and the Government.)

## The balance of payments current account

|  | (£ millions) |  |
|---|---|---|
| Visible exports | 80 157 |  |
| Visible imports | 100 714 |  |
| Visible balance |  | −20 557 |
| Invisible exports | 86 718 |  |
| Invisible imports | 81 098 |  |
| Invisible balance |  | 5621 |
| Current balance |  | −14 936 |

**Fig. 16.1** UK Balance of Payments 1988

Britain's current account for 1986 is illustrated in Figure 16.1. As can be seen, it consists of *visible* and *invisible trade*.

**Visible trade** Visible trade is trade in goods. The *visible balance* (also called the *balance of trade*) is equal to visible exports minus visible imports. Until the 1980s the UK generally exported more manufactured goods than it imported, but this was balanced by large imports of food and raw materials. There has therefore been a deficit in visible trade (imports greater than exports) in most postwar years.

|  | Exports (£ millions) | Imports (£ millions) |
|---|---|---|
| Food, drink & tobacco | 5 537 | 10 586 |
| Basic materials | 2 121 | 5 992 |
| Fuels | 5 818 | 5 058 |
| Manufactures | 66 681 | 85 078 |
|  | 80 157 | 106 714 |

**Fig. 16.2** The pattern of UK visible trade 1988

During the last 20 years the composition of visible trade has changed. Food and raw materials have fallen as a proportion of imports, because of an increase in agricultural production and the development of synthetic substitutes for goods such as wool and cotton. The production of North Sea oil since 1975 has also turned Britain from a net importer into a major exporter of fuel. However, the current low price of oil and running down of North Sea oil reserves may change this position after 2000.

|  | *(£ millions)* |
|---|---|
| Services | 3 248 |
| Interest, profits & dividends | 5 772 |
| Transfers | −3 579 |
|  | 5 621 |

**Fig. 16.3** Composition of invisible balance 1988

**Invisible trade** Invisible trade is trade in services such as those illustrated in Figure 16.3. Generally the UK has made a large surplus from invisible trade, particularly from financial services (the City of London is one of the world's major financial centres). British residents owned foreign assets of £90 billion at the end of 1987, and receive substantial income from these.

The *current balance* is the sum of the visible and invisible balances, that is:

**(visible exports + invisible exports) − (visible imports + invisible imports)**

Since the Second World War, the current balance has been in surplus about as often as it has been in deficit. In the early 1980s

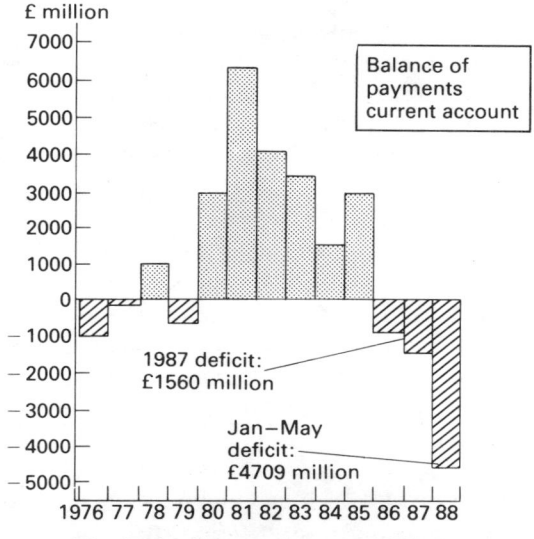

**Fig. 16.4** Current Account 1976–88

exports were consistently higher than imports, largely because of high earnings from North Sea oil exports.

From 1986, as can be seen from Figure 16.4, imports started to exceed exports. This was largely due to the rapid growth of the economy, combined with reductions in income tax. These meant that people had more money to spend upon imported goods and services such as cars and foreign holidays.

## Difficulties facing exporters

Firms trying to sell abroad face several special difficulties which do not apply to domestic sales:

### Language

Documents, advertising and trade names may have to be translated into other languages. This sometimes causes problems with brand names which may be offensive or silly in another language. For example, 'Nike' is an extremely rude word in some Arabic dialects, and the Volkswagen Rabbit had to be called the Golf in Britain because British consumers would be put off by the original name.

### Tastes and habits

These can vary considerably between countries. Rowntree Mackintosh had considerable problems when it tried to sell its sweets abroad. Smarties have different colour combinations for different countries. Kit-Kat did badly because French and German people do not have the British habit of a tea-break with a snack, and it goes badly with beer or wine. The French thought that combining mint and chocolate in After Eights was very strange (this difficulty was successfully overcome by advertising After Eights as 'so English').

### Information and distribution

It can sometimes be difficult to obtain information about how to sell products abroad, or to get adequate local agents. Delivery is also more complicated and expensive than for home trade.

### Credit risks

The risk of non-payment is much higher in many other countries, especially those which are politically unstable. Both banks and government departments such as the Export Credit Guarantee Department try to minimise these risks for importers (see 'Assistance for Exporters' below).

**Laws and regulations**
Most exporters face different technical and legal rules in other countries, such as left-hand drive and safety regulations for car manufacturers. The European Community is currently trying to get its member countries to agree upon similar standards for products to make trade within the Common Market easier for firms.

**Protectionism**
Protectionist measures such as those outlined earlier in this chapter may cause problems for exporters. Sometimes these are used deliberately to restrict imports.

**Currency changes**
The value of the currency may change, affecting both costs and income from exports. A fall in the value of the pound against the dollar would increase a British airline's costs because oil is priced in dollars. At the same time, it would be paid by its British customers in sterling, which would be worth less in other currencies. To protect against such changes, exporters can buy foreign currency on the *forward market*, which guarantees that they can buy at predictable prices.

## Assistance for exporters

Because of the importance of the export trade to the economy, firms can receive help from many sources, both Government and private:

**The British Overseas Trade Board (BOTB)**
The Department of Trade and Industry provides assistance for exporters, generally through the British Overseas Trade Board, in forms such as

*(a)* information and advice upon foreign markets.
*(b)* introductions to agents and business contacts.
*(c)* specialist library of statistics and intelligence.
*(d)* export market research.

*(e)* technical advice about foreign standards (run through the British Standards Institution).
*(f)* assistance with the preparation of documents.
*(g)* trade missions and promotions.

**The Export Credits Guarantee Department (ECGD)**
This is a separate Government department which is responsible to the Secretary of State for Trade and Industry. Its main function is to arrange insurance for exporters against the risk of not being paid by their customers. These risks include non-payment for reasons such as:

*(a)* bankruptcy or refusal to pay.
*(b)* failure to pay within six months.
*(c)* wars or political difficulties preventing trade.
*(d)* a foreign government preventing payments abroad, e.g. through exchange controls.
*(e)* cancellation of orders or export and import licences.

The ECGD covers a substantial proportion of Britain's exports – in 1986–87 it insured one-fifth with a total value of £13.8 billion, and paid £800 million to exporters to cover bad debts. The premiums paid by the exporter are based upon the particular risk involved in particular countries or industries.

**Non-Government aid to exporters**
There are many private-sector organisations which provide services to exporters, sometimes of a similar nature to those provided by the Government. The commercial banks have export departments to provide advice, finance and help with documentation. Merchant banks offer similar specialised services, and some *discount* or *accept* bills of exchange.

Many industries have trade associations which provide services to their members. Local Chambers of Commerce and the Confederation of British Industry can also help potential exporters.

# Financing of international trade

As explained above, there are greater dangers of non-payment for exports than for domestic trade. Cheques can be used, but the

*Overseas Trade* 177

---

£10 000

Canberra
1 January, 199–

Three months after date pay to our order the sum of £10 000 sterling for value received.

To: J. Smith
    London SW1.

(Signed) K. McGowran

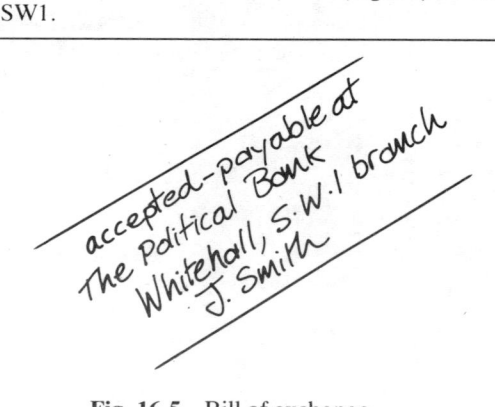

---

*accepted – payable at The Political Bank, Whitehall, S.W.1 branch*
*J. Smith*

**Fig. 16.5** Bill of exchange

exporter may not be prepared to accept these in case of default. There are therefore special methods of payment, most of which use banks as intermediaries between exporter and importer.

**Bills of exchange**
The traditional means of payment for international transactions is the *bill of exchange*, an example of which is shown in Figure 16.5.

This example assumes that three months credit is to be allowed to the buyer, but this period may vary. If the bill is payable 'on sight' there is no credit, and payment must be made immediately.

The bill of exchange is drawn up by the exporter and sent to the importer for agreement. Once it is signed by the importer it is a legally binding agreement to pay. A bill of exchange may be guaranteed by a bank or accepting house, and may be *discounted* (see Chapter 10).

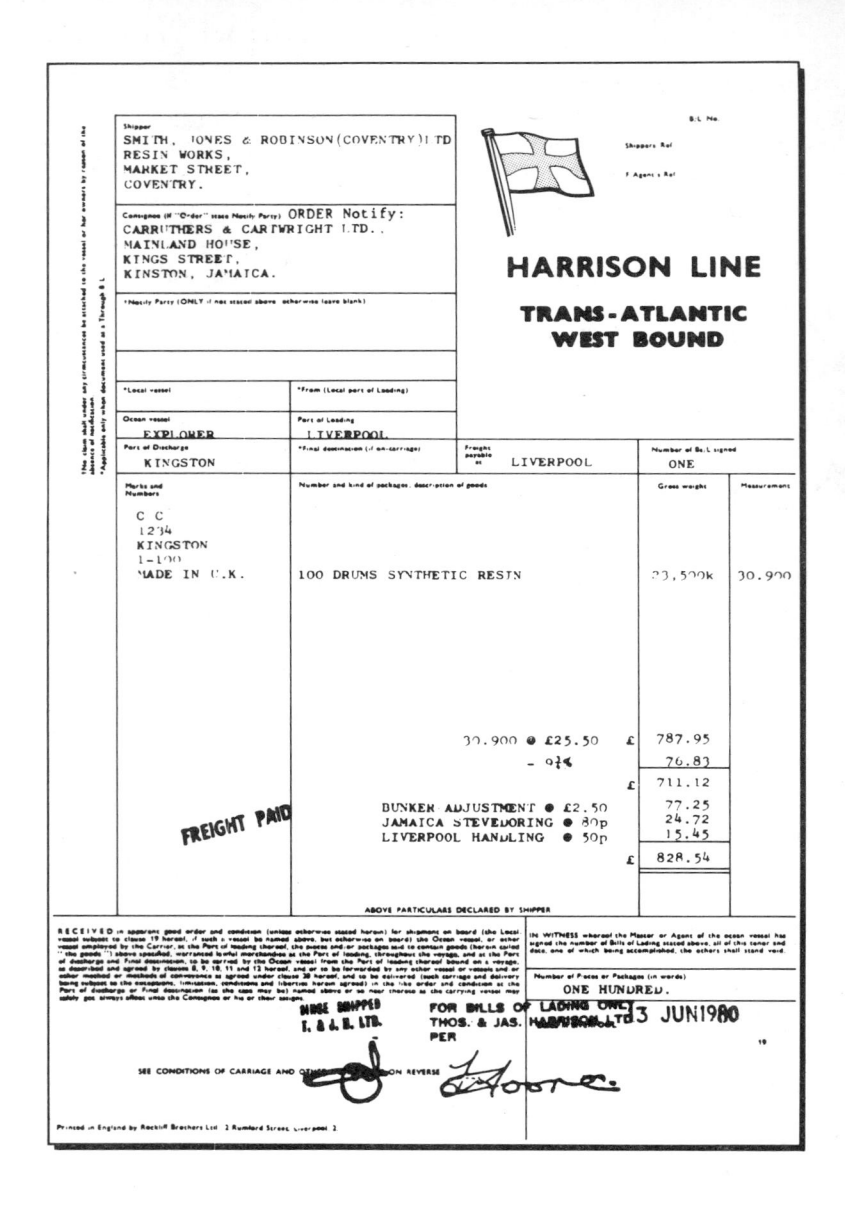

**Fig. 16.6** Bill of Lading

**The documentary credit system**

The documentary credit system works by the importer and exporter each nominating a bank to make and receive payments on their behalf. On despatching the goods the exporter will send the appropriate documents to the importer's bank. These will include a *bill of lading* (see Figure 16.6) which gives details of the goods and the prices and terms of payment. The importer's bank will arrange a credit for the amount with the exporter's bank.

When the goods arrive the importer will pay the amount agreed to its bank. The importer's bank will tell the exporter's bank to pay the amount, and will give the importer its copy of the bill of lading. This is then used to obtain delivery of the goods.

# Britain and the European Community

The European Community (EC) is an organisation of 12 countries – Belgium, France, West Germany, Italy, Luxembourg, Netherlands, Denmark, Republic of Ireland, United Kingdom, Greece, Portugal and Spain.

The first six of these countries were the original members who signed the Treaty of Rome, setting up the EC in 1957. Britain, Ireland and Denmark joined in 1973, Greece in 1981, and Spain and Portugal in 1986. The 12 members contain 320 million people, and are responsible for 20 percent of world trade, compared to the USA's 13 percent and Japan's 12 percent.

The EC is often known as the 'Common Market', because one of its central aims is to have free trade and movement of workers and capital between its members. This is still one of its main aims, although progress has been slow. In 1968, the original six members agreed to abolish tariffs between themselves, and to apply identical tariffs to all other countries.

In 1986 the 12 member countries signed the Single European Act, which was designed to remove all restrictions upon movement of goods, labour and capital between member states. Existing trade barriers are being abolished in stages, with the process being completed in 1992. By then it should be possible for an EC citizen to work anywhere in the twelve countries, and for any good which can be sold legally in one country to be sold in any of the others.

This process will involve tremendous change for people and

This . . .

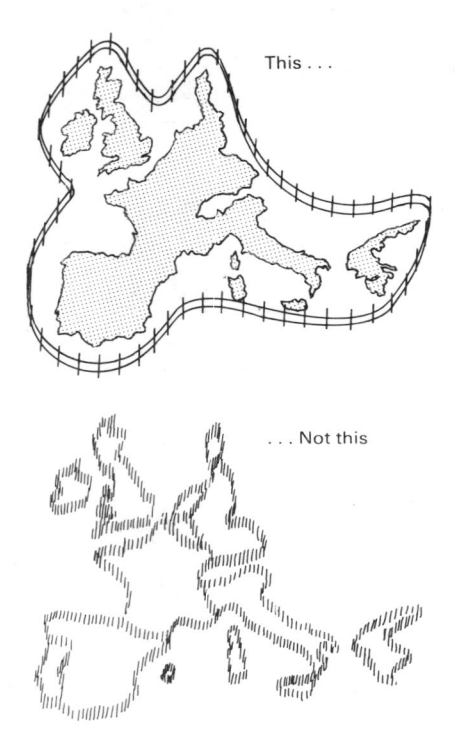

. . . Not this

The European Community arose from a desire to establish a peaceful prosperous Europe after the horrors of two World Wars. The twelve nations of the Community have agreed to merge their economic interests to form a 'common market' where trade may be conducted freely, people can work wherever they want, and money can be invested where it is most needed.

*The activities of the European Community encompass:*

- Industry
- Commerce
- Monetary cooperation
- Competition
- Transport
- Nuclear safety
- Environment
- Consumer protection
- New technologies
- Energy
- Professional training and job creation
- Regional development
- Aid to developing countries
- International cooperation
- Fisheries
- Agriculture

*The institutions of the European Community*

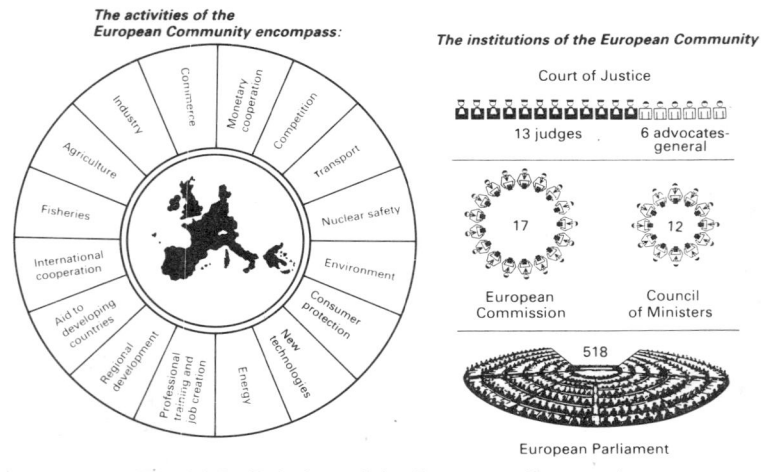

Court of Justice

13 judges    6 advocates-general

17 — European Commission

12 — Council of Ministers

518 — European Parliament

**Fig. 16.7**   Britain and the European Community

## General Community budget: 1985

### Receipts

| | |
|---|---|
| VAT | 55.5% |
| Customs duties | 29.6% |
| Non-repayable advances | 5.9% |
| Agricultural levies | 4.0% |
| Sugar and isoglucose levies | 3.8% |
| Miscellaneous | 1.2% |

### Expenditure

| | |
|---|---|
| Agriculture and fisheries | 72.9% |
| Regional policy | 5.9% |
| Social policy | 5.7% |
| Development cooperation | 3.9% |
| Research, energy, industry and transport | 2.6% |
| Administrative costs | 4.6% |
| Miscellaneous | 4.4% |

28 000 million ECU
(payment appropriations)

# Where does Britain fit in?

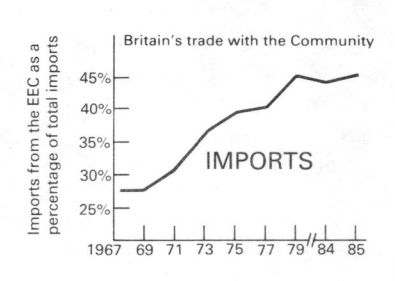

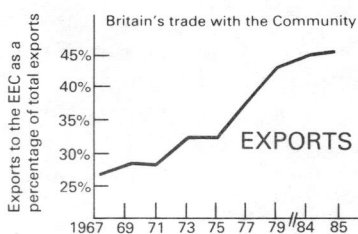

Britain's trade with the Community — IMPORTS (Imports from the EEC as a percentage of total imports, 1967–85)

Britain's trade with the Community — EXPORTS (Exports to the EEC as a percentage of total exports, 1967–85)

## What Britain puts into the Community

- A share of the running costs of the Community.
- Free access, for other Community countries, to Britain's market of 56 million people.
- Free access for Community citizens to jobs in Britain.
- Experience and traditions which result from being a stable, democratic nation.
- Experience of leading a multi-racial Commonwealth, and of helping many developing countries.

## What Britain gets out of the Community

- A share of the loans and grants from the Community for regional development, agricultural improvement, social aid, etc.
- Free access to the Community market of 320 million people.
- Free access for Britons to jobs anywhere in the Community.
- An opportunity to exert an influence on world affairs, with other Community countries, which Britain can no longer manage alone.
- An opportunity to offer more help to developing nations including those in the Commonwealth.

firms, and make competition within the EC more intense. It has also made it necessary for countries to agree upon basic standards for products, so that goods can be sold freely in all member countries. This is likely to be very important to British firms, as an increasing proportion of foreign trade is with EC countries.

## European Community institutions

The European Community is a political as well as an economic organisation, having been set up after the Second World War with the intention of uniting Europe. Its major institutions are:

**Council of Ministers** This is the Community's main decision-making body, with each member country having a seat on the Council. Usually a country will be represented by its Foreign Minister, but other Ministers are sometimes sent. The voting power of each member is based upon its population, ranging from 2 votes for Luxembourg to 10 for France, Germany, Italy and the UK. Generally, however, the Council tries to get a unanimous vote on important matters.

**European Commission** This has 17 members chosen by agreement between members. Each has responsibility for an area of Community policy such as competition or agriculture. Commissioners are meant to act on behalf of the EC and not for their own countries.

**European Parliament** The European Parliament has 518 members, who are elected directly by citizens of the Community. The number of members for each country depends upon its population, with the UK having 81. The Parliament has little real power apart from checking the work of the Council of Ministers and the Commission. However, it can sack Commissioners with a two-thirds majority vote, and has the power to reject the Community Budget.

**Court of Justice** This is the ultimate court of appeal in the Community, and can overrule national governments. For example, the abolition of corporal punishment in British schools occurred as the result of British citizens' cases in the European Court.

## Community expenditure

Most of the EC's income comes from VAT and customs duties imposed on its members, and by far the greatest item of expenditure is upon the *Common Agricultural Policy* (CAP). The aim of the CAP is to guarantee minimum prices to European farmers, so that the Community is as self-sufficient as possible in food.

The CAP has been heavily criticised because it causes higher prices for consumers. Foodstuffs such as sugar and butter can be produced far more cheaply in non-European countries, but imports from these areas are heavily taxed. Guaranteed prices also encourage farmers to produce as much as possible, which leads to 'butter mountains' and 'wine lakes' – massive surpluses of unwanted products.

To avoid these problems, the EC has introduced 'quotas' for products such as milk. These limit the amount which can be produced by farmers. Grants are also given to encourage use of farmland for other purposes, such as camping sites, etc.

The Community also spends large sums on regional and social projects in the poorer areas of member countries. These include new transport links such as railways and roads, job creation schemes and assistance with tourist developments such as theatres and museums.

# Commercial Abbreviations

The following abbreviations and terms are commonly used in business and commerce, and are listed here with their meanings.

**&** and (ampersand)
**@** at, for
**A1** first class, first rate
**a.a.r.** against all risks
**ab init.** *ab initio* (Latin), from the beginning
**abt** about
**a/c, acct** account
**A/C** current account
**ad., advt** advertisement
**ad val.** *ad valorem* (Latin), according to value
**AGM** Annual General Meeting
**agt** agreement, agent
**amt** amount
**ans.** answer
**A/P** accounts payable
**appro.** approval, approbation
**approx.** approximate
**A/R** accounts receivable
**A/S** account sales
**a.s.a.p.** as soon as possible
**asst** assistant
**av., ave** average

**bal.** balance
**b/d** bring (brought) down
**B/D** Bank Draft
**B/E** bill of exchange
**b/f** bring (brought) forward
**bk** book
**B/L** bill of lading
**B/P** bill payable
**B/R** bill receivable
**Bro., Bros** brother, brothers
**B/S** balance sheet; bill of sale
**bx, bxs** box, boxes

**c** cent(s)
**C** centigrade, celsius
**C/A** Capital Account
**CAP** Common Agricultural Policy
**carr. pd.** carriage paid
**carr. fwd** carriage forward
**cat.** catalogue
**CBI** Confederation of British Industry
**cc** cubic centimetre; carbon copy
**c/d** carried down
**cf.** compare
**c/f** carried forward
**C & F** cost and freight
**CGT** capital gains tax
**chq.** cheque
**c.i.f.** cost, insurance and freight

## Commercial Abbreviations 185

**cm** centimetre
**C/N** credit note
**Co.** Company
**c/o** care of
**COD** cash on delivery
**col.** column
**comm.** commission
**cont.** continued
**co-op** co-operative
**cr.** credit, creditor
**CS** Civil Service
**cum. div.** with dividend
**c.w.o.** cash with order

**D/A** Deposit Account
**DB** Day Book
**D/D** Demand Draft
**Deb.** Debenture
**dely, d/y** delivery
**dept** department
**dft** draft
**disc.** discount
**div.** dividends, division
**D/N** Debit Note
**do.** ditto (the same)
**doz.** dozen
**D/P** documents against payment
**dr.** debtor, debit
**d/s** days after sight

**ea.** each
**ECGD** Export Credit Guarantees Department
**EEC** European Economic Community
**EFTA** European Free Trade Association
**enc.** enclosure(s)
**entd** entered
**E&OE** errors and omissions excepted
**esp.** especially
**Esq.** Esquire
**est.** established; estimated
**ETA** estimated time of arrival
**ETD** estimated time of departure

**et seq.** *et sequentia* (Latin), and the following
**ex.** without
**exch.** exchange
**ex div., x. div.** without dividends
**ex int.** not including interest
**exors** executors
**exp.** express
**exs** expenses

**f, fr.** franc(s)
**F, Fahr.** Fahrenheit
**f.a.a.** free of all average (used in marine insurance)
**FAO** for the attention of
**f.a.q.** free alongside quay; fair average quality
**f.a.s.** free alongside ship
**fcp, fcap** foolscap
**f.d.** free docks
**f.i.f.o.** first in, first out
**FO** Firm Order
**f.o.b.** free on board
**f.o.r** free on rail
**fp.** fully paid
**fr.** from
**frt** freight
**ft** foot, feet
**fwd** forward

**g** gram(me)
**GA** general average (insurance)
**GDP** gross domestic product
**gen.** general
**GM** General Manager
**GMT** Greenwich Mean Time
**GNP** gross national product
**Gov.** Governor
**Govt** Government
**gr.** grain, grammar
**gr. wt.** gross weight

**HMSO** Her Majesty's Stationery Office
**HO** Head Office
**Hon.** Honorary, Honourable
**HP** hire purchase

## Business and Commerce

**HQ** headquarters
**hr, hrs** hour(s)

**i/c** in charge
**I/F** insufficient funds
**IMF** International Monetary Fund
**Inc.** incorporated
**ins.** insurance
**inst.** instant, current month
**int.** interest
**inv.** invoice
**IOU** I owe you

**J/A** Joint Account
**JP** Justice of the Peace
**Jun., Jr** Junior

**kg, kilo** kilogram(me)
**kl** kilolitre(s)
**km** kilometre(s)
**kw** kilowatts

**£** pound sterling
**l, lit.** litre(s)
**lat.** latitude
**lb** pound (weight)
**L/C** Letter of Credit
**Led.** Ledger
**LGA** Local Government Authority; Local Government Area
**l.i.f.o.** last in, first out
**long.** longitude
**Ltd** limited

**m** metre(s), minutes, million
**max.** maximum
**MC** Master of Ceremonies
**m/d** months after date
**med.** medium
**mem., memo.** memorandum
**Messrs** Messieurs (French), Gentlemen
**mfg** manufacturing
**mfr** manufacturer
**mg.** milligram

**mgr** manager
**min.** minimum, minute
**MIP** Marine Insurance Policy
**ml** millimetre(s)
**MP** Member of Parliament
**m.p.h.** miles per hour
**m/s** months after sight, metre per second

**n.a.** not available
**N/A** no advice, not acceptable (banking), not applicable
**NB** *nota bene* (Latin), mark well, note well
**nem. con.** *nemine contradicente* (Latin), no one contradicting
**N/F** no funds (banking)
**nil** *nihil* (Latin), nothing
**N/m** no mark
**N/O** no orders (trading)
**nom.** nominal
**NP** Notary Public
**NPV** no par value
**nr** near

**%** per cent
**%0** per thousand
**o/a** on account of
**o/c** over charge; out of charge
**o/d** on demand
**O/D** overdraft, overdrawn
**OK** all correct
**O&M** Organisation and Methods
**OPEC** Organisation of Petroleum Exporting Countries
**opp.** opposed, opposite
**OR** owner's risk
**ord.** ordinary
**o/s** out of stock, outstanding

**p.a.** *per annum* (Latin), yearly
**PAYE** Pay As You Earn (taxation)
**p.c.** per cent, post card
**p/c** price current
**p.c.b.** petty cash book
**pcl** parcel

## Commercial Abbreviations

**pcs**  pieces
**pd**  paid
**per**  by
**per capita**  by the head
**per pro, pp**  *per procurationem* (Latin), on behalf of
**pkg.**  package
**P & L**  Profit and Loss
**Plc**  Public Limited Company
**p/n**  promissory note
**P.O.**  postal order, post office
**pp.**  parcel post
**p. & p.**  postage and packing
**pr, pr.**  pair, price
**pref.**  preference, preferred
**prima facie**  at first sight
**PRO**  Public relations officer
**pro forma**  as a matter of form
**pro tem.**  *pro tempore* (Latin), for the time being
**PS**  postscript
**PSBR**  Public Sector Borrowing Requirement
**PTO**  please turn over
**PV**  per value

**qu.**  query, question
**quan.**  quantity
**qr**  quarter

**R/D**  refer to drawer (banking)
**re.**  with reference to, concerning
**rec(t)**  receipt
**recd**  received
**ref.**  reference
**reg., regd**  registered
**rep.**  report, representative
**retd**  returned
**rly**  railway
**rm**  ream
**R/p**  reply paid
**RSVP**  *Repondez, s'il vous plait* (French), please reply

**$**  dollar (money)
**SAYE**  Save As You Earn
**sch.**  school, schedule

**SDB**  sales day book
**sec.**  second
**sgn**  sign(ed)
**S/N**  shipping note
**soc.**  society
**spec.**  specification, speculation
**sq.**  square
**SS**  steamship
**St.**  saint, street, station
**std**  standard
**STD**  Subscriber Trunk Dialling
**stet**  let it stand
**stg**  sterling (money)
**stk**  stock

**TMO**  telegraph money order
**TO, t/o**  turnover
**Tr.**  Trustee
**TT**  telegraphic transfer
**TUC**  Trades Union Congress

**ult.**  *ultimo* (Latin), last month; ultimatum
**UN**  United Nations
**u/w**  underwriter

**v., vs**  versus; against
**var.**  variety
**VAT**  Value Added Tax
**via**  by way of, through
**viz.**  *videlicet* (Latin), namely
**vol.**  volume

**W/B**  Waybill
**w.e.f.**  with effect from
**whf**  wharf
**wk(s)**  week; weeks
**w.p.m.**  words per minute
**wt, wgt**  weight

**x.d.**  ex dividend (without dividend)
**x.int.**  ex interest (without interest)

**yr(s)**  year(s)
**yrs**  yours

# Glossary of Commercial Terms

In general, terms defined in the text are not included here. An asterisk indicates a cross reference.

**Air waybill**  A document made out by the consignor of goods sent by airfreight. It contains full details of the goods (their nature, weight and value), departure and arrival airports, and freight charges.

**Annual General Meeting (AGM)** (of a company)  The statutory meeting that each registered company is required to hold annually; the major item on the agenda is the approval of the Directors' Report and Accounts.

**Asset**  Anything with a money value (including debtors).

**Audit**  An examination of the accounts of an organisation (often by an independent firm of qualified accountants).

**Bankruptcy**  A situation when the High Court rules that a person is insolvent, i.e. unable to pay his/her debts.

**Bear market**  A situation when prices of stocks/shares on the Stock Exchange are generally falling (see also Bull market).

**Bill of Lading**  A document giving full details of goods being shipped, the name of the vessel and ports of departure and arrival. The holder of the bill is the legal owner of the goods for the time being.

**Blue chip**  A term given to ordinary shares of large and well established public companies (e.g. ICI).

**Bonus issue**  The issue of additional shares to existing shareholders without any payment being required; it will be made in proportion to existing shareholding, e.g. one new share for every three held. From the accounting point of view it is purely a book-keeping double entry, and makes no difference to the net asset value of the company as it is achieved by capitalising of reserves. The Stock Exchange market price will drop proportionately.

**Book value**  The present book-keeping value of an asset – generally it is the original cost less total depreciation* to date.

**Bull market**  A situation when prices of stocks/shares on the Stock Exchange are generally rising (see also Bear market).

**Capital taxes**  Taxes on capital transactions, e.g. capital gains tax, capital transfer tax, land development.

**Carriage forward**  When a seller quotes a price 'carriage forward' it means that delivery charges from his factory to the buyer's premises are to be paid by the buyer.

**Collateral**  The security for a loan that may be demanded by the lender (examples are property deeds, share certificates of public companies, and life assurance policies with a 'surrender value').

**Conglomerate merger**  see Diversification.

**Convertible loan stock**  A loan stock carrying a fixed interest but with the right to convert at a set date at a set price into ordinary shares.

**Corporation tax**  Tax on a company's profits.

**Cost, Insurance and Freight**  The term used when goods are being shipped or airfreighted from one country to another. It indicates that the seller will pay all freight and insurance costs up to the port/airport of destination (see also Free on board and Free alongside ship).

**Cover note**  A written confirmation of the proof of existence of an insurance contract pending issue of policy (common in motor vehicle insurance).

**Cum dividend**  The share price quoted includes the right to receive the dividend due shortly. Thus a company may declare a dividend on March 1st payable to all shareholders on the register on March 10th (see also Ex dividend).

**Debenture** (secured)  A loan made to a company whereby the lender has first legal claim on all or a stated part of what the company owns. Sometimes there is a public issue of debenture stock (generally in £100 units) and these will be traded on the Stock Exchange in the normal way. Debenture holders are creditors, not shareholders, and thus their interest is a charge against profits.

**Decreasing term assurance**  A life assurance with the sum assured reducing each year over a given period; it is very suitable to provide protection for mortgagors (house purchase).

**Deed**  A formal contract in writing, witnessed and 'under seal' (purely a formality nowadays – sealing wax is not required). Necessary for certain types of contracts (e.g. property sales, deeds of covenant,* etc.).

**Deed of covenant**  An agreement to make a gift of money regularly for a period of years. Subject to certain conditions this carries financial advantages to the recipient, as he can reclaim the tax that the donor himself had paid.

**Depreciation charge**  The amount a company takes from its trading profits each year (which sum it retains in the business) to pay for a replacement of its fixed assets (e.g. machinery costs £100 000, anticipated life 10 years, annual depreciation charge £10 000 so that the whole sum is written off over 10 years). Note that the charge need not be the same each year – under the 'reducing balance' system a much higher amount is charged in the early years. Whatever the method of calculation, the charge reduces profits, thus ensuring that the depreciation charge involved cannot be paid out as dividend (see also Wear and tear).

**Direct costs**  Costs that vary reasonably proportionately with volume of output: examples are production wages and raw materials. (See also Indirect costs.)

**Direct taxes**  Taxes paid by an individual or business (based on income) directly to the government: examples are income tax, corporation tax (paid by companies) and capital gains tax.

**Diversification**  A business in one trade which expands its activities into another and different trade, often in order to spread its risks. (Also referred to as a *conglomerate merger.*)

**Dividend cover**  The number of times a dividend payment can be met out of the after-tax profits of a company. The more times the profits cover (exceed) the dividend payment, the safer it is that the dividend will continue to be paid even if the company experiences a dip in trade.

**Documentary credit**  A method of making payments in the overseas trade whereby the importer provides funds through his bank which the exporter can draw upon.

**Double tax relief**  Bilateral agreements whereby a person earning a part of his income abroad is not taxed twice.

**Dow Jones Indices**  These indicate the general trend of share price levels on the New York Stock Exchange. See also Index numbers.

*Glossary of Commercial Terms* 191

**Drawback** If imported materials which have paid customs duties are re-exported (either as an 'entrepot'* transaction or after processing), the duty paid is reclaimable from HM Customs and Excise.

**Entrepot trade** Goods from overseas which enter the country purely for transhipment purposes (see also Drawback).

**Entrepreneur** The decision-maker and risk-taker in a business. The term is used mainly of sole traders and companies where one individual has the controlling interest and actively runs the business.

**Errors and Omissions Excepted (E & OE)** A term in common use at one time on accounting documents, with the intention of safeguarding the creditor in the event of there being mistakes on the document.

**Exchange control** Financial regulations imposed at the outbreak of World War II to control the flow of money out of the United Kingdom. After various relaxations they were finally abolished in 1980.

**Excise duty** The tax levied by HM Customs and Excise on a number of items, the main three being alcohol, petrol and tobacco.

**Ex dividend** The share price quoted excludes the right to the recently announced dividend. The price of the share usually falls by an amount equal to the amount of the net dividend after tax (see also Cum dividend).

**Fictitious assets** Assets appearing in a balance sheet for technical accounting purposes, e.g. a net loss; they have no realisable 'money' value (compare with Intangible assets).

**Finance Act** This is the Act of Parliament which makes the provisions announced in the Budget legally enforceable.

**Fiscal** Used in the terms 'fiscal policy' and 'fiscal year'. The former is concerned with government action to collect taxes and spend them. The latter refers to the tax year which runs from 6 April in one year to 5 April in the following year.

**Flag of convenience** A technique involving the registration of a ship in another country (e.g. Liberia, Panama) to reduce liability to taxation and to obtain the benefit of less stringent regulations about conditions affecting the crews.

**Free alongside ship** The seller undertakes to deliver the consignment to the quay at the port of loading. Not as commonly used as Free on board.*

**Free on board**  The seller undertakes to deliver the goods and pay all charges including the loading on to the ship at the port of *departure* (compare with Cost, Insurance and Freight).

**Freight**  Technically this means the cost of transporting a consignment for a particular journey, though in everyday language it is often used to refer to the goods themselves.

**Gearing**  If a company has a high level of borrowing or preference shares in relation to its total ordinary share capital, it is said to be highly geared. Low gearing is the reverse situation.

**Gilts**  see Government securities.

**Goodwill**  For accounting purposes the net worth of a business is the total of its assets less the total of its liabilities. Particularly when a business is being sold, a goodwill element is added to the purchase price because the buyer is acquiring an existing business – the expectation is 'that the old customers will come back to the old place'. Sometimes this goodwill item is shown indefinitely in the balance sheet as an intangible asset* but more often it is written off over a period of years.

**Government broker**  The stockbroking firm that acts on behalf of the Government when it deals in gilts (see Government securities).

**Government securities**  Commonly called gilts, because they are considered to be a 'risk free' investment. They bear a fixed interest and, with a few early exceptions, carry a repayment date. Other names they are given are Exchequer Stock, Funding or Redemption Stock. Sometimes a repayment *period* is given, e.g. 13 percent Exchequer Stock 2003–2005 – the Government will choose its own repayment date in this period.

**Gross Domestic Product**  The total income of residents arising from activities within the UK – effectively it is the gross national product* less any income from abroad.

**Gross National Product**  The total income of UK residents arising from activity anywhere.

**Hammering**  The announcement of the insolvency of a member of the Stock Exchange. Because of the existence of a guarantee fund, members of the public who suffer a loss from the insolvency are normally compensated.

**Hansard**  The Official Report of Parliamentary Debates, published daily. The records of both the House of Commons and the House of Lords for more than the last 400 years are available in the House of Commons Record Office.

**Holding (parent) company** A company that owns more than 50 percent of the share capital of another company, called a subsidiary. Often the latter in its turn controls its own subsidiaries.

**Horizontal integration** Mergers between businesses producing or distributing the same product or group of products, e.g. two publishers or two supermarket chains joining forces (see also Diversification and Vertical integration).

**Implied terms** (of a contract) Terms not specifically stated but which both parties would regard as 'taken for granted' (e.g. that the person offering to sell the goods is entitled to do so).

**Imprest system** An accounting system (commonly used for petty cash) whereby a 'float' is established and at regular intervals the cash paid is reimbursed so that the float is restored.

**Index numbers** These measure the average percentage change in the prices of a 'set' of items calculated in relation to a 'base' date. For example, the Retail Prices Index measures the retail prices of a group of major consumer goods, the prices being 'weighted' to allow for the relative importance of each item. Roughly speaking, 'weighting' takes into account what the average low-income family spends on the particular item out of every £ of its disposable income. Thus if 5p in every £ is spent on travel and 10p in the £ on heating, then an increase of 20 percent on the latter will have twice the effect on the Retail Price Index as the same percentage increase in the former. The 'weighted' price is assumed to be 100 at the base date, then if at a later date the price of the 'set' of items has risen by 10 percent the new index figure would be given as 110. There are also volume indices, such as the Index of Industrial Production.

**Indirect costs** Production costs that do not change very much (if at all) as production increases. Thus rent, rates and cleaning costs are good examples. (See also Direct costs.)

**Indirect taxes** A tax that is not paid direct to the Government by the taxpayer but is collected by an intermediary; examples are Value Added Tax and Excise Duty on alcoholic drinks and tobacco products. (See also Direct taxes.)

**Intangible assets** Assets for which the value cannot be accurately quantified in money terms, such as goodwill* and patent rights (see also Fictitious assets).

**Interim dividend** Many companies pay two dividends yearly; an interim one half way through the year and a final one when the year's financial results are known.

**Jobber's turn**  A stockjobber quotes two prices – the higher (or offer) price at which he is prepared to sell shares and the lower (or bid) price at which he will buy. The difference is his margin or 'turn'.

**Joint and several liability**  A situation where two or more persons accept responsibility together for the amounts owing and are also individually legally liable for the whole sum. The best example is the general partners in a business partnership.

**Joint stock bank**  A bank that is a public limited company (Plc).

**Joint stock company**  The original name for the type of business that is now known as a limited company; it is still used to some extent.

**Kaffirs**  A Stock Exchange term for South African gold mining shares.

**Legal tender**  The form of payment which a creditor *must* accept (note that cheques, postal orders, etc., are not legal tender but are called 'representative money'; in practice they are normally acceptable under certain conditions). Bank of England notes are acceptable up to any sum but there are maxima for the various denominations of coin.

**Letters of administration**  A High Court authority to deal with the property of a dead person who has not left a will or who has not nominated an executor in the will. In the former case the rules of intestacy, which set out a priority list of claimants according to the nearness of family relationship, must be followed.

**Liquid assets**  Those assets (including cash itself) with a fixed money value which can 'as of right' be easily and quickly converted into cash. Bank current and deposit accounts are the common ones; stock would not be included because there is no guarantee that a quick sale would be possible. There are degrees of liquidity, according to the speed with which the cash value can be realised.

**Liquidation**  The winding-up of a business, either because the members choose to do so or because it cannot meet its financial obligations (see also Receiver).

**Loss leader**  The practice of selling goods or services below cost to attract customers in the hope that they will purchase other items.

**Margin**  This has two meanings: (*a*) profit margin – see Mark-up; (*b*) dealing on the margin – a Stock Exchange term meaning dealing in shares on borrowed money.

**Marginal costs**  The additional costs per unit of production involved in increasing output. In many cases these decrease as many indirect costs* have already been covered and will not increase as production increases.

**Market capitalisation**  The value the Stock Exchange places on a company. Assume a company has one million £1 shares in issue and currently they are changing hands at 240p then the market capitalisation is £2 400 000; if its earnings (i.e. after-tax profits) for the year are £400 000, then its Price/Earnings ratio is 6 (2 400 000 divided by 400 000).

**Mark-up**  The gross profit on goods (e.g. cost price £25, selling price £30, mark-up £5 or 20 percent). Note that if expressed as a percentage of selling price (16⅔ percent) it is referred to as the *profit margin percentage*.

**Mergers**  Two or more companies combining to form one (see also Diversification, Horizontal integration, Takeover bid, Vertical integration).

**Minimum Lending Rate**  This used to be the interest rate fixed by the Bank of England which greatly influenced all other interest rates. It has now been abandoned.

**Naked debenture**  An unsecured debenture*.

**'Names'**  Members of Lloyds insurance underwriting syndicates who are 'sleeping' partners only; they contribute substantial amounts of capital but do not participate in business operations as they are not insurance professionals. However, they do have unlimited liability (refer to Chapter 2 for an explanation of this term).

**National Debt**  This reflects government expenditure over the years that has been financed by borrowing; currently the UK national debt is around £12 000 per head of population. The amount owing to other countries (the external debt) is a burden on the UK balance of payments both as far as interest and capital repayments are concerned. The amounts owing to residents and institutions (e.g. from the issue of Government securities, Treasury bills, National Savings, etc.), though having the effect of materially increasing taxation, do not in the end make the community any poorer as only transfer payments are involved (i.e. moving money from one group of people to another).

**National income**  The money value of all the goods and services produced in any year. It is the same amount as national output because all the factors of production – land, labour (including the entrepreneur*), capital – are paid a reward in the form of rent, salaries and wages, profits and interest; and it is the factors of production which are used in producing goods and services. (See also Gross Domestic Product and Gross National Product.)

**Offer for sale**   A public issue of shares involving an Issuing House buying the entire issue and then re-selling to the public through the issue of a prospectus. The majority of public issues by public limited companies nowadays are made this way.

**Official List**   The daily list published by the Stock Exchange giving, amongst other information, the bid and offer prices of all quoted securities (see also Jobber's turn).

**Oncosts**   see Indirect costs.

**Operating costs**   see Direct costs.

**Parent company**   see Holding company.

**Patent**   A licence from the Patent Office giving the applicant (generally for 16 years) the sole rights to an invention or new process. The Patent Office also deals with registration of trade marks and trade names.

**Pay As You Earn**   Since 1942 employers have had the statutory duty to collect income tax by deduction from pay from their employees. The employer is advised by the Inspector of Taxes how to calculate these deductions, which have to be sent to the Collector of Taxes at fixed intervals. The employer is purely the collecting agent: he has no power to amend the basis of calculation, which is a matter between the taxpayer and the Inspector. Though deductions are made each time an employee is paid, it is the total earned in the tax year which ends on 5 April that is important.

**Payment in kind**   The Truck Acts forbid payment of total wages in kind (as occurred last century in some industries). However, many employees do receive fringe benefits which are of course payments in kind. Examples are luncheon vouchers, use of company cars for private purposes and free living accommodation. Generally these give the employee some income tax advantage.

**Per capita**   Per head, as in per capita income.

**Per pro (pp)**   This indicates that a person is signing correspondence on behalf of his employer or principal. However, it only gives limited authority and the principal will not be bound if the person signing exceeds his authority. Much less use is made of 'per pro' in correspondence nowadays than hitherto.

**Plimsoll Line**   The load line on the side of a ship that shows it is not overloaded; the Department of Trade administers this and many other Merchant Shipping Acts regulations.

**Preferential creditor**  One who is entitled to be paid before other creditors (e.g. Debenture holders*).

**Preliminary expenses**  All the expenses incurred in forming a company, which can be very substantial in the case of a public limited company. They appear initially in the Balance Sheet as an asset but are often written off out of profits (as with Goodwill*).

**Price/Earnings Ratio**  see Market capitalisation.

**Price Index**  see Index numbers.

**Pro-forma invoice**  Strictly speaking, this is not a demand for money but an advice. It is used: (*a*) when goods are sent to an agent abroad who hopes to sell them, where invoice indicates the anticipated price the supplier hopes to receive; (*b*) when goods are sent on a 'sale or return' basis – if the goods are retained then the payment becomes due; (*c*) when a payment is requested before goods will be despatched.

**Public Sector Borrowing Requirement**  The amount that a government has to borrow to cover the excess of the expenditure of the entire public sector over its receipts from various forms of taxation.

**Receiver**  An accountant appointed to run a company which is in financial trouble. He will also be responsible for winding up the company if it has to go into liquidation*.

**Redundancy payments**  The compulsory compensation paid by an employer to an employee whose job has disappeared because of reduction of demand or introduction of new technology. Payment is based on salary and length of service and a proportion of the sum is met by the Government from the National Insurance Fund.

**Refer to drawer (RD)**  The paying bank may 'mark' a cheque in this way if it is not prepared to pay it. There could well be a technical error (e.g. if the cheque is signed by an unauthorised individual); or if there are insufficient funds to meet the payment, the cheque is said to be dishonoured.

**Resale Price Maintenance (RPM)**  Until 1964 the supplier could nominate the price at which the retailer had to sell a product to the final consumer, even though there was no contract between the supplier and the retail customer. Under the Resale Price Act 1964 this practice was made illegal unless the Restrictive Practices Court agreed that the 'price fixing' was in the public interest (and it has done so in very few cases).

**Retail Price Index**  see Index numbers.

**Revenue reserves**  The portion of the profits of a company that are retained in the company (ploughed back) so as to provide funds for future operations.

**Revolving loans**  A service provided by banks, retail stores, etc., whereby the customer is allowed to owe his creditor up to a specified limit without having to ask permission each time he borrows (by issuing a cheque or buying goods). The loan is often tied in with a budget account whereby in return for a fixed monthly payment the customer can have credit up to $X$ times that sum.

**'Rights' issue**  A company needing more capital may offer existing shareholders the right to purchase more shares, usually at a price below the current market price.

**'Spot'**  This refers to a currency or commodity price. For example, 'spot' sterling is the price of the £ today.

**Stagging**  'Stagging' means applying for shares in a new share issue of a company (which the applicant thinks will be a popular one and therefore over-subscribed) not with the intention of retaining the shares as an investment but in the hope that it will be possible to sell them at a profit when dealings on the Stock Exchange commence a few days later. 'Stags' apply for more shares than they want because they are anticipating that there will be a 'scaling down' when the allotment takes place.

**Stock valuation**  Unsold stock is normally valued at cost price (or replacement price if this is less). However, difficulties arise where there are large numbers of different stock items, possibly purchased at different prices from several suppliers, and it may not be practicable to keep each batch separate. Two methods of valuation in use are:

*FIFO (First in, first out)*  This assumes that the oldest stock is sold first, therefore unsold stock will have come from the newer deliveries. If prices are rising, this method tends to push up the valuation.

*LIFO (Last in, first out)*  The reverse assumption is made: that the newest stock is sold (or used) first, therefore unsold stock will be deemed to have come from the oldest batches.

**Takeover bid**  One company offering to buy a controlling interest in another company. They may offer cash to the latter's shareholders, or shares in their company in exchange or a combination of both (see also Mergers).

## Glossary of Commercial Terms

**Tax avoidance** The (legal) arrangement of one's financial affairs so as to minimise tax liability.

**Tax evasion** The (illegal) non-payment of tax (e.g. as a result of providing false information on a Tax Return).

**Taxable income** The amount remaining after deducting the tax-free allowances from total pay.

**Time and motion study** see Work study.

**Trade association** A voluntary body of firms in the same line of business which seeks to protect its members' interests and keep them informed of any developments likely to affect them (e.g. new legislation).

**Trustee status** Certain trust funds can by law only invest in companies with trustee status, i.e. those with over £1 million share capital and which have paid a dividend for at least the last five consecutive years. Building societies' funds normally also have this status.

**Variable costs** see Direct costs.

**Vertical integration** The taking over of a business which either supplies a company with its industrial needs or buys its products. Examples would be a company operating paper mills gaining control of a newspaper, or a soft drinks manufacturer taking over a business which manufactures cans. In the last few decades not a great deal of vertical integration has taken place. (See also Horizontal integration.)

**Wear and tear** The loss in value which an asset (e.g. machinery) suffers as a result of its normal use in business activities (see also Depreciation charge).

**White Paper** An official statement of Government policy on some important economic or social issue. These are published by HM Stationery Office.

**Winding-up** (of a company) see Liquidation, Receiver.

**Work study** An analysis to discover working methods that will use labour as economically as possible, thus reducing costs; this involves timing employees on particular tasks and sometimes causes resentment amongst them.

# Multiple-Choice Test

In each of the following questions there is only one correct answer. The answers are given on page 207.

1 Mass production is possible only if
   a   the raw materials required are found locally.
   b   consumers will pay a high price for the product.
   c   there is a wide market for the increased production.
   d   many skilled workers live near to the factories.

2 Which one of these statements is *false*?
   a   Commercial services cannot begin until the manufacturing processes have been completed.
   b   If there were no commercial services most goods would not be produced.
   c   Commercial services add values to products.
   d   Every stage of production employs commercial services.

3 The term 'producer' in its true economic meaning refers to one who
   a   grows crops or manufactures goods.
   b   advertises goods or services for sale.
   c   adds value to a product.
   d   provides raw materials or food.

4 A and B are in a formal partnership having contributed capital of £20 000 and £10 000 respectively. Profits will therefore be
   a   divided in a 2:1 ratio.
   b   shared equally, as under the 1890 Partnership Act all partners are equal.
   c   divided according to the amount of business each has obtained.
   d   divided according to the provisions of the Deed of Partnership.

## Multiple-choice Test 201

5 Each year every limited company sends to the Registrar of Companies a copy of its

    *a*   register of shareholders.
    *b*   memorandum of association.
    *c*   directors' report and accounts.
    *d*   sales forecast for the year to come.

6 When the ordinary shares of a limited company have a face value of £1.00 and a market value of 95p

    *a*   the company has made a trading loss.
    *b*   the shares are said to be at a premium.
    *c*   the stockbroker and jobber between them lose the 5p
    *d*   the capital of the company has not been reduced by the fall in the value of the shares.

7 If a shareholder in a limited company has received no dividends for some years he may well

    *a*   vote for any resolution proposed at the Annual General Meeting for a change in the Board of Directors.
    *b*   ask the company to buy back his shares.
    *c*   appeal to the Department of Trade and Industry.
    *d*   ask the Registrar of Companies to investigate the company's affairs.

8 One advantage enjoyed by sole traders over limited companies is that

    *a*   they find it easier to raise more capital.
    *b*   the personal assets of proprietors are not at risk.
    *c*   they do not pay VAT.
    *d*   decisions are more quickly and flexibly made.

9 A limited company made a profit of £100 000 last year. This profit

    *a*   must be paid to shareholders as dividends.
    *b*   may be paid to shareholders as dividends if the Board of Directors decide to do so.
    *c*   must be applied partly to the payment of dividends and partly to the 'ploughing back' of reserves to meet next year's expenses.
    *d*   must be paid according to the wishes of the ordinary shareholders as expressed in their votes at the Annual General Meeting.

10 Shares in co-operative societies differ from those in public limited companies in that:

    *a*   shares are quoted on the London Stock Exchange.
    *b*   there is no maximum shareholding.
    *c*   shares can be paid for by instalments.

## Business and Commerce

**11** If there are too few retail shops, prices may rise because

    *a*   bigger shops spend more on advertising.
    *b*   more shop assistants are needed for the bigger shops.
    *c*   there is too little competition.
    *d*   customers must buy more goods per customer-visit.

**12** A retail co-operative society

    *a*   passes on its profits to its customers.
    *b*   has its shares quoted on the Stock Exchange.
    *c*   passes on its profits to its employees.
    *d*   must buy all its goods from the CWS.

**13** A multiple shop organisation

    *a*   has many departments in one place.
    *b*   owns many shops in different parts of the country selling the same goods.
    *c*   has uniformity of name and style throughout the country.
    *d*   must be owned by a co-operative organisation.

**14** Wholesalers in general

    *a*   need a considerable amount of working capital.
    *b*   incur very little risk.
    *c*   deal only with the manufacturers.
    *d*   have very high overhead costs.

**15** Which one of these statements is *true*?

    *a*   A wholesaler sells cheap goods to the householders on their door steps.
    *b*   A wholesaler is a connecting link between the retailer and manufacturer.
    *c*   A wholesaler only deals in goods which can be sold in very large quantities.
    *d*   A wholesaler insists on cash payment from his customers.

**16** As a retailer I receive a trade discount of 20 percent and a cash discount of 5 percent (one month) from my supplier, so that

    *a*   goods catalogued at £100 will cost me £76 provided I pay within a month.
    *b*   neither discount will be received unless I pay my account promptly.
    *c*   goods catalogued at £100 will cost me £75 provided I pay within a month.
    *d*   both discounts will be shown on the advice note.

**17** When I receive a statement of account from a wholesaler this tells me how much

  *a*  is owed to me by my customers.
  *b*  I owe the supplier.
  *c*  money I have in the bank.
  *d*  I have sold in the past month.

**18** A UK bank note can legally be

  *a*  refused by a creditor who would prefer a cheque.
  *b*  exchanged for gold at the Bank of England.
  *c*  printed by any UK commercial bank.
  *d*  tendered in payment of a debt.

**19** Which one of the following is *not* a function of the Bank of England?

  *a*  Running the bankers' clearing house.
  *b*  Acting as the bankers' bank.
  *c*  Acting as the government's bank.
  *d*  Producing notes and coins.

**20** Banks make regular payments on a customer's behalf by means of

  *a*  standing orders.
  *b*  cheques.
  *c*  bankers' draft.
  *d*  credit cards.

**21** A cheque I have paid into my bank is returned to me by my bank marked 'Refer to drawer'. This means that

  *a*  the cheque was incorrectly drawn, e.g. the date is missing, or the words do not agree with the figures.
  *b*  I neglected to endorse it before paying it in.
  *c*  the drawer did not have sufficient money in his account to meet it, and has made no overdraft arrangements with his bank.
  *d*  the drawer wishes to see me before the debt is settled.

**22** Which one of the following best defines a cheque?

  *a*  An order by a drawer requiring a banker to pay the payee.
  *b*  A promise by a banker to pay the payee.
  *c*  A promise by a drawer to pay the drawee.
  *d*  An order by a bank requiring another bank to pay the payee.

**23** I receive an open cheque in payment of a debt. I draw two parallel lines across its face, write my name on the back, and then send it to another person to whom I owe money. In doing so, I

204  *Business and Commerce*

    *a*  have acted correctly, since my creditor can pay it into his account.
    *b*  have acted wrongly, since I had no right to cross the cheque.
    *c*  need not have endorsed it.
    *d*  have prevented my creditor from passing it on again to his creditor.

**24**  Your organisation wishes to make an urgent delivery of samples from London to Glasgow. Which of the following services would be the most suitable?

    *a*  Freepost.
    *b*  Datapost.
    *c*  Datel.
    *d*  Recorded Delivery Service.

**25**  A business wishes to circularise potential customers about a 'special offer' involving filling up a form and returning it. The facility most useful for this purpose is

    *a*  an advertisement (with coupon) in books of stamps.
    *b*  the Business Reply Service or Freepost.
    *c*  Datel.
    *d*  cash on delivery.

**26**  Given that a trading company in a given year had:

| Opening Stock | £400 | Closing Stock | £600 |
| Purchases | £5200 | Sales | £10 000 |

its rate of stock turnover for the year is

    *a*  100 percent
    *b*  200 percent
    *c*  10 times
    *d*  20 times

**27**  Most trading businesses in UK aim to have

    *a*  low expense rate, short period of credit allowed, low rate of stock turnover and negligible working capital.
    *b*  low expense rate, high rate of stock turnover, short period of credit allowed and adequate working capital.
    *c*  short period of credit allowed, high working capital, high gearing of capital and low rate of stock turnover.
    *d*  high working capital, long period of credit allowed, low rate of stock turnover and high capital gearing.

**28**  An average stock of £20 000 (at cost) being turned 10 times a year at a gross profit rate of 20 percent on sales, with expenses of 10 percent on turnover, would show a net profit of

*a*   £16 000
   *b*   £26 000
   *c*   £25 000
   *d*   £20 000

**29** 'Tramp' vessels are those ships that provide a

   *a*   coastal service only.
   *b*   service that is at owner's risk, i.e. no marine insurance company will undertake to insure the cargo being carried.
   *c*   regular, scheduled service between ports, i.e. to a published timetable.
   *d*   service that can be chartered.

**30** Containerisation involves the

   *a*   standard sizing of transport units.
   *b*   preparation of goods for deep freeze storage.
   *c*   attractive packaging of goods.
   *d*   selling of pre-packed goods in supermarkets.

**31** If an insurance company calculates that there is one chance in ten that a certain event will occur in the course of a year, it will

   *a*   charge a premium of rather more than 10 percent of the value of the goods insured.
   *b*   pay out not more than nine-tenths of the value of the goods in any claim.
   *c*   give back one-tenth of the value of the goods if the event does not occur this year.
   *d*   refuse to pay out on more than one claim per ten years.

**32** A trader insures his plate-glass windows against damage. If he receives £100 from the insurer to make good some damage, this payment is

   *a*   indemnity.
   *b*   insurable interest.
   *c*   premium.
   *d*   capital gains.

**33** Those who accept risks at Lloyd's are known as

   *a*   actuaries.
   *b*   agents.
   *c*   underwriters.
   *d*   jobbers.

## 206  *Business and Commerce*

**34** A basic principle of insurance is that the insured must not fail to disclose any material fact. This principle is known as

   *a*   utmost good faith.
   *b*   insurable interest.
   *c*   proximate cause.
   *d*   indemnity.

**35** An invisible import is

   *a*   purchase of goods and services by Americans on holiday/business in the UK.
   *b*   natural gas.
   *c*   purchase of goods and services by UK citizens on holiday/business in America.
   *d*   illegal immigrants.

**36** Entrepot trade relates to goods

   *a*   entering the country illegally.
   *b*   to be re-exported.
   *c*   to be processed.
   *d*   on which tax has to be paid.

**37** The terms of trade show the

   *a*   relationship between exports and imports by value.
   *b*   change of export prices over time.
   *c*   value of exports in any one year.
   *d*   value of exports minus imports in any one year.

**38** If Britain devalues her currency against the US dollar

   *1*   my holiday in the United States will cost me more.
   *2*   the price of British cars in American showrooms will go up.
   *3*   American imported goods will cost more in British shops.
   *4*   the British Terms of Trade with the United States will become unfavourable.

   *a*   All of these are true
   *b*   Only *1*, *2* and *3* are true
   *c*   Only *1*, *3* and *4* are true
   *d*   Only *3* and *4* are true

**39** This table shows a country's balance of payments for 1990

| | |
|---|---|
| Exports | £250 million |
| Imports | £280 million |
| Invisible Surplus | £20 million |
| Capital Account Surplus | £25 million |

Which one of the following is *false*?

- *a* The country has a visible deficit for 1990.
- *b* The country has a current account surplus for 1990.
- *c* The country has a balance of payments surplus for 1990.
- *d* The country has a balance of trade surplus for 1990.

**40** In which one of the following methods of obtaining goods on credit does ownership of the goods *not* pass immediately to the purchaser?

- *a* Credit sale
- *b* Hire purchase
- *c* Budget account
- *d* Bank credit card

# Answers to Multiple-Choice Test

| | | | | | | | |
|---|---|---|---|---|---|---|---|
| **1** | *c* | **11** | *c* | **21** | *c* | **31** | *a* |
| **2** | *b* | **12** | *a* | **22** | *a* | **32** | *a* |
| **3** | *c* | **13** | *b* | **23** | *a* | **33** | *c* |
| **4** | *d* | **14** | *a* | **24** | *b* | **34** | *a* |
| **5** | *c* | **15** | *b* | **25** | *b* | **35** | *c* |
| **6** | *d* | **16** | *a* | **26** | *d* | **36** | *b* |
| **7** | *a* | **17** | *b* | **27** | *b* | **37** | *a* |
| **8** | *d* | **18** | *d* | **28** | *c* | **38** | *b* |
| **9** | *d* | **19** | *d* | **29** | *d* | **39** | *d* |
| **10** | *b* | **20** | *a* | **30** | *a* | **40** | *b* |

# Examination Questions

The author and publishers are grateful to the following examination boards for permission to reproduce questions:

Institute of Export (Export); London and East Anglian Group (LEAG/GCSE); Midland Examining Group (MEG/GCSE); Northern Examining Association (NEA/GCSE); Royal Society of Arts (RSA); Southern Examining Group, (SEG/GCSE).

The following abbreviations are used for subjects:

British Industrial Society (BIS)
Industry and Society (IS)
Understanding Industrial Society (UIS)
(Note: After 1990 it is intended that the last two examinations will be renamed 'British Industrial Society'.)

The term 'specimen' refers to papers that were prepared by GCSE boards as an example of the type of question which might be asked in the first GCSE examinations in 1988. The GCSE questions which are not thus described are from the actual papers for 1988.

### Chapter 1

1 *(a)* Explain the meaning of
(i) production, (ii) commerce.
*(b)* Describe how commercial activity helps to satisfy wants.
(*LEAG/GCSE Commerce*)

2 'Commercial workers produce nothing.' Examine the rôle of commercial workers in the light of this statement. (*LEAG/ GCSE Commerce specimen*)
3 Set out carefully the principal divisions and sub-divisions of commerce and give an idea of the relative importance of each. (*RSA*)
4 The United Kingdom has a 'mixed economy'. Explain the meaning of this statement. Do you consider any alternative system to be superior?
5 What is meant by 'commercial activities'? Discuss their importance to the economic life of the country.
6 What are 'direct service' occupations? Why is it that under-developed poor countries can only afford to spend proportionately small sums of money on them?
7 In what ways does the British Government provide direct financial aid to industry?

## Chapter 2

1 Discuss the advantages and disadvantages of the public joint stock company as a type of business organisation. (*Export*)
2 Which form of business unit would you commonly expect to find engaged in the production and/or sale of each of the following? Give a reason for your choice in each instance.
   *(a)* electronic accounting equipment costing from £5000 upwards.
   *(b)* dental services in a medium-sized town.
   *(c)* sale of newspapers and periodicals with delivery over a fairly small area.
   *(d)* building and decorating services with an annual turnover of £200 000.

## Chapter 3

1 Explain why good internal communications are essential for a business when dealing with suppliers and customers.
2 Some companies are multinational, operating in many different countries. What advantages and disadvantages is this type of

210  *Business and Commerce*

organisation likely to have over a company based in one country?
3 Why are the vast majority of cars produced by a small number of very large firms? Explain why it is still possible for small firms to exist in the car industry.
4 What advantages would a large firm such as IBM have over smaller competitors in the computer industry? Given these advantages, how could a small business survive in the industry?
5 Why are some businesses concentrated in a few areas of Britain, whilst some are spread throughout the country? Use examples to illustrate your answer.
6 'About half of British firms are *footloose*'. Explain what is meant by 'footloose'. If this statement is true, why do many firms stay in high-cost areas such as South-East England?


**Chapter 4**

1 A public limited company wishes to increase its capital. Discuss three possible methods of doing this.
2 How can I purchase the ordinary shares of a public company? What risks am I taking in buying these shares? What rights do I possess as a shareholder? If a company does not pay a dividend, due to poor financial results, is there any way I can get my money back?
3 Assess the importance of the services rendered by the Stock Exchange to the investor, the general public and the government. (*Export*)
4 Describe how a large public limited company might undertake any three of the following:
   *(a)* raise an extra £1 million of share capital.
   *(b)* take over a smaller business.
   *(c)* borrow an extra £1 million for working capital.
   *(d)* replace its managing director.
   *(e)* deal with the profit for the year just ended. (*RSA*)
5 What influences affect the value of securities dealt with on the Stock Exchange? (*Export*)
6 *(a)* (i) Name the company opposite whose shares are available for purchase.

# LONDON AND EAST ANGLIAN GROUP PLC

Offer for Sale

by

**Board, Stephenson and Thompson Limited**

on behalf of

**London and East Anglian Group PLC**

of 1,500,000 ordinary shares of 25p each
at 100p per share
of which 50p is payable on 1 July 1990
and 50p is payable on 1 December 1990

*The Offer for Sale in the U.K. has been underwritten by Stephen Bowler and Associates, Merchant Bankers.*

*Note 1*
Successful applicants for shares will be entitled to receive, free of charge, a loyalty bonus of one extra share for every ten shares continuously held from allocation to 30 September 1992.

*Note 2*
If you wish to apply for shares, you must complete and return an application form. A cheque or banker's draft for the amount now payable at 50p per share must be pinned to the completed application form. Your cheque or banker's draft must be made payable to 'LEAG Share Offer' and crossed 'not negotiable'.

*Note 3*
The basis of allocation of shares will be announced on 5 July 1990. If there has been heavy demand for shares, you may not receive all or any of the shares for which you have applied.

A final share certificate will be sent to you after payment of the second instalment.

(ii) State the type of shares being issued.
(iii) What is the nominal value of each share?
(iv) State the issue price when fully paid.
(v) How much will be raised from the issue if all shares are sold?

Nashima Khan applied successfully for 400 shares. Stock Exchange dealings began on 7 July and at the close of business on that day the price of the shares was 60p.

*(b)* (i) How much did Nashima pay on 1 July?
(ii) State which methods of payment may be used by Nashima.
(iii) Explain the difference between these methods of payment.
(iv) Name the crossing required and state a reason for its use.
(v) Which document will Nashima receive if she keeps her shares and pays the second instalment?

*(c)* (i) What is the market value of Nashima's shares on 7 July?
(ii) What is the gain or loss from selling the shares at that date?
(iii) How could Nashima sell the shares?
(iv) State any advantage to Nashima of keeping the shares instead of selling them quickly.

Nashima kept her shares and after six months she received from the London and East Anglian Group a cheque for £30. Six months later a further cheque for £50 was received.

*(d)* (i) What is the name given to these payments?
(ii) Suggest why the cheques were for different amounts.
(iii) Calculate the percentage return to Nashima from buying 400 shares.

*(e)* (i) State the method used to issue London and East Anglian Group shares.
(ii) Explain briefly how this method operates.
(iii) Why might Nashima's application for shares have been unsuccessful?
(iv) State three other methods which could have been used to issue London and East Anglian Group shares.
(*LEAG/GCSE Commerce*)

## Chapter 5

1. *(a)* List two industries which have been privatised by the Government.
   *(b)* Give two reasons why some people would disagree with privatisation.
   *(c)* Briefly describe the process by which an industry is privatised.
   *(d)* What reasons can be given in support of the privatisation of education? (*LEAG/GCSE UIS specimen*)
2. Although the majority of our goods and services are provided through private enterprise, a substantial proportion are provided through state-controlled institutions. Explain why this is so.
3. 'Local authorities can only do what the law allows them to do.' Explain this statement, illustrating your answer with examples of services provided by local authorities which impinge on the life of the local business community.
4. Conshire Council are proposing that all the authority's cleaning services be privatised, in line with council policy to reduce the number of services provided by the local authority.
   *(a)* In addition to cleaning services, what other services could a local authority privatise?
   *(b)* How do local authorities raise the money necessary to provide their services?
   *(c)* Many people are angry at the proposal to privatise cleaning services. Describe the generally accepted methods which they could use to influence the Council's final decision on the matter?
   *(d)* What arguments are there for and against privatising local authority services? (*SEG/GCSE BIS Specimen*)
5. Name four industries controlled by public corporations. State the arguments for and against nationalisation.

## Chapter 6

1. *(a)* What is the importance of cash discount and trade discount to the retailer and wholesaler?

(b) On June 1 Albert sells goods to John at £720 less 25 percent trade discount;
On June 12 John returns one half of the goods;
On June 14 Albert sells further goods to John at £900 less 30 percent trade discount;
On June 30 John pays the amount owing less 5 percent cash discount.
How much does John pay Albert?

2. Show how the VAT system of taxation illustrates the true meaning of the word 'production'. Give an example starting from the manufacturing cost of £100 and allow for 15 percent VAT, to bring out this true meaning clearly. (*RSA*)

3. List not more than five documents used in connection with purchases and sales on credit (home trade), describing clearly the purpose of each document. (*RSA*)

4.

**ORDER FORM 1275**

J Allen and Co Ltd
Field Road
Newcastle
NE5 5JZ

Date: 1 April 1990

To: Northern Office Products plc
Church Road
Preston
PR4 8RT

Please supply and deliver:

| Cat No. | Quantity | Description | Cost per unit |
|---------|----------|-------------|---------------|
| OD 832–7 | 5 | Office Desks | 100.00 |

Signed ................
    Purchasing Officer

## INVOICE

No. 1811

Northern Office Products plc
Church Road
Preston
PR4 8RT

To: J Allen and Co Ltd
    Field Road
    Newcastle
    NE5 5JZ

VAT Reg No: 123 7541 04

Date: 21 April 1990

| Order No 1275 | Date 1 April 1990 | Date Despatch 21 April 1990 | Terms 2½% 28 days |
|---|---|---|---|
| Quantity | Description | Unit Price | Goods value £    p |
| 5 | Office desks OD 832–7 | £100 | (i) |
|  | Less 20% Trade Discount |  | (ii) |
|  | Amount excluding Tax |  | (iii) |
|  | Add 15% VAT |  | (iv) |
|  | TOTAL |  | (v) |

(a) What business documents may have been used before the order was sent?
(b) What information will J Allen and Co Ltd need before deciding to make an order with Northern Office Products?
(c) Calculate the missing amounts which are marked (i) to (v) on the invoice.
(d) Write a description and explain the purpose of the following terms used in the invoice.
    (i) Terms 2½ percent 28 days.
    (ii) 20 percent Trade Discount

    (iii) VAT
 (e) How might the invoice be useful to both buyer and seller?
 (f) In this transaction Northern Office Products plc is a wholesaler for office equipment, while J Allen and Co Ltd is a retailer. What advantages and assistance might J Allen and Co Ltd expect to obtain by buying from a wholesaler instead of going directly to a manufacturer? (*NEA/GCSE Commerce*)

## Chapter 7

1 How does a sole trader's balance sheet differ from a statement of profit and loss? Explain the various entries one might expect to see included in a typical balance sheet. (*RSA*)
2 What is meant by 'rate of turnover'? Why is it important? Work out the annual rate of turnover from the following information.

| | |
|---|---|
| Net sales for the year | £20 000 |
| Gross profit | £5000 |
| Cost price of average stock held | £1500 |

Are you able to say that this is a fast or a slow turnover rate? (*RSA*)
3 The following information was extracted from a firm's books for the year to 31 December 19—.
  Opening stock: £2500; Closing stock: £3000;
  Purchases: £21 000; Sales: £30 000; Expenses: £6000.
Find (i) cost of goods sold; (ii) gross profit; (iii) net profit; (iv) gross profit as a percentage of turnover.

## Chapter 8

1 'The distribution of goods is just as important as the production of them.' Discuss.
2 Describe the ways in which a retail co-operative society differs from a multiple store organisation. (*RSA*)
3 What factors have brought about the great changes in the pattern of retail trade in recent years? (*Export*)
4 How would you account for the large number of retail concerns

in the UK? Do you think their number could be reduced without inconvenience to customers?

5 Sharon Wilson owns a self-service grocery store and wishes to expand by opening a similar shop in a different area.
  (a) (i) What is meant by self-service?
      (ii) State *two* advantages and *two* disadvantages to Sharon of selling through self-service.
  (b) What factors should Sharon consider when choosing a site for the new shop?
  (c) (i) Why might it be to Sharon's advantage to form a partnership before opening the new shop?
      (ii) How are profits allocated in a partnership? (*SEG/ GCSE Commerce specimen*)

6 (a) (i) What is the *basic* function of a retailer?
      (ii) Name *two* retail outlets other than shops
  (b) Describe and contrast the chief characteristics of *two* of the following types of retail outlets: retail co-operative stores, department stores, supermarkets, multiple shops.
  (c) Despite charging higher prices than large scale retailers, some independent traders still continue to compete successfully. How do you explain this situation? (*LEAG/GCSE Commerce specimen*)

7 (a) Explain why some retailers prefer to open shops in suburban areas rather than in town centres.
  (b) Show the distinctive advantages to consumers of shopping at each of the following:
      (i) a small local shop,
      (ii) a hypermarket,
      (iii) a multiple shop. (*LEAG/GCSE Commerce*)

8 (a) Give four services a retailer may provide for his customers.
  (b) Describe two main features of a supermarket which are not usually found in a small shop.
  (c) What do you consider to be the advantages and disadvantages of purchasing goods by mail order?
  (d) What are the reasons for the decline of the wholesaler in recent years? (*LEAG/GCSE UIS specimen*)

9 Blackmore and Webb PLC own a number of supermarkets in the West Country supplying food, drink and household goods. They are planning a new hypermarket for one of the larger

towns in which they do not have a shop at the moment. At a recent meeting of the Board of Directors the agenda included the following items:

*Location*    There are two good sites available. One of them is in the centre of the town and the other is out of town at the junction of two main roads.

*Branding*    The firm has its own label on all the commonly purchased goods and they intend to continue this policy but they have to decide which other brands to stock.

*Self-service*    Some members of the Board think that the store can be entirely self-service. Others maintain that customers like service for some of the goods they buy and also that there are other goods that the firm must serve.

*Credit sales*    The firm offers credit facilities in some of their shops but most members of the Board would prefer cash sales alone. The Managing Director thinks it would be important to offer hire purchase on some of the goods sold and to permit the use of credit cards.

*(a)* (i) What are the essential features of a supermarket?
    (ii) In what ways is the proposed hypermarket different?
*(b)* (i) What does 'PLC' mean in the firm's name?
    (ii) What does it tell you about the firm's main source of capital?
*(c)* (i) What are the advantages of the town centre site?
    (ii) What are the advantages of the out of town site?
    (iii) Which would you vote for?
*(d)* Why is it that the firm has a wide range of goods carrying its own brand label?
*(e)* State, with reasons, what kinds of goods customers
  (i) prefer to be served by an assistant.
  (ii) prefer to serve for themselves.
*(f)* How would unit retailers in the town be affected by the hypermarket? If you were a unit retailer selling groceries, describe with reasons the actions you might take to keep your customers. (*MEG/GCSE Commerce specimen*)

## Chapter 9

1 Direct selling by manufacturers to consumers is increasing. Explain why this is so, illustrating your answer with examples.
2 'The wholesaler is a useful though not indispensable link in the chain of production.' Explain fully the meaning of this statement, stating whether you agree or disagree with the view expressed.
3 'Middlemen are performing a useful function which helps everybody'; 'middlemen are more likely to help themselves than help the public'. Discuss these contrasting views of the activities of middlemen.

## Chapter 10

1 Why is the Bank of England of such importance in the British monetary system?
2 *(a)* Write a paragraph on the 'impracticability of barter';
  *(b)* Describe the desirable characteristics of a good money material.
3 What is *(a)* the discount market; *(b)* an accepting house? Describe their functions.
4 Describe the services of the commercial banks which are of especial value to the business world.
5 Describe the various means by which payments can be made through the commercial banks.
6 Describe the work of the bankers' clearing house. Draw a diagram showing how a cheque is cleared.
7 'A bank is an institution that holds an umbrella over the trader while the weather is good but takes it away as soon as it starts to rain.' Discuss this statement with reference to overdrafts. (*RSA*)
8 *(a)* Distinguish between the use of barter and money as a means of exchange.
  *(b)* State three functions of money.
  *(c)* Describe briefly three services (other than lending money) which a bank provides for a business.
  *(d)* What are the factors that a bank manager would take into consideration when lending money to a small business?
  (*LEAG/GCSE UIS specimen*)

9 Read the following information carefully and then answer the questions which follow.

> 'For many people the key service offered by a clearing bank is the current account. This account provides a convenient way of paying others and of receiving payment of a wage or salary by credit transfer. The current account, together with
> 5 a number of other types of account, provide the banks with the funds to lend to industry and commerce. The traditional form of bank lending for business customers is the overdraft which is particularly suitable for meeting fluctuating working capital requirements. The clearing banks, through
> 10 subsidiaries, also provide facilities such as leasing and factoring.'
>
> Adapted from *The Clearing Banks: Their role and activities* (Banking Information Service).

(a) (i) Name the type of bank account referred to in the passage.
   (ii) State *two* ways in which payment can be made from this type of account.
(b) Name and describe the system, referred to in the passage, which is used for payments such as wages.
(c) Name *one* type of bank account *not* mentioned in the passage.
(d) (i) Define *working capital*. (lines 8 & 9)
   (ii) Why is the overdraft 'particularly suitable for meeting fluctuating working capital requirements'? (lines 8 & 9)
(e) Show how business can benefit from the facilities provided by banks for
   either  leasing (line 10)
   or     factoring (line 11). (*SEG/GCSE Commerce specimen*)

## Chapter 11

1 Study the graphs opposite and answer the questions which follow.

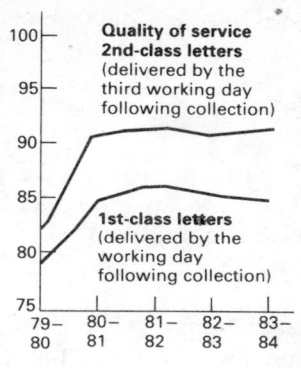

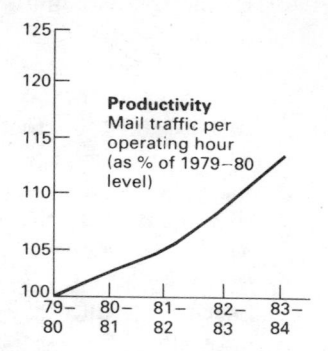

Financial years

The Post Office, faced with competition from electronic mail and the telephone service, wants to make its letter service more efficient. It is trying to reach agreement with the Union of Communications Workers (UCW) on changes which will cut costs and get letters delivered more quickly. The proposed changes include the following.
- More use of mechanical letter sorters. New Optical Character Recognition machines can sort letters with typed addresses at the rate of 500 a minute.
- More use of part-time workers for sorting and delivering mail.
- A new productivity bonus scheme. This would increase earnings by between 5% and 10%. It would be paid for out of the savings made by the changes proposed.

The UCW welcomes the extra pay that its members might receive. However, it is worried that the use of part-time workers will lead to the use of casual and unskilled workers.

*(a)* In 1983–84
  (i) what percentage of first-class letters were delivered within 1 day?
  (ii) what percentage of second-class letters were delivered within 3 days?
*(b)* By how much did productivity rise between 1979–80 and 1983–84?
*(c)* Why is it so important to the Post Office to increase productivity and improve the speed of delivery? *

222  *Business and Commerce*

    *(d)* Explain the benefits that the Post Office wishes to gain from the following:
       (i) mechanisation
      (ii) more use of part-time workers
     (iii) a new productivity bonus scheme.
    *(e)* The Post Office argues that the changes are essential and that the workers will benefit. The UCW disagrees. Outline the arguments of the management and the union.
      (i) management
     (ii) union
    *(f)* Discuss the differing opinions about how new technology may affect the British economy and society in the near future. (*NEA/GCSE IS specimen*)

2  Write notes on any four of the following: (i) Telex; (ii) Registered and Recorded Delivery; (iii) Subscriber Trunk Dialling (STD); (iv) Business Reply Service and Freepost; (v) Cash on Delivery (COD); (vi) Datel; (vii) Datapost.

3  *(a)* State one advantage and one disadvantage of communication by telephone.
   *(b)* State three advantages of telex.
   *(c)* State three ways in which registered post differs from the recorded delivery service.
   *(d)* State two differences between freepost and the business reply service.

## Chapter 12

1  In what ways are railways trying to meet the competition of the roads? To what extent have they already succeeded, and are likely to succeed in the future? Give your reasons.

2  Discuss the importance of transport to commerce with particular reference to surface transport within the United Kingdom.

3  *(a)* Why have passengers taken to the air so readily, whilst freight is much less easily persuaded into the sky?
   *(b)* Describe the effects, current and future, of the large-scale use of containers in transport.

4  What facilities and equipment must be available for the efficient functioning of a modern commercial port? (*Export*)

5  Discuss the importance of 'containerisation' in road, rail and sea transport. (*Export*)

6 Computex is a United Kingdom manufacturer of home computers. Most deliveries within the United Kingdom are made using Computex's own fleet of vehicles while deliveries abroad are usually made by air.
 (a) (i) Give *four* reasons why Computex uses road transport for most deliveries in the United Kingdom.
  (ii) What might be the advantages and disadvantages to Computex of having its own fleet of vehicles for such deliveries?
 (b) Why does Computex normally use air transport for deliveries overseas?
 (c) (i) Name *two* telecommunication services.
  (ii) Briefly show how *each* of these services might be used by Computex to meet customers' orders more quickly.
  (*SEG/GCSE Commerce specimen*)

7 (a) What are the reasons for the increase in the commercial use of air transport during recent years?
 (b) Why is it likely that other types of transport will continue to carry a larger volume of goods than air transport? (*LEAG/GCSE Commerce specimen*)

8 Lindens Industries Ltd produces typewriters and office supplies. Deliveries of orders within the United Kingdom are made by Lindens Industries' own fleet of vans, while deliveries overseas are sent by air.
 (a) State two reasons why Lindens Industries uses road transport rather than rail for deliveries in the UK.
 (b) Explain (i) the advantages and (ii) the disadvantages to Lindens Industries of having its own fleet of vans for deliveries.
 (c) Comment on the benefits to Lindens Industries of using air transport for deliveries overseas.
 (d) Select two telecommunications services and indicate how each service could be used by Lindens Industries in dealing with orders from customers. (*LEAG/GCSE Commerce*)

## Chapter 13

1 (a) Explain the purpose of insurance.
 (b) Describe the stages in taking out a new motor insurance policy.

224  *Business and Commerce*

    *(c)* John Stephens aged 20 years passed a driving test last month and wishes to insure a new car. Comment on the importance of the principle of utmost good faith when John applies for insurance.

    *(d)* A retailer's stock is insured against the risk of fire for £15 000. The stock is actually worth £12 000. State how much compensation the retailer will receive in the event of total loss and explain your answer. (*LEAG/GCSE Commerce*)

2  *(a)* Why is insurance based on statistics?

    *(b)* Compare the risks which are likely to be insured against by (i) a department store, and (ii) an exporter of machine tools, and explain which risks are common and which are specific to each business. (*LEAG/GCSE Commerce specimen*)

3  Explain fully the meaning of the statement: 'Insurance is a pooling of risks'.

4  Suppose a business man has insured his premises against fire for a premium of 2% of their value, and in 20 years he has had no fire and claimed no compensation. What benefits have been received by each party to the contract?

5  *(a)* State two examples of risks that a business owner might wish to insure against.

    *(b)* Suggest two risks against which a business owner could not insure.

    *(c)* Explain the meaning of 'insurable interest'.

6  Explain by reference to a fire insurance contract, what is meant by the terms *insurable interest*, *utmost good faith*, *indemnity* and *premium*.

7  Look carefully at the information in the box opposite before answering the questions below.

    *(a)* What is the name, given in the data, for
        (i) a payment to an assurance company
        (ii) a contract of assurance?

    *(b)* Why does the table in Figure 1 contain different rates of premium?

    *(c)* Calculate, showing workings, the total annual premium which John would have to pay to Western Assurance for the policy required.

Western Assurance plc has prepared the following data for those wishing to take out a 20-year with-profits endowment policy.

*Figure 1*

| Age of insured person | Annual premium per £1000 assured |
| --- | --- |
| below 25 years | £30 |
| between 25 and 30 years | £35 |
| between 31 and 35 years | £40 |
| between 36 and 40 years | £45 |
| over 40 years | on request |

John Adams, who is 28 years of age and married, wishes to take out a 20-year with-profits endowment policy for the sum assured of £5000. He has been sent the following graph by Western Assurance to illustrate the likely returns on this type of policy.

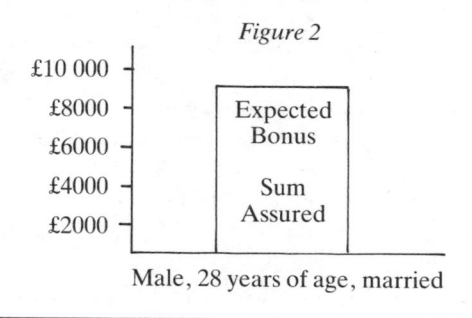

*Figure 2*

```
£10 000 ─
 £8000 ─   ┌─────────────┐
           │  Expected   │
 £6000 ─   │   Bonus     │
           │             │
 £4000 ─   │    Sum      │
 £2000 ─   │  Assured    │
           └─────────────┘
    Male, 28 years of age, married
```

(d) How do assurance companies decide rates of premium such as those shown in Figure 1?

(e) Give details of the benefits which John and his family might obtain by taking out the endowment policy.

(f) John decides he cannot afford the endowment policy quoted but he still wants to obtain £5000 life cover for his family. Name and briefly describe the other types of life assurance policy which could give him the cover he requires. (*SEG/ GCSE Commerce specimen*)

## Chapter 14

1 'Without advertising, the consumer would be better off'. Explain whether you agree with this statement.

2 It has been argued that advertising encourages competition in some industries, but discourages competition in others. How can both of these statements be true?
3 How does advertising affect the type of broadcast and reading material available to the public?
4 *(a)* What is the difference between informative and persuasive advertising?
   *(b)* State two benefits which advertising brings to a company.
   *(c)* Describe the work of an advertising agency.
   *(d)* How would you carry out a market research survey? What are some of the problems you face? (*LEAG/GCSE UIS specimen*)
5 'About half of all advertising is wasted, but the problem is that we don't know which half'. Explain what is meant by this statement.
6 Why might some advertisers prefer a local paper with a circulation of 50 000 to a television advert viewed by 15 million?

## Chapter 15

1 What legislation has been introduced in the post-1970 period to protect consumers against unsatisfactory purchases? Under what circumstances may a customer legally return goods and require the seller to refund the money paid? (*RSA*)
2 'There is no real need for Consumer Protection. People only have themselves to blame if they do not choose wisely.' Outline a reply to this argument.
3 In addition to government activity in the area of consumer protection a number of voluntary agencies assist the consumer in various ways in the provision of informed advice. Write an account of the work of some of these agencies. Do you think they serve a useful need?
4 Explain what is meant by *(a)* criminal law; *(b)* common law;

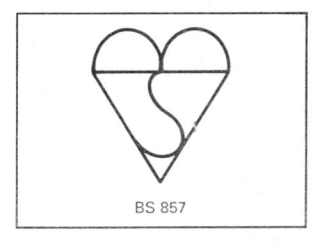

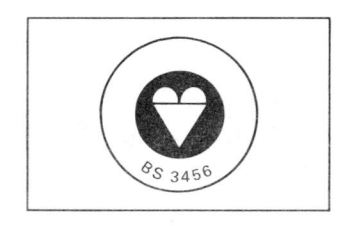

*(c)* statute law; *(d)* a legal contract. Give illustrative examples where possible.
5  *(a)* Identify the labels on p. 226 used in consumer protection.
   *(b)* Give two examples of national pressure groups.
   *(c)* Explain, with examples, the work of the Advertising Standards Authority.
   *(d)* In what ways does the Consumers Association help to protect the consumer?
   *(e)* In what ways does the Government help to protect the consumer? (*LEAG/GCSE UIS specimen*)

## Chapter 16

1  What problems face the exporter which do not exist in the home trade? Show how the Government assists exporters to overcome their difficulties. (*Export*)
2  What are the chief items which make up the 'invisible exports' of the UK at the present time? Why is it so important for the UK to have a favourable balance on 'invisibles'?
3  The United Kingdom (and other countries) often imports raw materials, food and finished goods it is capable of producing itself. Explain why this happens and illustrate your answer with specific examples.
4  Organised commodity markets have existed in the UK for a very long time. What purposes do these markets serve?
5  Discuss the various ways in which overseas debts may be settled. (*Export*)
6  *(a)* (i) What is meant by specialisation?
       (ii) Name *two* countries and state the good or service in which each specialises.
   *(b)* What is meant by international trade?
   *(c)* Show that specialisation by countries results in the need for international trade.
   *(d)* (i) What particular difficulties might firms come across when they take part in international trade?
       (ii) Describe the ways in which the United Kingdom government helps United Kingdom firms to overcome some of these difficulties.
7  Look carefully at the table below relating to foreign trade and then answer the questions which follow.

| *Goods* | £m |
|---|---|
| Total goods exported by the United Kingdom | 900 |
| Total goods imported from other countries | 1000 |
| Balance of trade | ? |

| *Services* | |
|---|---|
| Total services exported by the United Kingdom | ? |
| Total services imported from other countries | 240 |
| Balance on services (favourable) | 160 |

*(a)* (i) Calculate the balance of trade figure.
    (ii) Is the balance of trade figure favourable or unfavourable?
    (iii) Comment on the meaning of your answer above.
    (iv) Calculate the figure for total services exported by the UK.
    (v) What is the amount of surplus on the balance of payments?
    (vi) Comment on the significance of a balance of payments surplus.
*(b)* State the area of the world with which the UK does most visible trade.
*(c)* Explain three difficulties (compared to home trading) faced by exporters. (*LEAG/GCSE Commerce*)

8. Jones and Sahni Ltd produce parts for washing machines. Until now, they have sold all their output in this country. They receive three large orders from firms overseas which would be profitable. The firm is concerned at the time it will take to receive payment and the possibility that they will not be paid at all. They know very little about overseas markets and do not want to bother with the orders unless there is a prospect of more business overseas.

*(a)* Which government department might be able to help the firm?
*(b)* (i) What transport arrangements would you use to get the parts from Birmingham to Australia?
    (ii) Explain why you have chosen this method.
*(c)* Mr Sahni has been reading about our foreign trade and is anxious to make a contribution to improving our balance of

payments although he doesn't understand some of the things he reads. Explain to him:
  (i) the difference between the balance of trade and the balance of payments.
  (ii) how the exports from the firm might affect the balance of payments.
  (iii) what 'invisible' exports are, giving *two* examples of each to make the meaning clear.
(d) The orders are welcomed because the firm will make better use of their resources and obtain economies of scale.
  (i) Explain what is meant by 'economies of scale'.
  (ii) Give *two* examples of economies of scale.
(e) Why is international trade very important for Britain? (*MEG/GCSE Commerce specimen*)

9 (a) The following table of figures relates to a country's current trade account.

|  |  | £ million |  |  |
|---|---|---|---|---|
|  |  | 1984 | 1985 | 1986 |
| Visible Trade | —Exports | 560 | 790 | 680 |
|  | —Imports | 760 | 770 | 800 |
| Invisible Trade | —Exports | 300 | 350 | 360 |
|  | —Imports | 180 | 220 | 260 |

  (i) Calculate the visible balance (balance of trade) for 1985.
  (ii) Calculate the current balance (balance of payments on current account) for 1986.
  (iii) State whether the current balance for 1986 was favourable or unfavourable.
  (iv) Explain clearly the difference between visible and invisible trade. Give two examples of each.
(b) Describe the additional costs and difficulties a business might have when exporting overseas rather than selling within its own country.
(c) In the 1970s Britain had a surplus in trade in manufactured goods and a deficit in primary products. At the present time this situation has been reversed, with a deficit on manufactured goods and a surplus on primary goods.

(i) Giving examples, distinguish between primary and manufactured goods.
(ii) Explain why Britain's pattern of trade has changed in the way stated above. (*NEA/GCSE Commerce*)

The practice in modern examinations, particularly for GCSE, is to set questions which test a wide range of topics, often in the form of 'case studies' of a particular firm or situation. The following questions cover subjects from several chapters in the book.

1  *(a)* Running a successful sole proprietor business making pine furniture, you decide to form a private limited company:
   (i) Explain *two* important advantages to be gained by changing to a private limited company.
   (ii) Name *two* documents which must be sent to the Registrar of Companies.
   (iii) What is the minimum number of shareholders allowed in this form of business?

   At the end of your first year's trading you produced the following information explaining how your total income for the year was distributed:

   | | |
   |---|---:|
   | Raw materials and components | £120 000 |
   | Wages | £60 000 |
   | Tax | £9 000 |
   | Dividends | £1 000 |
   | Retained profits | £15 000 |

   Using the above figures, calculate your company's:
   (iv) Total revenue for the year
   (v) Costs of production for the year
   (vi) Total profit (gross profit) for the year.
   (vii) If the company only issued 2000 ordinary shares and you own 500, what dividend shall you receive at the end of the first year? (Show your working)
   *(b)* Briefly describe ways in which the firm might now try to increase profits. (*MEG/GCSE UIS specimen*)

2  'In the UK the nationalised industries employ over two million people'.
   *(a)* Give the names of *two* nationalised industries.

*(b)* Explain *one* difference between a private enterprise and a nationalised industry.
*(c)* How does a nationalised industry:
   (i) raise capital?
   (ii) dispose of any profits?
   (iii) attempt to be accountable to consumers?
*(d)* (i) Give *two* advantages to a firm setting up in an enterprise zone.
   (ii) When setting up a new firm describe the other factors you would consider when deciding its location.
*(e)* What are the arguments for and against 'privatisation'? (*MEG/GCSE UIS specimen*)

3 *(a)* Who awards the 'Kitemark'?
*(b)* (i) Give the name of the organisation that publishes the magazine *Which?*
   (ii) Explain two ways that *Which?* magazine can help the consumer.
*(c)* Mrs Grange is cutting bread for tea. She finds a nail in the loaf.
   (i) Which public official should she complain to?
   (ii) Describe the action that is likely to follow.
*(d)* A firm sends you a set of encyclopaedias, that you had *not* ordered, and demands that you either pay for them immediately or send them back. Explain what your rights are.
*(e)* Argue the case for buying goods by credit card rather than by hire purchase.
*(f)* Explain the factors that firms must consider when launching an advertising campaign. (*MEG/GCSE UIS specimen*)

4 *(a)* Outline the main features of mail order trading.
*(b)* Why are the prices charged by mail order firms often higher than the prices of similar goods in shops?
*(c)* Name and briefly describe *three* Post Office services which allow payment to be made by mail order customers who do not possess bank accounts.
*(d)* (i) Distinguish between gross profit and net profit.
   (ii) Show that a mail order firm's advertising campaign could result in a lower level of net profit for the firm. (*SEG/GCSE Commerce specimen*)

## 232  Business and Commerce

5  Examine the chart below and answer the questions that follow:

**Summary of forms of private sector enterprise**

| Form of Business Enterprise | Ownership and Control | Advantages | Disadvantages | Capital Source |
|---|---|---|---|---|
| One-man Business (small shop) | One person | a Personal control<br>b Easy to start<br>c Easy to make decisions<br>d Incentive to work | a Limited skill<br>b Limited capital<br>c Unlimited liability | |
| Partnership (professions) | | d Same as to c above<br>e Additional capital<br>f Additional skill | d Same as to c above<br>e Each partner responsible for the acts of the other partners | a Partners' savings<br>b Loans from banks<br>c Ploughed back profits |
| Private Company (small family firm) | | a Limited liability<br>b Continuity | a Corporation tax<br>b Shares cannot be offered to public<br>c Capital still limited | a Shareholders' capital<br>b Private placing<br>c Loans from banks<br>d Ploughed back profits |
| Public Company (large national companies) | shareholders + 2 directors | a As above<br>b Additional capital as shares can be sold to the public | a As above<br>b Publication of accounts<br>c Gulf between management and shareholders | a Stock Exchange placing<br>b Offer for sale<br>c Public issue<br>d Rights issue<br>e Ploughed back profits |

  (a)  List three sources of capital used by the one-man business.

(b) Briefly state who is responsible for the ownership and control of:
   (i) a partnership
   (ii) a private company.
(c) Which types of business organisation raise capital through the issue of shares?
(d) Explain the advantages of the one-man business.
(e) Explain what is meant by the term 'ploughed back profits'.
(f) What are the differences between ordinary shares and preference shares? (*LEAG/GCSE UIS specimen*).

6. Linford Moore thinks his firm, which produces and sells a range of office furniture and equipment, ought to be able to increase its sales and its net profit. The pie chart below shows how his sales are divided between different sectors of the economy. The 24 percent miscellaneous sales includes many small orders on which the firm makes a loss. Linford is looking for a way to keep that market but make it profitable.

(a) What is meant by the term 'net profit'?
(b) (i) From the pie chart give an example of an industry which has recently been privatised.

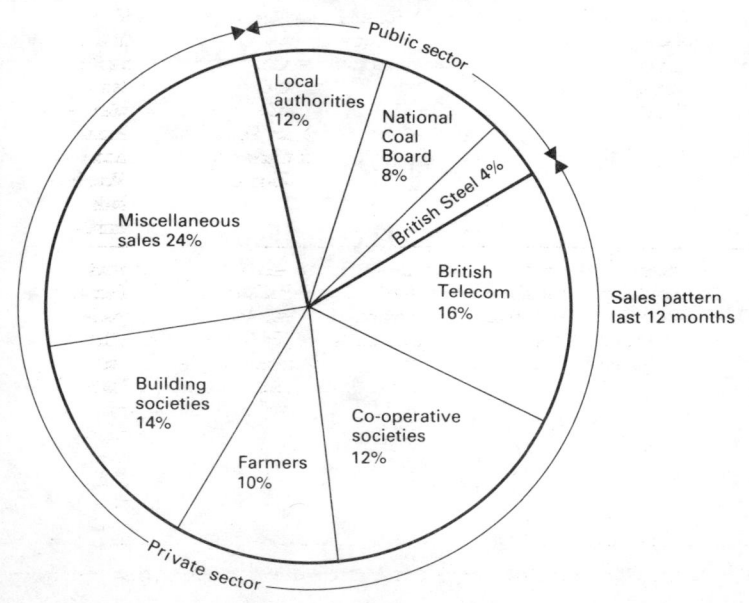

Public sector

Local authorities 12%
National Coal Board 8%
British Steel 4%
British Telecom 16%
Miscellaneous sales 24%
Building societies 14%
Farmers 10%
Co-operative societies 12%

Sales pattern last 12 months

Private sector

(ii) What is the meaning of the word 'privatised'?
- (c) From the pie chart,
    - (i) find what percentage of total sales was to the public sector.
    - (ii) give an example of
        1. a service industry.
        2. an extractive industry, saying what is meant by 'extractive'.
- (d) State *two* ways in which co-operative societies differ from PLCs.
- (e) State and explain *two* ways by which local authorities might have obtained the money to buy the office furniture.
- (f) In what way does the pie chart show that Britain is a mixed economy?
- (g) How might Linford make the miscellaneous sales profitable? (*MEG/GCSE Commerce specimen*)

7  Study the extract from the prospectus for BAA given below, and answer the questions which follow.

---

# B·A·A

## Offer for Sale

BY

## County NatWest Limited

ON BEHALF OF

## The Secretary of State for Transport

OF UP TO

500,000,000 Ordinary shares of 25p each in BAA plc
(at a fixed price of 245p per share, 100p being payable on application).
125,000,000 of these shares may alternatively be purchased by tender
(at or above the fixed price, with part payable on application).

The second instalment of 145p per share is payable on 19 May 1988.

(a) Complete the specimen cheque below as if you were applying for 150 BAA shares on 12 July 1987.

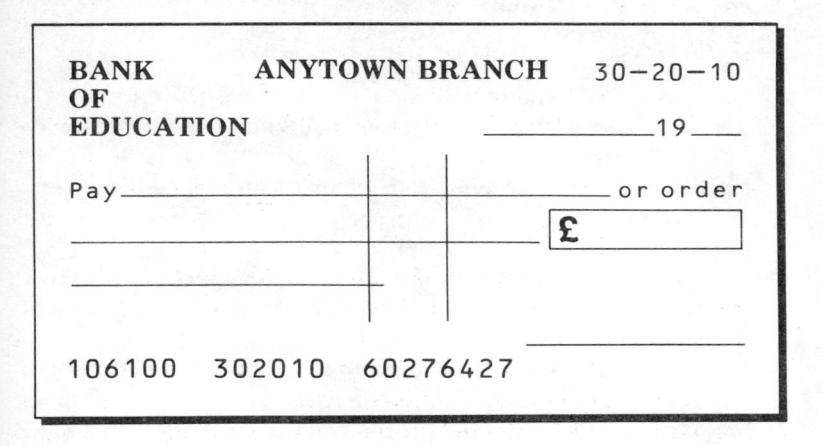

```
BANK            ANYTOWN BRANCH      30-20-10
OF
EDUCATION                        _____19___

Pay_____ or order
_____   £
_____

106100   302010   60276427
```

(b) A friend of yours had a small amount of money but could not decide between buying some BAA shares or opening an account with a building society. Advise your friend, pointing out the differences between these two methods of investing.

(c) The sale of BAA shares was an example of privatisation. Giving examples of other privatised companies, explain what privatisation means and how the ownership and control of the business will change. (*NEA/GCSE Commerce*)

8  You have designed a new board game and you are thinking of setting up a small business to produce it.
   (a) Give *three* advantages of setting up your own business rather than working for someone else.
   (b) Give *three* sources of capital for your small business.
   (c) Explain how you could find out whether the board game would be likely to sell.
   (d) Give *two* ways in which, as a small business, you are likely to advertise your product and explain why you have chosen each method.
   (e) The board game is a great success and orders come in fast.

Discuss the problems which might result from the rapid growth of your business under the following headings.
(i) Production
(ii) Finance
(iii) Government regulations. (*NEA/GCSE IS specimen*)

9 Geoffrey has some spare capital which he wishes to invest. He is undecided whether to invest in a building society, a bank or on the Stock Exchange.

*(a)* If the capital is invested in a bank, should it be placed in a deposit account or a current account? Give a reason for your answer.

*(b)* Explain *two* different types of investment which Geoffrey could make in a public limited company and the degree of risk attached to each.

*(c)* How does the Stock Exchange assist (i) companies, and (ii) investors? (*MEG/GCSE Commerce specimen*)

10 Read the following conversation and answer the questions which follow.

---

Mary was doing her course work for GCSE Commerce and interviewed Peter, who was about to open a new butcher's shop.

*Peter* 'I can't wait to open the shop next week. I've really worked hard getting all the counters in position and arranging all the cold storage equipment.'

*Mary* 'How do you think you will benefit from Commerce? I mean all the Aids to Trade which you learned about at school.'

*Peter* 'Well it's only a very small business so I don't think I will be involved with them much. I suppose I will need a bank to keep my takings and somewhere to store my meat but that's about it really.'

*Mary* 'What about your van? I thought you were going to deliver some large orders? How are people going to get to know about this shop? There don't seem to be many people walking past.'

*Peter* 'I wouldn't worry about that. When my mum gets talking everybody is bound to find out about it!'

*Mary* 'I see you've got something in the fridge already – isn't it a bit soon? It might go off!'

*Peter* 'Oh that's alright, it's only a few pork sausages, and there isn't much pork in them anyway.'

*(a)* Peter says that he will only need a bank for keeping his takings. Explain the services that a bank provides which Peter may find useful for his business.

*(b)* Apart from banking and storage, Peter says that he will not be very much involved with the Aids to Trade. Say whether you agree with this statement, explaining your answer in relation to Peter's business.

*(c)* (i) Describe the work of an organisation which exists to protect consumers from Peter selling meat which has gone off.

(ii) Describe the legal protection for consumers against Peter advertising his sausages as '100 percent pork'.

*(d)* Peter finds that there is a lot more competition in selling meat than he first imagined. State what types of retailer might be competing with Peter, and advise him on the steps he could take to attract customers and make his business profitable.

11  Ten years ago, Dave Ascot and Pete Newbury set up Racing Circuits, a limited company, in the South East of England. Both men used to work for a large firm, but wanted to start their own business. They felt they would get more job satisfaction from the extra responsibility and freedom to take their own decisions, and it would be worth the risk of giving up safe jobs.

Each year has seen a growth in profits and sales. Last year the firm earned a net profit of 10 percent on sales which were £2 million. Racing Circuits Ltd had done very well in European markets because the value of the pound has been helping British exports. Its sales promotion at overseas trade fairs and exhibitions has made more people aware of its products.

The company has an authorised capital of £250 000 and up to now it has issued £100 000 of ordinary and preference shares. It has a good relationship with its bankers, Barminster Bank PLC. According to its most recent Balance Sheet, it is owed £175 000, whilst its creditors are owed only £50 000. It has no cash-flow problems and its order book for the next 18 months is nearly full.

The Board of Directors have been called to a meeting to discuss company expansion. A new vacant factory, ideal for the firm's requirements, has just become available at a cost of £100 000.

(a) Explain the meaning of the terms
   (i) limited company;
   (ii) creditor;
   (iii) cash-flow.
(b) (i) Give *two* reasons why Dave Ascot and Pete Newbury wished to start up their own business.
   (ii) State *one* disadvantage of giving up a job with another firm in order to start your own business.
(c) Give *two* reasons why the firm's overseas sales have increased in recent years.
(d) (i) Calculate from the information the net profit made by Racing Circuits Ltd last year.
   (ii) If the company decide to finance the new factory from last year's profits, how much money would remain for distribution to shareholders?
(e) (i) State *one* disadvantage of using profit to finance the new factory.
   (ii) From the information in the text, suggest *two* other ways Racing Circuits Ltd could finance the new factory. (*SEG/GCSE BIS specimen*)

12 Look carefully at the information opposite and then answer the questions which follow.

(a) Name the company whose shares are being offered for sale.
(b) State (i) the type of share being issued
   (ii) its issue price when fully paid.
(c) An investor wishes to buy 300 of these shares. Calculate, showing workings, the value of the cheque that would have to be enclosed with the application.
(d) Describe the possible ways in which Kleinwort Benson Limited and Lazard Brothers & Co. Limited could have helped in the issue of these shares.
(e) If applications for 700 million shares are received, comment on
   (i) the possible ways in which the available shares could be distributed amongst applicants.

# British Aerospace
Public Limited Company

**Offer**
by
**Kleinwort, Benson Limited**
and
**Lazard Brothers & Co., Limited**
on behalf of
**British Aerospace Public Limited Company**
and
**The Secretary of State for Trade and Industry**
of
**146,852,746 Ordinary Shares
of 50p each at 375p per share**
200p is payable on application
175p is payable by 10th September 1985
underwritten by

Kleinwort, Benson Limited    Lazard Brothers & Co., Limited
Hill Samuel & Co. Limited            Morgan Grenfell & Co. Limited

J. Henry Schroder Wagg & Co. Limited

(ii) the likely share price when these shares are first quoted on the Stock Exchange. Give a reason for your answer.

*(f)* (i) What is meant by privatisation?
(ii) What evidence is there in the data that this issue of shares is an example of privatisation? (*SEG/GCSE Commerce specimen*)

# Sources of Information

Leaflets and other useful information may be obtained from the following:

Advertising Association
Abford House
15 Wilton Road
London SW1V 1NJ

Advertising Standards Authority
Brook House
2/16 Torrington Place
London WC1E 7HN

Association of British Insurers
Aldermary House
Queen Street
London EC4N 1TT

Bank of England
Information Division
Threadneedle Street
London EC2R 8AH

Banking Information Service
10 Lombard Street
London EC3V 9AT

British Overseas Trade Board
1 Victoria Street
London SW1H 0ET

British Standards Institution
2 Park Street
London W1A 2BS

British Telecommunications PLC
81 Newgate Street
London EC1A 7AJ

British Waterways Board
Melbury House
Melbury Terrace
London NW1 6JX

Building Societies Association
3 Savile Row
London W1X 1AF

Confederation of British Industry
Centre Point
103 New Oxford Street
London WC1A 1DU

Co-operative Development Agency
21 Panton Street
London SW1Y 4DR

Consumers Association
14 Buckingham Street
London WC2N 6DS

Co-operative Wholesale Society
New Century House
Corporation Street
Manchester M60 4ES

European Commission Information Office
8 Storey's Gate
London SW1P 3AT

Electricity Consumers' Council
Brook House
2/16 Torrington Place
London WC1E 7LL

Export Credit Guarantees Department
PO Box 272
Export House
50 Ludgate Hill
London EC4M 7AY

Equal Opportunities Commission
1 Bedford Street, Strand
London WC2E 9HD

Lloyds of London
Publicity and Information
1 Lime Street
London EC3M 7HA

National Consumer Council
20 Grosvenor Gardens
London SW1N 0DH

Office of Fair Trading
Field House, Breams Building
London EC4 1PR

Post Office
31 Grovesnor Place
London SW1X 1PX

Post Office Users' National Council
Waterloo Bridge House
Waterloo Bridge Road
London SE1 8UA

Stock Exchange
London EC2N 1HP

Trades Union Congress
Congress House
Great Russell Street
London WC1B 3LS

# Index

accepting houses  100
acknowledgement  56
ACORN system  85
advertising  1, 149–57
  advantages &
  disadvantages  150
  control of  155–7
  media  151–3
  types  149–50
Advertising Standards Authority
  (ASA)  155–7
advice note  56
aids to trade  8
Annual General Meeting
  (AGM)  15
Articles of Association  18–19
assets  62–5
Assisted Areas  28–9
auctions  87–8
authorised capital  40
automatic vending  88
average stock  70

balance of payments  171–4
balance sheet  62–5
Bank of England  97–9, 108
banking services  27, 30–3,
  99–112
banks
  commercial (joint-stock)  31,
  100–1

  consortia  32–3
  international  32–3
  merchant  40, 100
  origins of  96–7
barter  95
'Big Bang'  35–7, 111
bill of exchange  108, 177
borrowing  30–3
brand names  149
British Overseas Trade Board
  (BOTB)  175–6
British Rail  49, 131–3
British Standards  165–6
British Telecom  51–3, 124–5,
  127
budget accounts  103
building societies  97, 112–14
business names  10, 18–19

capital
  liquid  65
  owner's  62–4
  return on  64–5
  working  65
capital goods  *see* producer goods
cash dispensers  105
*caveat emptor*  158
Certificate of Incorporation
  18
Certificate of Trading  18
chain of distribution  71

# Index

Channel Tunnel (Eurotunnel)   53, 136–7
cheque cards   105
cheques   103–9
command economy   *see* planned economy
commercial services   8
commodity money   94–5
Common Market   *see* European Community
communication   22–3
communications   1, 48, 115–27
Companies Acts   10–11, 18
Company Secretary   23–4
Consumer Credit Act   161–2
consumer law   7, 158–62
consumer organisations   164–6
Consumer Protection Act   162
Consumers Association   164–5
containerisation   136
contracting-out   51
control, span of   23
Co-operative Development Agency (CDA)   20–1
Co-operative Retail Society (CRS)   20–1, 82–4
Co-operative Wholesale Society (CWS)   20–1, 82–4
co-operatives   20–1, 82–4
cost of sales   66
credit note   58–9
creditors   63
current accounts   101

debentures   32, 34
debtors   64
delivery note   57
demand   3
denationalisation   51
department stores   81
deposit accounts   102
deregulation   51
direct debits   110–11
direct mail   85–6
direct services   8
discount houses   99–100
diseconomies of scale   26

distribution   1, 23, 25
dividend   14, 34, 37, 41
documentary credit system   177–9

economies, types of   2–7
economies of concentration   29
economies of scale   25–6
enquiry   54
Environmental Health Department   164
European Community (EC)   14, 179–83
expenses   67–9
Export Credit Guarantee Department (ECGD)   176
extractive industries   *see* primary industry

Fair Trading Act   162
finance houses   100
fixed assets   62–3
fixed-term loan   31–2
footloose industries   26
franchises   32, 74–5
free market economy   2–4

giro credit system   108, 110
Girobank   51, 123
Government
  assistance to business   26, 28–30, 34
  control over business   6–7, 10, 18, 162
  finance   42–3
  local   43–5
gross profit   62–9
gross profit margin   66–7

health and safety   5
holding company   25–6

incorporation   11
Independent Broadcasting Authority (IBA)   155, 157
independent retailers   *see* unit shops

industrial inertia 29
insurance 1, 138–48
  cost of 138–9
  Ombudsman 145–6
  re-insurance 145
  terms 140–1
  types 141–3
  uninsurable risks 139
international trade  *see* overseas trade
invoice 57–8
issued capital 40
issuing house 40

joint-stock companies  *see* limited companies

leasing 32
liabilities 62–5
limited companies 9, 11, 14–19
limited liability 9–19
limited partnerships 12–13
loans for business 30–4
local authorities 43–5, 164
location of industry 26–9

Marketing Boards 21, 94, 149
Memorandum of
  Association 18–19, 40
merchant banks 40, 100
Mercury Communications 126–7
mixed economy 3, 5–7
money
  functions 95–7
  types of 95–7
monopolies
  control of 162
  natural 47–8
  statutory 49
Monopolies and Mergers
  Commission 162
multinational companies 22
multiple stores 78, 80

National Consumer Council 166
nationalisation 43, 45–51, 164, 166

nationalised industry consumer councils 164, 166
net profit 62–9
net worth 64
night safe 111

Office of Fair Trading (OFT) 162
order 56
ordinary shares 34, 40–1
organisation 22–5
organisation charts 23–5
overdraft 31
overseas trade 167–83
  balance of payments accounts 171–4
  European Community (EC) 179–83
  payments 176–9
  problems of exporters 174–5
  protectionism 176–9
oversubscription 40

Partnership Act 11–13
Partnership Agreement (partnership deed) 12–13
partnerships 11–13
party-plan selling 88
Personnel Officer 24–5
planned economy 3–6
Post Office 49–51, 116–23
preference shares 34, 40–3
primary industry 7–8
private limited company 9, 14–15
privatisation 44, 46–7
profit
  distribution of 9–21, 30–1
  gross 62–9
  importance of 3–5, 30, 37, 46–7, 49
  net 62–9
  retained 10, 30–1
profit and loss account 67–9
pro-forma invoice 57
protectionism 169–71
public corporations 44, 50–1; *see also* nationalisation

public limited companies  15–19
purchases, in accounts  66

quotation  54–6

regional policy  28–9, 34
Registrar of Companies  14, 18, 40
registration of companies  18–19
remittance advice note  59
resale price maintenance (RPM)  76
research and development  25
retained profit  10, 30–1

Sale of Goods Act  159–60
sales, in accounts  66
scarcity  2
secondary industry  7–8
service industries  see tertiary industry
shares
  buying and selling  35–9, 111
  new issues  34, 39–41
  prices of 37–9, 41
  types of  34
small firms
  assistance for  26
  problems of  11, 26, 73–4
  reasons for survival  11, 26, 74
sole proprietor  see sole trader
sole trader  9–11, 17
span of control  23
standing orders  110
statement of account  58–9
stock  64–7, 69–70
Stock Exchange  14–15, 17–18, 32, 34–9, 41, 111
Stock Exchange Automated Quotation System (SEAQ)  35–7

stock turnover  70
supermarket  74, 76–8
superstores  79–81
supply  3
Supply of Goods and Services Act  160

takeovers  39
Takeovers Panel  18
tertiary industry  7–8
Third Market  35
Trade Descriptions Act  160
trading account  65–6
Trading Standards Department  160–1, 164
transport  1, 27, 48, 128–37
  choice of  127–9
  containerisation  136
  inland waterways  134–5
  pipelines  135–6
  rail  131–3
  road  130–1
  sea  133–4

undersubscription  40, 53
undistributed profit  see retained profit
Unfair Contract Terms Act  161
unit shops  73–4
Unlisted Securities Market (USM)  35
Unsolicited Goods and Services Act  161

Value Added Tax (VAT)  60–1
variety chain store  78
voluntary chains  74–5

Weights and Measures Act  161
*Which?*  163–4
wholesaling  1, 89–94
working capital  65